The

Legal Mind

How the Law Thinks

Daniel W. Park

About the Author

Dan Park is a graduate of Yale Law School. He holds a B.A. from Swarthmore College and an M.A. from Stanford University. Dan has practiced law for over 15 years and currently is the Chief Campus Counsel for the University of California, San Diego. Since 2005, he has taught Introduction to the Legal System at UC San Diego Extension. He is a member of the American Law Institute, and his scholarly work has appeared in academic journals published by Stanford and Gonzaga Law Schools and legal newspapers like *The Los Angeles Daily Journal*. In 2011, *The Daily Transcript* recognized Dan as one of the top in-house attorneys in San Diego. Dan lives in San Diego with his wife, two children, and two dogs. You can follow Dan on Twitter at @danparkathome.

For Deborah, Andrew, and Eric.
Always.

CONTENTS

Prologue

WHY IS THE law so complicated, and why do lawyers always find something to argue about? People exposed to the legal system for the first time always seem to ask these same two questions. When disputes arise, most people tend to have a clear sense of the right outcome. The legal mind has a lot more doubts.

Everyone has a little bit of lawyer in them. Every day, in ways both large and small, we argue, analyze, and persuade the people around us—or we attempt to do so—and the people around us attempt to do the same to us. Arguments and information bombard us from every corner, from family, friends, and co-workers to journalists, politicians, and salesmen. We debate about everything from sports and movies to politics and justice. We all argue, but we could do it better.

Most of us are amateurs when it comes to arguments, disputes, proof, and making a case, because most of the time we don't actually need to win our arguments. We can agree to disagree and continue about our lives, holding fast to our opinions whether or not anyone else agrees with us.

1

When disputes bubble over into the legal system, things are different. In a legal dispute, there is no avoiding the deep and difficult problem of how to persuade others of the truth of what we think and the justice of what we want. The legal system takes our most deeply held beliefs and puts them to the test of determined adversaries and skeptical judges. This can be treacherous territory.

Learning the ways of the law is important. The law governs every moment of our lives from our first breaths to our last. The law controls

- when and how we can get married,
- how we educate our children,
- how, when, and who can start businesses or practice certain professions, and
- what happens to our property after we die.

The law is everywhere around us, but often invisible, like gravity or the air we breathe. Despite its fundamental importance, the law can seem incomprehensible. The incomprehension goes beyond simply not knowing all of the law's innumerable rules. The system itself, its inner logic, its vital core, can be baffling. The law appears mysterious, counterintuitive, and sometimes even nonsensical. To those locked in its processes, the law can be positively maddening.

Steve Jobs, the legendary founder of Apple, once observed that one of the most important insights he ever had was that "everything around you that you call life was made up by people who were no smarter than you—and you can change it."[1] The same is true about the law. Unlike the laws of nature, which spring from the Universe, the laws of society are composed by people—people no smarter than you—and as a consequence, the law is understandable, accessible, and changeable. The key is knowing how the law thinks.

The way the legal mind thinks about and approaches problems often takes people by surprise. They don't understand how false allegations can be taken seriously. They don't understand why lawyers argue over seemingly petty points or why judges entertain those arguments. They don't understand why the law punishes one person and lets another seemingly similar person walk away. And they definitely don't understand why everything takes so long. More than anything, they want to know what the law is thinking.

"The life of the law," wrote Oliver Wendell Holmes Jr. more than 120 years ago, "has not been logic; it has been experience."[2] This is not the way most people approach problems, but it is a powerful method for resolving disputes, and you can learn and apply it. By understanding the problems the law confronts, you will appreciate the law's methods and arm yourself to face disputes and win arguments. Mastery begins by getting inside the law's head.

* * *

In the late 1980s, Seiji Ogawa, a researcher working at the renowned Bell Laboratories—the same think tank that gave the world transistors and fiber optics—had a problem. He wanted to see what was going on inside the brains of mice, but he didn't want to have to cut them open to do it.

Then Ogawa and his colleagues noticed something no one else had noticed before. The blood flowing into the rats' brains could be measured by magnets using magnetic resonance imaging (MRI). The MRI could show the parts of the brain that were active at any given moment by identifying areas where blood was carrying higher levels of oxygen.[3] For the first time, scientists could see what parts of the brain were working the hardest while animals (and later people) were actually thinking. Ogawa's work led to the development of functional magnetic resonance imaging (fMRI) and gave the world the first pictures of real brains at work in real time. Since Ogawa's discovery, more than twelve thousand scientific papers have been published based on information gathered from fMRI's.[4]

This book attempts to be an fMRI for the legal mind. At any given moment, different parts of the legal system perform different functions, and different regions are more active for certain activities than others. But at all times the whole system is working together to produce a unified outcome. This book identifies the problems the legal mind faces and explains how the legal mind confronts those problems, the solutions it offers, and how those solutions fit together to form a coherent whole.

The legal mind aims for justice in a complicated and uncertain world, and it faces some profound and formidable obstacles to achieving that lofty goal. Part one looks at two of the deepest problems that the legal system must confront and overcome:

- Figuring out what really happened in the past; and
- Figuring out what are the right rules to apply.

Solving those problems is complicated by the fact that people will deeply and vigorously disagree about the right answer to both questions.

Anyone who has watched a baseball game has had the experience of the crack of a bat, the blur of a ball, a racing fielder, a hard throw, and an arm outstretched to make a catch while a runner charges up the line to first base. The umpire makes a call—safe or out—and the crowd erupts, some in cheering delight, others in outraged protest. Even though fifty thousand people witnessed the play that just happened, violent disagreements can break out over whether the umpire's call was right or wrong.

In the days before instant replays, disputes over whether the runner was safe or out might never be definitively settled despite the thousands of witnesses who saw everything unfold right before their eyes. If definitive resolutions about what happened are elusive with thousands of witnesses, imagine how much more difficult finding resolutions is when only a handful of biased people with an interest in the outcome are on hand to give an account of events. The problem for the legal system is how to gather and present the evidence needed to reach a reliable and convincing conclusion about past events when people deeply disagree.

This problem of proof is rooted in the limitations of our ability to perceive and remember; it is complicated by our tendencies toward bias and occasional outright deception; and it is further deepened by the need to overcome traps of false logic and unreliable assumptions. We may think we know whether the baseball runner is safe or out, but it can be hard to be absolutely sure and even harder, if not impossible, to convince the skeptical fans of the opposing team.

Even if the facts are established beyond dispute, figuring out the right rules presents challenges of its own. Just formulating clear and understandable rules is hard. Rules are composed with words, and like all words, rules are susceptible to ambiguity, misinterpretation, and misapplication. Words are slippery because they often mean different things to different people. To communicate what we mean, we must routinely refine our ideas and the words we use to express them to approach bit by bit the rules that we truly intend.

It is hard enough to be clear when we know exactly what we want to say. The challenge becomes exponentially more difficult when we are not entirely sure what we think but need to formulate rules anyway. The world is a complicated place, so it is hard to anticipate all the circumstances in which a rule might be applied. Our sense of what is right or wrong can depend on seemingly small differences, the importance of which we appreciate only when we confront them in real life.

The problem of rules is finding the right rule for the right situation expressed in the right way so that the rule can be understood and correctly applied. No easy feat.

Part two describes how the legal system attempts to solve the problem of proof and the problem of rules.

To address the problem of proof, written records and oral testimony must be stitched together into a coherent whole. Contradictions and inconsistencies must be identified and explained. And above all, corroboration must be sought out and evaluated.

For the problem of rules, the law depends heavily on the doctrine of *stare decisis*. The doctrine of *stare decisis* requires courts to follow and obey the prior decisions of earlier courts. Even within this system cracks emerge that require further interpretation and elaboration, leaving ample room for attorneys to argue.

Part three describes the mechanics of the legal system and the process it uses to come to conclusions about facts and rules. Two different types of courts—trial courts and appellate courts—exist to address these problems. Trial courts specialize in finding facts. Appellate courts specialize in expounding the law. The procedures these courts employ reflect the specialized problems they are designed to solve and are themselves critical components of the law's solutions to the problems of proof and rules.

Finally, part four looks at the two cornerstones of legal thinking: the law of agreements (contracts) and the law of accidents and injuries (torts). Although the modern legal system is a vast thicket of rules and regulations, most legal rules can be understood as variations of either agreements or accidents. We will explore the major features of contracts and torts with the aim of understanding their fundamental principles. Once understood, these principles can be applied to almost any legal question.

Every day, each of us must choose what to believe and what not to believe. The law and the legal system face the exact same challenges. While the vocabulary and structure of the law may be unfamiliar, their purpose is the same as ours: to discover truth and do justice. By the end of this book, the law won't be less complex and lawyers won't be less argumentative, but you will understand how the legal mind thinks and the evidence and arguments most likely to persuade others, no matter what the problem, disagreement, or dispute.

Sun Tzu, the ancient Chinese military strategist, wrote in *The Art of War*, "If you know the enemy and know yourself, you need not fear the result of a hundred battles."[5] By understanding the legal mind, there is no need to fear the legal system. When you know how the law thinks, you will be prepared to respond to—and win—any argument. Let's get started.

Part One

Facts and Laws

EVERY LEGAL DECISION has two essential ingredients: facts and laws. Together they comprise the foundation upon which the entire legal system is built.

First facts. Life happens. We eat, sleep, and work. We make friends and enemies. We talk, we move, we interact. Often, too often, we stumble and bump into others, and others stumble and bump into us. Our lives are the sum total of our experiences. These experiences can be good or bad, welcome or unwelcome, fortunate or spectacularly cruel, but the events themselves do not depend on what we think of them. They are real. They are hard. These tangible experiences are what the law calls facts.

Yet facts can be slippery things. We know them through our senses. We remember them with our memories. We understand and interpret them with our minds. Facts exist, but at the same time they are also a product of the human mind, and like all things human, our understanding of facts is prone to error and failure.

In the legal system, the term "facts" does not necessarily refer to established, known truths, like the Earth orbiting the Sun, but rather facts include our personal points of view on our experiences. Facts are things that we have seen, heard, felt, smelled, or tasted (sight and sound being the most dominant). Our thoughts, our intentions, our plans, and our purposes are facts. Our actions are facts. And so are the thoughts and actions of others.

Our ability to know and establish for others facts is constrained by the limits of the human mind. When filtered through human eyes and ears, facts take on a shade of uncertainty. Different people may perceive the same event very differently, and so facts can be, and very often are, highly disputed. Facts happen, but people will disagree, vehemently at times, about what happened and what didn't. The first great problem the legal mind must grapple with is finding facts in the face of vigorous conflict and controversy over the truth.

Facts are the first step, but alone they are not enough for a legal decision. The legal significance of a person's thoughts and actions is only clear when we know the rules that apply to those thoughts and actions.

Human beings love rules. We create rules for everything. The law is just another set of rules, but with this distinction: the law's rules will be enforced by the coercive power of the government.

The multiplicity and complexity of rules mean that we must always be asking what our rules really mean and which of the many possible rules applies in any given situation. The challenge is understanding and applying the right rule at the right time.

The problem of proof and the problem of rules arise from different sources. The problem of proof is rooted in the difficulty of knowing the past. The problem of proof is rooted in the difficulty of reducing our sense of justice into understandable words that can be applied consistently.

Although we will discuss these two problems separately, it is important not to lose sight of the fact that a legal decision emerges only when facts are combined with laws to produce a judgment.

Take a simple situation: Darryl hits Paul. That's a fact (or would be, if this weren't a hypothetical example). Understanding the legal meaning of this act requires more information. We need to know the rule. In this example, the general rule is simple and intuitive: one person cannot hit another person. Putting the fact (Darryl hit Paul) together with the rule (hitting is forbidden) yields the legal decision that Darryl is in the wrong.

Yet even this simple scenario quickly gives way to complexity if we add more information. What if the blow was an accident? For example, what if Darryl stumbled and collided with Paul in the midst of his fall? What if Darryl was pushed by another person and fell into the collision through no fault of his own? What if Darryl had been trying to push Paul out of danger and inadvertently hit him in the rush to save his life?

So maybe we amend the rule to fit our sense of when hitting someone is just and when it is unjust. Once down this path, the exceptions keep piling up. What if Darryl hit Paul as part of a boxing match? Consent seems to matter, so we amend the rule again. What if Paul was threatening Darryl and Darryl struck his blow only to save himself from serious injury? So maybe we add another exception, this time for self-defense.

Our simple rule has multiplied into half a dozen more detailed rules, and each of these sub-rules points in a different direction on the question of whether Darryl is in the wrong. Paul and Darryl have every incentive to try to spin the facts of their encounter to fit the most favorable rule. And so a legal dispute is born.

Our intuitions about right and wrong and justice and injustice are highly sensitive to the particulars of a situation and not always consistent or clear. The dance between facts and laws can produce an infinite variety of combinations. It is against this chaotic backdrop that the legal system must confront the problem of proof and the problem of rules.

I

The Problem of Proof

The enemy of knowledge is not ignorance. It is the illusion of knowledge.
—Stephen Hawking

MOUNTAINTOP TROUBLES

Imagine you are returning home from a trip to Tanzania, Africa. Although the flight from Dar es Salaam to Amsterdam back to the United States is long and exhausting, you are sustained by the thought of regaling your friends and family with stories of your travels when you get home.

You arrive tired, jet-lagged, and grungy, but after a short rest and shower, you gather your friends from the neighborhood to triumphantly tell them that on your trip you ascended to the summit of Kilimanjaro, one of the world's highest peaks. Your beaming smile of pride fades as you see that your neighbors' faces are a mix of raised eyebrows and half-suppressed smirks. Your confusion quickly slips to anger, and you ask what's going on.

Your neighbors look at one another not sure who should speak for the group. Finally, one of them shrugs sheepishly and says that your climbing Kilimanjaro is a nice story, but frankly, not one of them believes you. Your eyes widen in disbelief. You know what you know. You saw what you saw. You did what you did. You protest their skepticism. The spokesperson holds up an empty hand and speaks the two-word mantra of every person who wants convincing: "Prove it."

Now what?

You've already told them your story (given your testimony, so to speak), but that was not enough to win over the skeptics. What's your next move?

After a moment, you go for your camera and show them the pictures you took from the summit, a glorious view down the forested slopes of the mountain, falling away to the vast African plains below. Distant peaks are lined by the bluest sky and adorned with picturesque wisps of white clouds adding delicate contrast and dimension. You point to the photograph and say, "There's your proof!"

Your neighbors nod their heads. They agree that it's a pretty picture. The only thing, says one, is that picture could have been taken anywhere. How can they be sure that it is from the summit of the tallest freestanding mountain in the world and not from some other, less prestigious peak? Also, even if this is a picture from the top of Kilimanjaro, how can they be sure that you were the one who took it?

You raise a finger to ask for a moment. You disappear and return with your airline tickets and passport. You show them the dates of the tickets and stamps on the passport, conclusive proof that you spent the last ten days in Tanzania. Then you show that the camera has time-stamped the photo from the summit with a date and time. The date lines up with the ticket and passport. This photo, you declare, was without doubt taken in Tanzania.

Your neighbors respond tentatively. One questions whether the time stamp is accurate. Couldn't the camera have been programmed to show any date? Even assuming the date is accurate, it is not clear that the camera was in Tanzania, even if they accept that you were there. Another neighbor points out that even if we assume that the date is right and the camera went to Tanzania with you, there is no definite proof that the photo is from Kilimanjaro and not some other place in that beautiful country. And even if this were Kilimanjaro, another chimes in, who's to say that someone didn't take the picture for you while you waited lazily at the bottom?

Your frustration grows as you cast about for more evidence to convince your neighbors (whom you are beginning to think of as inquisitors rather than friends). You search through your things and come up with the following: a hiking permit you purchased (with dates matching those of the photograph), a receipt from a guide who helped you with the climb, and a postcard from a fellow hiker making reference to seeing you on the summit of Kilimanjaro.

This is all you have. You rest your case. A line of sweat stretches across your hairline. You look expectantly at your neighbors. Slowly, one by one they begin to nod. You've done it. They're convinced.

You start to tell them about your excursion to the Serengeti, but then stop. It's a great vacation story, but who has the energy to prove it?

Congratulations. You've just experienced the problem of proof.

THE RARITY OF PROOF

We tell each other stories every day, and yet we often have very little experience with proof.

We rarely need to prove a fact to another person. In many cases, no proof is necessary because we've shared our experiences with the people around us. Our friends and family have seen what we've seen, so we don't have to convince them that what we've collectively experienced is real. In other cases, because our relationships with our friends and family are built on bonds of trust, our word is proof enough that what we say happened is, in fact, a true and accurate account.

Frequently, proof doesn't matter much because the stories we tell and the stories we're told don't matter much. Demanding proof from our friends, families, acquaintances, and co-workers serves no useful purpose because it makes no difference whether their stories are true or false or whether we believe or disbelieve them. Did your co-worker really run the Boston Marathon in under three hours or catch a giant fish or read the complete works of Shakespeare or meet the president of the United States or win the Medal of Honor for uncommon valor under enemy fire? You can choose to credit these stories as impressive accomplishments or dismiss them as exaggerations and lies. Either way, neither view will stock a refrigerator, patch a leaky roof, or put gas in a car. You do not need to demand evidence because the truth of the matter doesn't meaningfully change your everyday life.

Even proof about the great events of history, for the most part, doesn't trouble most of us most of the time. Any minimally authoritative account will do. Major world-shaking events—like the Battle of Waterloo or the attack on Pearl Harbor or the assassination of President John F. Kennedy—

may be dramatic turning points in history, but for most people outside a small circle of professional historians and conspiracy theorists, any plausible account is acceptable. In the end, the wisdom of Napoleon's battle plans or the details of the Japanese assault or the questions about how one shooter could accomplish the assassination of a president just don't make much difference in how we live our lives.

This is not to say that history holds no lessons. On the contrary, history is often essential to understanding why the world is as it is, but such understanding—like the ability to appreciate the nuances of a Chopin nocturne or the turn of the Mona Lisa's smile—while enlightening, enriching, and elevating, has no practical consequence for most people most of the time. And so, we make no systematic inquiry into the facts; we take our histories as they are told to us and then get on about our business.

In legal disputes the precise facts of an event matter very much (at least to the people involved) because what happened will dictate whether and how much someone has to pay another person. What exactly did the car dealer promise to fix under warranty if my car breaks down? What exactly was the driver's blood alcohol level at the time of the accident? What color was the light at the time the car entered the intersection? Who would be the better parent in a divorcing couple? Will a patient ever be able to walk again after a surgical accident? When facts change people's lives, the problem of proof becomes acute.

When facts really matter, our ability to produce, interpret, and evaluate proof takes center stage. Reconstructing the past requires searching for the tracks people's actions have left behind. The people who directly experienced the events and the records they produced must be analyzed, weighed, and ultimately presented to a decision-maker who will make a judgment about what really happened.

The process of proving what happened in the past is fraught with fallibility. Four major problems stand as imposing obstacles to definitively and unequivocally knowing what happened in the past:

1. The problem of deception;

2. The problem of forgetting;

3. The problem of perception (and, in particular, the problem of eyewitness testimony); and

4. The problem of fallacies.

The problem of proof is the sum of all of these challenges. Before exploring these problems, it is useful to pause briefly to think about how we know anything at all.

KNOWING WHAT WE KNOW

All of us have our different understandings, opinions, and beliefs about what the world is really like, and these differences lead us into disputes. Resolving disputes requires convincing another person, and convincing another person requires proof. So how do we know what (we think) we know?

The first source of our knowledge of the world is our own direct experience. If you take a sip of a hot drink and it scalds your tongue, you know that hot liquid burns. You know the sky is blue because you've seen it. You know where you live, how to drive a car, the names of your family and friends, and you know all of these things from your personal perception.

Yet what each of us knows from our direct experiences is just a small fraction of the sum of all the knowledge we have about the world. You know that the Earth revolves around the Sun without personally witnessing the movement from space.

You know that George Washington was the first president of the United States without having been present at his inauguration in 1789. We know our history, science, and culture because other people told us, either in person or in the media, and we believe them.

It is not uncommon for what we think we know to be the subject of intense controversy and dispute among experts. Sometimes, what was unquestioningly believed in one era is flatly rejected as superstition and quackery in another. At one time, the scientific consensus was that the Sun revolved around the Earth. Now we know that the Earth revolves around the Sun. At one time, people thought human beings were made up of tiny versions of their larger selves (called homunculi).[6] Now we know that humans are made up of cells. At one time, people thought that nothing was smaller than an atom. Now we know about quarks and other subatomic particles.

It is not only scientific thinking that evolves. Slavery was once the law of the land in America, and a long and bloody civil war was required to rip it out of the fabric of society. There was a time when respectable, law-abiding Americans hanged men and women for being witches.[7] Today hanging witches seems bizarre and incomprehensible, and yet in other parts of the world, witchcraft accusations, even against children, are not uncommon.[8]

One interesting thought experiment is to ask yourself which of your most strongly held beliefs will be repudiated by a future age as ignorant, misguided, disgusting, or appalling, just as we reject so many of the beliefs of our ancestors.[9] The possibility that even our firmest convictions might turn out to be wrong is a sobering reminder that a great deal of our knowledge and beliefs about how the world works is built on a foundation of shifting sands.

The classic statement of this observation comes from John Stuart Mill, the great nineteenth-century, English philosopher. In chapter 2 of *On Liberty*, Mill wrote,

> Yet it is as evident in itself, as any amount of argument can make it, that ages are no more infallible than individuals; every age having held many opinions which subsequent ages have deemed not only false but absurd; and it is as certain that many opinions, now general, will be rejected by future ages, as it is that many, once general, are rejected by the present.[10]

In a legal dispute, the objective is to persuade another person that what we think we know is in fact the truth. The people we are trying to persuade (*e.g.*, judges and juries) do not have direct, personal experience with the events. They do not share bonds of trust with us that vouch for our words. And they do not have access to neutral, authoritative statements of fact. Their personal understanding, knowledge, and beliefs must be gleaned from secondhand sources with varying degrees of accuracy and bias.

In broad terms, there are two classes of evidence that can be advanced to convince a third party that one version of events is an accurate description of the truth: direct evidence and circumstantial evidence.

Direct evidence is evidence that a person has directly experienced through his or her senses. It is what the person saw, heard, smelled, touched, or tasted. It is the immediate experience that we all have every day of our lives.

To understand **circumstantial evidence**, we will put on our detective hats and solve the mystery of the missing slice of cake.

It is the day of Ted's spouse's birthday, and to celebrate the occasion, Ted has stretched far out of his normal culinary comfort zone and baked a cake. Not a pre-made mix simply stirred and popped in the oven, but something made from scratch. Hours go into the effort, but when it is done, no one is more surprised than Ted to see that he has created a real treat that his spouse will long remember. Satisfied, Ted retires from the kitchen to get cleaned up before dinner.

Ted returns to find that his confectionary masterpiece has been prematurely carved. A triangular hole gapes out at him where once perfectly frosted contours lay. Ted searches furiously for the culprit and settles on his two children, ages ten and eight, seated angelically at the kitchen table. Ted's eyes narrow to an angry bead. He points an accusing finger in the children's direction and demands to know who ate the cake. Both children immediately deny any involvement in the cake-consumption caper.

I invite you to stand in Ted's shoes for a moment and play the role of judge and jury in this small, but important (to Ted at least) drama by considering the direct evidence. We have testimony from not one, but two, witnesses who were in a position to observe the events. In fact, the sweet, innocent children are the only two witnesses with any direct knowledge because they were the only ones there, and they say they didn't do it.

There is reason, however, to be suspicious of this testimony. It is self-serving, meaning that the children's testimony benefits them. Just because testimony is self-serving doesn't mean it's not true—otherwise no innocent person could ever defend a charge by denying it—but it does raise questions about its accuracy.

Ted is suspicious, but the direct evidence isn't there to support a definitive conclusion. Next, let's consider the circumstantial evidence that might cast doubt on the testimony of our youthful witnesses. First, a piece of cake is missing. That is an irrefutable fact. So someone took it.

Second, while the children were the only ones in a position to see who took the cake, they were also in a position to take the cake. In other words, they had the *opportunity* to commit the crime.

Third, Ted knows that children love cake, especially his children, so they had a *motive*—a self-interested reason—to take the cake. They also have a motive to lie about taking the cake to avoid getting in trouble.

This circumstantial evidence is enough to cast suspicion on the children, but let's add one more circumstantial detail to close the case. Dark chocolate is smeared around the lips of the children's adorable faces. The children have no plausible explanation for how this unusual marker got on their faces. The residue has the same color and texture as the frosting from the chocolate cake. No objective fact (besides the children's denials) suggests a source for the chocolate other than the prematurely cut-up cake. Indeed, the only explanation consistent with a plausible story is that the frosting came from the cake. The inescapable conclusion is that the children are indeed the guilty culprits.

Ted furrows his eyebrows and wrinkles his nose. He was not present at the scene to witness directly whether or not his beloved kids ruined his cake, but he has seen and heard enough. The children are sent to their rooms without dessert—

that is, without any *more* dessert—and Ted rolls up his sleeves and sets to work baking another cake.

Circumstantial evidence is the product of logic, as opposed to the immediate experience of direct evidence. The confectionary caper pits direct evidence (the children's testimony) against circumstantial evidence (the cake frosting on their lips). Both have strengths and weaknesses.

In popular culture, circumstantial evidence is often equated with weak, maybe even fabricated evidence, but direct evidence is equally susceptible to fabrication. In the example, the testimony from the children was direct evidence, but their testimony was false. The cake frosting smeared on the children's lips was circumstantial evidence. A strong inference could be made that the frosting got on the children's faces when they ate the cake. The circumstantial evidence trumped the direct evidence.

Much of what we know about the world comes from circumstantial evidence—that is, from logical inferences that we make from other known facts. All of your friends receive an invitation to a wedding, but you don't. It's possible that your invitation got lost in the mail, but the lack of an invitation is good circumstantial evidence that the bride or groom (or both) don't want you there. A colleague asks to take a day off to watch his favorite sports team play, but his request is turned down. When he calls in sick the morning of the game, that's circumstantial evidence that he's playing hooky. Your spouse meets an old flame for lunch and together they disappear into a hotel only to emerge an hour later with mussed hair and rumpled clothes. You don't need to have been a fly on the wall to make the logical inference of what happened behind closed doors. We rarely catch people with their hands in the cookie jar, but the crumbs on their clothes are often evidence enough to form a judgment.

Despite the fact that circumstantial evidence can be every bit, if not more, convincing than direct evidence, many of us don't believe it. In one study, even after the differences between direct and circumstantial evidence were explained, only 62 percent of the study participants correctly identified whether evidence was direct or circumstantial. The most common error was to classify unreliable evidence as "circumstantial" and reliable evidence as "direct."[11]

Logic is often more reliable than testimony. In the case of the missing cake, the inference that comes from the frosting on the children's faces is much more powerful, credible, and convincing than the contradictory direct evidence of their full-throated denials. A circumstantial case, yes, but still a compelling one.

If only the children had known!

THE PROBLEM OF DECEPTION

This may come as shock because I hardly know you, but the people closest to you are liars. This may come as more of shock, but so are you. So am I. Human beings lie. All of us—and a lot more frequently than we care to admit.

Nobody likes a liar. "A classic survey," reported Megan Garber in *The Atlantic*, "asked participants to rank the general desirability of 555 different personality traits. The one that ranked at the very bottom, dead last out of 555, was 'liar.'"[12] Nevertheless, it has been estimated that typical Americans tell somewhere between two and fifty lies each day.[13]

In one research study, in a ten-minute long conversation, more than three quarters of the people told at least one lie.[14]

In another study where people were asked to keep a journal of their social interactions, people disclosed that they lied to more than one out of every three people that they had talked to.[15] We may say that we don't like lying, but we do it—a lot.

People lie for all sorts of reasons, some good, some bad. In many cases, we mean no harm by our everyday deceptions. In the right context, lies can serve useful social functions. For example, lies may be appropriate

> in social contexts, where they may prevent embarrassment, protect privacy, shield a person from prejudice, provide the sick with comfort, or preserve a child's innocence; in public contexts, where they may stop a panic or otherwise preserve calm in the face of danger; and even in technical, philosophical, and scientific contexts, where (as Socrates' methods suggest) examination of a false statement (even if made deliberately to mislead) can promote a form of thought that ultimately helps realize the truth.[16]

The range of our everyday deceptions can be much broader than most of us care to admit. Although noble justifications exist for telling less than the whole truth, we often aim our most convincing lies at ourselves. We may tell ourselves that our motives for clipping the truth are pure, but in many cases, the person we're really trying to protect is ourselves.

Other times, of course, liars act deliberately and self-consciously, with no pretense of a higher motive. They are frauds, cheats, charlatans, and shysters, peddling falsehoods to part us from our money or to shield themselves from the consequences of their own actions. They trick others for personal profit.

But not all of these tricksters are wicked devils. The *Harvard Crimson* surveyed the incoming class of 2017, and ten percent admitted to cheating on an exam. Forty-two percent admitted to cheating on a homework assignment.[17] These Harvard students are not alone. "According to the behavioral economist Dan Ariely, the author of *The (Honest) Truth About Dishonesty: How We Lie to Everyone–Especially Ourselves,* 'Everybody has the capacity to be dishonest, and almost everybody cheats'–but 'just by a little.'"[18] Like the famous Pogo comic strip, when it comes to lies, we have met the enemy, and he is us.[19]

With lying being so common, and each of us having more than a little experience with the act, it is tempting to think that we would be pretty good at figuring out when people were telling the truth and when they were lying. That would be wrong. Wildly wrong, if we believe the social psychologists who study lying for a living.

One professor of psychology and a team of researchers tested 13,000 people to measure how good they were at spotting lies. Out of 13,000 people, how many scored well at lie detection? Only 31 people. That's only two out of a thousand.[20] If your car only started once out of every 500 tries, you probably would be taking the bus to work every day.

Detecting a lie can be difficult because good liars are often the most convincing people. They possess qualities that tend to take us in. They're manipulative, excellent actors, expressive, and often physically attractive. They're eloquent, intelligent, and quick to detect and address suspicion.[21] As Jean Giraudoux quipped, "The secret of success is sincerity. Once you can fake that you've got it made."[22]

Not only are liars good at lying, collectively we are pretty bad at spotting lies. In one study, 2,000 people from over 60 countries were asked what they look for to tell if someone was lying. Most people answered, "Liars won't look you in the eye."[23] Despite this widespread vote of confidence, so-called gaze aversion "is not a reliable way to spot lying behavior."[24] Researchers have not found any significant correlation between eye movements and lying or truth telling.[25]

In fact, despite decades of scientific research into lie detection, research has found that "not a single nonverbal, verbal, or physiological response is uniquely associated with deception."[26]

Upon reflection, it is perhaps not so surprising that we are not particularly good at spotting lies. If you could tell people were lying just by looking at them, lying would die out. People don't mind lying, but they don't want to be known as liars. Lies only work because they are hard to catch.

Because deception comes naturally and all of us are practiced in its art, filtering truth from lies is a significant obstacle to knowing what really happened. In legal disputes where people are driven by self-interest, deceptions large and small are pervasive.

In situations where a person has a lot to gain by lying, most people are instinctively on guard against deception. Paid advocates, like marketers, salesmen, and lawyers, are commonly regarded with suspicion.

This caution is helpful because it offers some protection against being taken in by the unscrupulous and untrustworthy. At the same time, when we are on the other side of the equation and are the ones trying to convince others, that cautious attitude can make it difficult to convince a skeptical audience that we are telling the truth. We are wise to discount other people's protestations of innocence, but when we're the ones accused, you can be sure that other people discount our own protestations exactly the same way.

In a dispute, both sides have an interest in having their particular version of the truth believed. Both sides have a motive to lie. Both sides want to convince whoever is making a decision that they are telling the truth, but decision-makers are not very good at distinguishing between liars and truth tellers.

The dilemma for the legal mind then is this: either side in a dispute could be lying. It's entirely possible that both sides are lying. There is no reliable way to tell the difference between truth and lies just by looking at someone. Yet a dispute requires a resolution. There must be a winner and a loser.

The problem of deception is a thorny one, but as we shall see in the next section, an even greater challenge to knowing the past lurks in the recesses of our minds.

THE PROBLEM OF FORGETTING

Jorge Luis Borges, an Argentinian writer from the middle of the twentieth century, wrote a short story called "Funes, the Memorious" about a young man whose infallible memory was so prodigious that every detail of every event was perfectly preserved in his mind. If Funes were to tell you everything that happened to him the previous day, it would take an entire day or more. Every detail of every thought, perception, or sensation that coursed through his body etched itself permanently in his mind.

Funes's memory was a miracle, and yet his fantastic recall did not empower him to do great things. It paralyzed him. While Funes could recall everything, he was unable to think. As Borges put it in the story, "To think is to forget differences, generalize, make abstractions. In the teeming world of Funes, there were only details."[27]

Funes's tragedy of remembering is a reminder that we forget much more than we remember, and that's not always a bad thing. Our capacity to forget is a strength. It allows us to focus on the moment, to distance ourselves from painful or irrelevant events, to distill the important from the trivial, to find patterns, to understand concepts, to see the forest and not just an unending collection of trees. Yet, we often forget our own forgetting and believe that we, and those around us, remember far more than we really do. So complete is our forgetting of our own forgetting that sometimes we cannot distinguish between memories that are real and those that are merely imagined.

On January 28, 1986, at 11:37 a.m. the space shuttle *Challenger* sat on a launch pad in central Florida poised to make history. On board the space craft, in addition to the usual complement of astronauts who had been journeying into space for the previous quarter century, was Sharon Christa McAuliffe, a woman who was to be the first schoolteacher to fly in space. McAuliffe had been selected for the mission from among more than 11,000 educators who had applied for the honor. After a year of intensive training by the National Aeronautics and Space Administration (NASA), McAuliffe was strapped into the shuttle, alongside six crewmates, waiting for her chance to make space-age history.

Seventy-three seconds into the flight, the O-ring seal in the right solid rocket booster failed. The broken seal allowed pressurized hot gas from within the solid rocket motor to compromise the external fuel tank. The solid rocket booster pulled away from the spacecraft, obliterating it. By 11:40 a.m., less than three minutes after takeoff, *Challenger* had fallen from the sky and was swallowed by the sea. All seven members of the crew died instantly. Millions of Americans of all ages, including schoolchildren, watched the disaster unfold on live television with horror.

The day after the *Challenger* accident, with memories of the tragedy still fresh on the country's collective mind, an enterprising researcher at Emory University named Ulric Neisser seized the moment by asking a group of university undergraduates to write a description of how they heard about the disaster, things like where they were, what time of day it was, what they were doing, thinking, feeling, etc. Then, he waited.

Two and a half years later, Professor Neisser approached these same students and asked them the same questions about how they had heard about the *Challenger* disaster. His results were shocking.

First, a quarter of the accounts were "strikingly different from their original journal entries."[28] More than half had errors in their recollection, and only a mere 10 percent had all the details correct. The failure of memory only 30 months later for an event as vivid and gripping as the *Challenger* disaster was a stunning demonstration of the unreliability of even our most deeply felt memories.

But that was not all Professor Neisser found. Most of the people in the study were confident that their recent recollections of the event were more accurate than the account they themselves had recorded two and a half years earlier, one day after the tragedy. Even after Professor Neisser showed the study participants how they had changed their stories, several refused to admit that they had made a mistake and insisted that their current memory was the correct one. "A couple of these subjects," Professor Neisser reported, "were so confident about the accuracy of their current recollections that, in order to discredit their [own] responses to the questionnaires, they argued that people sometimes misreport events at first!"[29] Forgetting is bad, but thinking that fabricated memories are real is indisputably chilling.

The upshot of this research is that "however much people think they are remembering actual events, they are really remembering memories—and probably memories of memories. The mind, [Professor Neisser] said, conflates things."[30] It is troubling enough to think that much of what we remember may only be an imperfect, and potentially highly inaccurate, reconstruction of events as they actually happened. "The process of calling [a memory] into conscious awareness," observes Elizabeth Loftus, one of the country's leading experts on memory and its failings, "can change it, and now you're storing something that's different."[31] It is even more troubling to think that most of us, most of the time, have no idea that this reconstruction is happening. In fact, the majority of people don't believe that it happens at all.

To see how difficult remembering can be, examine the following list of words: *bed, rest, awake, tired, dream, wake, snooze, blanket, doze, slumber, snore, nap, peace, yawn, drowsy.*[32] Take your time to make sure you have looked at every word and convince yourself that there are no tricks or traps. When you're finished, read on.

Memory studies have shown that most people have trouble remembering more than seven or eight things in their short-term memories (sometimes called "working memory").[33] Even this limited amount of information typically doesn't last long. Some studies have suggested that memories start fading in as few as thirty seconds, or fewer.[34] As someone who forgets telephone numbers and names only a moment after I hear them, I have no doubt that fast forgetting is an all-too-real phenomenon

Most people, however, think that their memories are great. One study found that fully 77 percent of people believed that the phrase "I have an excellent memory" applied very or fairly well to them.[35] According to another survey, almost half of the respondents believed "once you have experienced an event and formed a memory of it, that memory doesn't change."[36] Almost two-thirds of the people believed that "human memory works like a video camera, accurately recording the events we see and hear so that we can review and inspect them later."[37] In general, we are pretty confident in our memories.

Yet this confidence flies in the face of common experiences when our memories fail us. Who hasn't spent frustrating minutes (or hours) looking for misplaced keys? We've all been there; the keys were in your hands at some point and at some point you put them somewhere, and yet your memory of your own actions can sometimes be a complete and utter blank. The lost-and-founds of museums and parks and schools throughout the world are a testament to how easily things slip our minds. In one sense, we all know this. Yet in another, we don't really believe it.

A failure of memory is often met with skepticism, especially if the event in question turns out, with the benefit of hindsight, to have been significant. But is this skepticism misplaced? Let's test ourselves. Without looking, try to recall as many of the words in the list that you read a few paragraphs back. I encourage you to write down the words that you can remember. Take your time, but don't cheat. I'll wait.

If you are like most people, you will have remembered fewer than half of the words on the list. (If you remembered them all, you might want to consider signing up for the U.S.

Memory Championship.)[38] What happened? Perception does not seem to be the root of the problem. The lighting was good. Your view of the words was unobstructed. There was no time pressure and no particular stress to distract you. Assuming you're reading this section in one sitting, no more than a couple of minutes at most passed between the time you read the list and your attempt to recall it. Remembering is much harder than it seems.

For most people, the frailty and fallibility of memory can be quite surprising, but if our memories are failing us every moment of every day with every recollection that we try to dredge from the recesses of our minds, it is more surprising that collectively we tend not to be more aware of the limits of our recall. One reason that we rarely notice the errors of our memories is that we rarely receive direct feedback on whether our memories are right or wrong. Outside of tests and quizzes in school, very few of our memories are subjected to rigorous scrutiny. But when facts matter, as they do in the legal system, vigorous challenges of memory are the norm.

Before we move on, take a second look at the words you wrote down when you attempted to recall the original list of words. (Or try to remember what you remembered, but by this point, you already know how prone to error that would be.) Does your recalled list contain the word "sleep"? There is a good chance that it does. About 40 percent of people who have done this exercise put the word "sleep" on their remembered lists. But wait, was the word "sleep" on the list? How sure are you (without going back to double-check)? Are you sure enough to send a person to jail if her guilt or innocence turned on the certainty of your recollection?

As it happens, "sleep" was not among the words on the list. It is one thing to forget what was on a list. At some level, we all know that details can be hard to remember. It is quite another thing to insert something onto a list that was never there in the first place. This is not merely a mundane forgetting of a small detail, but the manufacturing of something that did not exist. Forgetting did not just lead to a straightforward failure to recall, but to the creation of a memory of something that never happened. This is scary and sobering stuff.

If you had "sleep" on your list, don't feel bad. The list is filled with words associated with sleep. It is more than fair to categorize the list in your memory under the general heading of "sleep" and in that way improve your ability to recall (or guess) the words that were actually on the list. At the same time, in recalling words associated with a broad category like sleep, the mind often inserts something that was not there, but that logically makes sense. Guessing is useful in everyday life because you will likely be right much more than you are wrong, but we like to think of our memories as something more solid than high-probability guesswork.

Even if we acknowledge that our memories are imperfect, we like to think that at least we remember the most important things. If an event is particularly impactful, memory research shows that while we are more likely to have a vivid picture of the event in our minds, overall our memories are still highly unreliable. Following in the footsteps of the Challenger study, researchers J.M. Talarico and D.C. Rubin examined people's recollections of the extremely emotional events of September 11, 2001, when terrorists hijacked airplanes and crashed them into the World Trade Center and the Pentagon, killing thousands and catapulting the United States into a global war on terror.[39] The researchers found that the emotional power of that terrible day caused people to have more vivid and detailed recollections, but these highly developed memories were no more accurate than any other memories.

What's worse, even though people's memories of the events were uneven at best, the strong emotions that they felt that day made them feel more certain that their memories were correct, even though their confidence was misplaced. Our intuition that vivid events create vivid memories is right. Our intuition that vivid memories are highly likely to be true and accurate is wrong.

All of this discussion is not to say no one ever remembers anything. That's obviously not the case. The point is that memory does not work the way most of us think it works. Memory is not simply a replay of a video stored perfectly and pristinely in the mind. In many cases our brains record only the gist of an experience rather than the specific details. Our heads are filled, writes author John Medina, "with generalized pictures of concepts or events, not with slowly fading minutiae."[40]

The reason for this extended discussion is that we don't believe our memories are as fallible as they are or that memory works in the strange way that it does. Even in classrooms, where people are paying money to learn, forgetting is shockingly common and fast. Most people forget 90 percent of what they learn in a class within 30 days, and the majority of this forgetting occurs within a few hours after class ends.[41] (I hope at least some of the lessons of this book will last longer!)

Thus, the problem of forgetting has two parts. First, a person may sincerely have no recollection of an event, even if we expect them to remember. Second, a person may confidently believe he or she recalls the event, but the memory is incorrectly reconstructed. The first case is problematic because it forces us to turn to alternate sources to figure out the truth. The second case is positively pernicious because the misleading information—though honestly given—actively moves us away from the truth.

This second problem—thinking we are remembering when in fact we're piecing together the past from general memories and educated guesses—has altered how scientists think about how the human mind works. Daniel Gilbert, in his book *Stumbling on Happiness*, summarized the research this way.

> The general finding—that information acquired after an event alters memory of the event—has been replicated so many times in so many different laboratory and field settings that it has left most scientists convinced of two things. First, the act of remembering involves 'filling in' details that were not actually stored; and second, we generally cannot tell when we are doing this because filling in happens quickly and unconsciously.[42]

This forgetting about forgetting has important consequences for the legal mind. If a person says that they do not remember the details of an event, it is plausible that they have indeed forgotten. There is no reliable way to know whether they are feigning ignorance or whether the memories have truly slipped away. This uncertainty should give us pause before judging people who say they have forgotten details that later turn out to be important to resolving a dispute.

In a dispute, a single moment in time can be so important that to someone considering the case the moment can seem to occupy the whole world to the parties involved, when in reality it is just another moment in a sea of moments whose significance was underestimated until after the memory of the event had long since faded.

At the same time, if someone professes to have a sharp recollection, even if the person has no reason to lie, caution is still very much in order. In many cases, the firmness of memory is just a trick of the mind.

Without some external way to check the accuracy of memory, a person's uncorroborated recollection is a shaky foundation upon which to build a case.

THE PROBLEM OF PERCEPTION

The American songwriter Paul Simon once wrote, "A man hears what he wants to hear and disregards the rest."[43] A variation of this observation might be: a woman kisses whomever she wants to kiss and disregards the rest.

A group of young women were brought into a television studio to film a commercial for a new lip balm. The angle for the ad campaign was that the new lip balm would be the most kissable on the market. To prove the point, two handsome male models sat on raised stools, separated by a small table. One had the new balm on his lips, the other the competitor's brand. The women were asked if they would mind kissing the two models to see which lip balm was more kissable. Giddy with the idea of kissing these wildly attractive men, the young women happily agreed.

To make the test fair, the women were blindfolded so they wouldn't know whether the model they were kissing had the new lip balm or the competitor's. When the blindfolds were secured, the two male models silently slipped off the stools and crept offstage. A trainer emerged from backstage with two chimpanzees in tow. The chimps climbed onto the stools and puckered up.

The blindfolded women were led up to the stools and were asked to kiss the models. Without hesitation, they leaned in—and kissed the chimps. Not just small pecks, but full-on, lip-smacking kisses. To complete the prank, while the women were in mid-kiss, the producers of the television show stripped off the blindfolds. The women opened their eyes and leapt back in shock, horror, and dismay. They had no idea that they were kissing chimpanzees instead of supermodels. A triumph of the mind over the senses.[44]

Our senses are our windows into the world, but they are not always as reliable as we imagine. We do not see what we think we see. It's a physiological fact.

Sight is produced from light hitting over 125 million receptors on the retina at the back of the eye. The two main types of light receptors are rods and cones. Rods mostly process dim light, capturing images in black and white. Cones work in bright light and help us perceive color.[45] But part of the retina lacks light-sensitive receptors. In one spot (called the optic disc) nerves connect the eye to the brain so that the images captured in the eye can be processed in the brain.

What this means is that every time we look at something, there is a hole in the picture that we literally cannot see because there are no light receptors in that part of our eyes. This gap in our ability to see the world is called the blind spot.[46] Everyone has one—two, actually, one in each eye. Yet, we don't walk around seeing a darkened patch of emptiness every time we open our eyes. What's happening?

The mind is a beautiful and supple thing. It is always working, burning energy at a fast and furious pace. In the average adult, the brain represents approximately 2 percent of the total body weight but accounts for 20 percent of all the energy consumed.[47] Much of that energy is being used to process visual images from the eyes. According to some estimates, 90 to 95 percent of all information received in our brains courses through the visual pathways.[48] With our brains' heavy reliance on sight, it is no surprise that phrases like "seeing is believing" are ingrained in our cultural language.

Our eyes are never still. They constantly flicker and flit, capturing light from many different directions simultaneously. The brain stitches these images together instantaneously, or at least fast enough that the conscious parts of our brains don't notice. The images we see are composites, formed from all of our many unconscious, rapid eye movements. Our minds fill in missing information from our blind spots perfectly.

Despite the amazing work of our brains in piecing together light into coherent images, our eyes regularly deceive us. Optical illusions delight in showing off the eye's mistakes. Yet the errors of the eye are not merely the products of misfires in our rods and cones.

Of the neural pathways that lead to the visual centers of our brains, only 20 percent come from our eyes. The other 80 percent come from where we store our memories.[49] Seeing is more than registering stimulation from waves of light. Seeing requires processing, recognizing, categorizing, understanding, comparing, predicting, and reacting.

The eyes provide an image, but in the words of the Enlightenment philosopher John Locke, "the mind furnishes the understanding with ideas of its own operations."[50] Putting the same point in more contemporary terms, "[t]hough seeing and hearing and touch seem simple and direct, they are not. They are fallible inferences based on knowledge and assumptions which may not be appropriate to the situation...Perceptions are 90 percent or more stored knowledge."[51]

To know that a flutter of motion is a bird swooping through tree branches requires more than just perceiving one shape moving through another shape. It requires knowing and remembering about birds and wings, branches and leaves, their differences and their connections. That additional information comes from our minds and memories, not from our eyes.

Even experts are vulnerable to mind and memory dominating perception. In 2001, researcher Frédéric Brochet brought together 54 wine experts for a wine tasting. The experts were asked to compare two different wines, one red and one white. The experts described the red wine with traditional terms associated with red wines, words like "jammy." What the experts did not know was that the two ostensibly different wines were exactly the same. They were both white wines, with one dyed red. The experts were tricked by their eyes. They saw a red wine, and so they described a red wine, even though it was really white. Their expectations about what a red wine should taste like were so strong that they ignored everything else.[52]

The physiology of the eye demonstrates that seeing is not as simple as it seems. One critical issue in collecting proof of any fact is always whether the information provided was properly perceived in the first place.

Perception is an issue with any testimony about what someone saw or heard. Where was a person relative to the event? Did he or she have a good and clear vantage from which to see or hear? Were there distractions, stress, or other things that could impair perception? The classic example is the eyewitness who wasn't wearing his glasses, but even with perfect eyesight, our vision is more limited than we often think.

In one experiment, researchers Geoffrey Loftus of the University of Washington and Erin Harley of the University of California, Los Angeles, asked people to identify pictures of famous celebrities at different distances. They found that the eye could make a reliable identification up to about 25 feet, but then the ability to discern faces begins to degrade. At 110 feet, the reliability of people's identifications was essentially zero.[53] In other words, in less distance than it takes to make a first down in football, our ability to perceive faces and details begins to decline, entirely disappearing long before we're anywhere near the end zone.

The problem of perception can skew any witness's testimony, but nowhere is it more prevalent and more dangerous than in the criminal justice system when a person stands accused of a crime solely on the strength—or weakness—of uncorroborated, eyewitness testimony.

THE PROBLEM OF EYEWITNESS TESTIMONY

On February 12, 1998, just before 4:00 p.m. in the afternoon, Arthur Carmona, a sixteen-year old Hispanic boy from a poor neighborhood in Orange County, California, was riding his bicycle to a friend's house without a helmet, when he spotted a police car nearby.[54] A few months earlier, Arthur had gotten a ticket for not wearing a helmet, so he ducked down a side street, stashed his bicycle, and continued to his friend's house on foot. Moments later, he was swarmed by police officers with guns drawn, barking orders to freeze and keep his hands where they could see them.

Arthur was stunned. He could not believe that not wearing a helmet could possibly generate a police reaction like this, but his nightmare was just beginning. Unbeknownst to Arthur, approximately twenty minutes earlier, at around 3:30 p.m., a man wearing a black Lakers cap and brandishing a gun had burst into a local juice bar and demanded that the cashier fill a backpack with money from the cash register while he held the customers at gunpoint. The cashier complied, and moments later, the robber fled with $340 in cash, jumped into a truck waiting outside, and sped off. The police were called, and a massive manhunt ensued.

The getaway driver was quickly found. An alert bystander had taken down the truck's license plate number. Within the hour the police raided the getaway driver's apartment. They captured the driver and found a gun, a Lakers cap, and a backpack full of money.

Tracking the gunman was trickier. Different reports had the gunman jumping out of the truck at various locations. The description was extremely sketchy: Hispanic male, between 20 and 30 years old, between 5'5" and 6', wearing jeans and a black Lakers cap. Arthur was Hispanic, wearing jeans, and between 5'5" and 6' tall, but so are a lot of people in Southern California, and that's where the similarities ended. Arthur was 16, not 20 to 30. He didn't have a Lakers cap, a gun, or a backpack full of money, and he was found nowhere near the vicinity of the crime. Nevertheless, a partial fit with a vague description was enough to make Arthur the prime suspect for the police.

The police brought two clerks and a customer from the juice bar to see if they could make a positive identification. There was no line-up. The only suspect offered by the police was Arthur. Still, the witnesses hesitated. They just weren't sure. The officers on the scene called for the black Lakers baseball cap that had been seized from the getaway driver's apartment. The police put the cap on Arthur's head, and the witnesses, seeing the cap that they had seen before, pointed at the hat and declared that Arthur was the gunman.

Arthur was charged with armed robbery. On the strength of the dubious eyewitness identifications, Arthur was convicted and, because he had turned sixteen just days before the juice bar robbery, he was tried as an adult and sentenced to twelve years in state prison. For two and a half years, Arthur languished in jail, until attorneys from the international law firm of Sidley Austin filed a massive 350-page brief demonstrating that Arthur had been wrongfully convicted by sloppy police work and doubtful eyewitnesses who recanted their identifications when they learned the full story of Arthur's arrest.

The case was scheduled for a hearing to determine whether Arhtur had truly received a fair trial. The morning of the hearing, rather than try to explain to a judge why Arthur should stay in jail based on flimsy and dubiously procured evidence, the District Attorney agreed to let Arthur go. Arthur Carmona walked out of prison a free man and added his name to the list of people wrongfully convicted based on erroneous eyewitness testimony.

While we should celebrate the legal system for correcting a grievous error in the case of Arthur Carmona, we have to ask how the judge and jury could have gone so wrong. Cases like Arthur's are frighteningly common.[55] In the United States, estimates put the number of innocent people convicted of crimes that they did not commit at between 25,000 to 50,000 people *every year*.[56] Erroneous eyewitness identifications play a large role in producing that number.

Eyewitness identification requires three distinct acts.[57] First, the witness must accurately perceive the event. Psychologists call this the "encoding" or "acquisition" stage.

Second, the witness must retain what he or she perceived. Finally, the witness has to recall the original perception. This is called the "retrieval" stage. An error at any one of these three stages (encoding, retention, and retrieval) will mean that the identification is probably not right.

We rely on sight above all other senses, so it is little surprise that when someone says they saw something with their own eyes, we are inclined to believe them. In a criminal trial, one of the most dramatic moments that can take place is when a prosecutor asks a witness if she sees the perpetrator of the crime in the courtroom. The witness will straighten herself in her seat, fix a steely stare at the defendant, raise a condemning finger, and declaim, "That's him. That's who did it. I saw him with my own eyes, and I will never, ever forget his horrible face."

The strength of such testimony is devastating to any claim of innocence. According to researchers, "mistaken eyewitnesses account for more convictions of innocent persons than all others combined."[58] Numerous studies have found that jurors routinely overestimate the accuracy of eyewitness identifications.[59] The power of the eyewitness's condemnation comes from our collective confidence that we can trust our eyes to tell us what we see and our memories to recall those images upon demand.

Our confidence in the power of vision, however, is misplaced. In 1997, two Harvard psychologists, Dan Simon and Christopher Chabris, conducted what has become one of the most famous experiments in human perception of all time.[60] The researchers videotaped two teams of actors simultaneously passing basketballs back and forth. One team was dressed all in white. The other team was dressed all in black. The video was less than a minute long. The researchers asked people to count the number of passes made by the white team, without counting any passes made by the black team. The researchers then asked people to report how many passes they had counted. Seems simple, right? Mostly it was, except the experiment wasn't really about counting passes.

About 30 seconds into the video, a female actor dressed in a full-body gorilla suit walked into the middle of the basketball players, stopped at the center of the action, faced the camera, thumped her chest, and then walked out of the picture. In all, the gorilla-suited actor was on screen for about eight seconds, more than ten percent of the total length of the video.

The people counting the passes were asked if they had noticed anything unusual about the video. How many people saw the gorilla? 80 percent? 90 percent? 100 percent? (It was a gorilla in the middle of a basketball court, after all.) Shockingly, only about 50 percent of the people saw the gorilla. The other 50 percent hadn't noticed it at all.

When the researchers played the video a second time, some of the people were so surprised by their own failure to see what was right in front of their eyes that they accused the researchers of switching the videos to trick them. Not only had half the people not seen what, in retrospect, seems obvious and unmistakable, many of these same people refused to accept the fact that they had made a mistake even when presented with incontrovertible proof.

If people have trouble noticing the unexpected when counting basketball passes in a safe, secure, unpressured laboratory environment, imagine how much more difficult it is to make accurate observations when the stakes and tensions are much higher. Rather than admit that their perceptions and memories are simply not clear enough to make a positive identification, people will just take a guess.

In one study, 350 people were shown a grainy surveillance video of an armed robbery that ended with a security guard being shot and killed. They were then shown either a lineup or photographs of possible perpetrators and were asked to identify the robber. Every single person—all 350 of them—picked someone from the lineup or the photographs. By now, you can guess the trick. The gunman wasn't in any of them.[61] That's 350 eyewitness identifications—and all of them wrong. Think about what might happen if the photo that had been picked were yours!

In another study, people were presented with various crime scenarios taken from prior empirical studies and were asked to predict the accuracy of the eyewitness identifications in those earlier studies. Nearly 84 percent of the people overestimated the accuracy of the eyewitnesses. The people were not just off base. They were way off base. On average, the people estimated that the eyewitnesses had picked the right person 71 percent of the time. In fact, the eyewitnesses were right only 12.5 percent of the time. Seven out of eight times, the eyewitnesses had gotten the identification wrong, even though the vast majority of people figured that they had gotten it right.[62]

Errors are worrisome. The fact that we don't even recognize our own errors, even when they have been pointed out, is downright terrifying. When deciding whether to believe an eyewitness identification, studies have shown that jurors pay the greatest attention to the witness's degree of confidence.[63] Yet, as we've seen, people frequently believe that they are right when they are wrong. Confidence is a poor predictor of accuracy.[64]

Few people know this better than Jennifer Thompson-Cannino and Ronald Cotton.[65] In 1984, Jennifer was a 22-

year old college student at home alone when a man entered her apartment. The intruder told her that he was there to rape her, and if she cooperated, she wouldn't be hurt. Jennifer screamed.

A knife was suddenly at her throat. The man was on top of her, pushing her down, and pinning her arms above her head. "Shut up or I'll cut you," he yelled. And then he raped her.

Throughout the ordeal, Jennifer focused on her assailant's face, determined to memorize his every feature so that he could be brought to justice for the heinous crime he was committing.

A few days later, Jennifer was at the police station looking through photographs when she saw the face of her rapist. It was Ronald Cotton. A few days after that, Jennifer picked Ronald again, this time out of a line-up.

There was no doubt in Jennifer's mind. They had caught the right man. "I was absolutely, positively, without-a-doubt certain he was the man who raped me when I got on that witness stand and testified against him," Thompson later recalled. "And nobody was going to tell me any different."[66]

In 1985, Ronald Cotton was convicted for the rape and spent the next eleven years of his life in jail. Ronald always maintained his innocence, and in 1996, DNA evidence conclusively demonstrated that he was not the man who had raped Jennifer.

No one was more surprised than Jennifer Thompson. She had done everything right. She had concentrated on studying her attacker's face. She had picked his picture out of an array of photographs, and again out of a line-up, and a third time at a trial in front of a judge and jury. She was absolutely certain.

But she was also wrong. Nevertheless, the strength of her confidence convinced a jury to convict Ronald Cotton of a crime he did not commit.

Other problems with eyewitness identification abound. For example, numerous studies have shown that most people have trouble identifying people from other races, with one study finding that "the chance of a mistaken identification is 1.56 times greater in other-race than in same-race conditions."[67] Witnesses are also easily swayed by suggestion from seemingly authoritative sources like prosecutors or the police or other witnesses.[68]

The Supreme Court has acknowledged the many causes of mistaken eyewitness identifications.

> External suggestion is hardly the only factor that casts doubt on the trustworthiness of an eyewitness's testimony ... many other factors bear on "the likelihood of misidentification"— for example the passage of time between exposure to and identification of the defendant, whether the witness was under stress when he first encountered the suspect, how much time the witness had to observe the suspect, how far the witness was from the suspect, whether the suspect carried a weapon, and the race of the suspect and the witness.[69]

Nevertheless, despite the dubious reliability of many eyewitnesses, for the most part, the legal system relies on traditional safeguards to guard against convicting the innocent. These safeguards are things like the right to confront and cross-examine witnesses, the right to assistance from an attorney (in criminal cases), instructions to the jury cautioning about the potential unreliability of eyewitnesses (in some jurisdictions), the right to present expert witnesses on the dangers of eyewitness testimony, and in criminal cases, the requirement that guilt be proven beyond a reasonable doubt.[70]

Seeing may be believing, but belief and truth are not always the same thing. As Oliver Wendell Holmes Jr. put it, "Certitude is not the test of certainty. We have been cocksure of many things that were not so."[71] Guarding against human errors, especially errors in eyewitness testimony, is one of the greatest challenges for the legal system.

THE PROBLEM OF FALLACIES

"To err is human," wrote Alexander Pope three hundred years ago, and modern cognitive psychology and behavioral economics have demonstrated this in spades.[72] While we like to think of ourselves as rational, logical beings, making reasoned decisions based on facts, evidence, and common sense, social scientists have catalogued a dizzying array of mental errors and judgmental biases that distort how we make up our minds.

The problem of proof is not limited to ferreting out lies, fighting forgetting, or battling the limits of perception. Proof must also contend with biases and fallacies that lead us to jump to conclusions that seem reasonable but are quite often wrong.

The Rooster that Called Out the Sun

Linus Pauling was one of the most important scientists of the twentieth century. Pauling's discoveries in chemistry and biochemistry won him the Nobel Prize in Chemistry in 1954. He was also a devout pacifist, and his advocacy against war eight years later won him another Nobel Prize, this time in Peace, making Pauling one of only four people in history to win two Nobel Prizes. Scientific luminary Francis Crick, one of the discoverers of the structure of DNA, recognized Pauling as the "father of molecular biology."[73] And Linus Pauling really liked orange juice.

In the 1960s, Pauling began taking three grams of vitamin C every day to prevent colds, and every day he didn't get sick he became more convinced that vitamin C was a wonder drug. In 1970, he published a book called *Vitamin C and the Common Cold*. In 1971, Pauling began a collaboration with a cancer researcher to prescribe vitamin C as a therapy for cancer patients, claiming that cancer patients who took vitamin C had a survival rate four times as great as patients who didn't. Regrettably, later research refuted Pauling's claims that vitamin C was a cure-all. The prestigious Mayo Clinic conducted a clinical trial and found that vitamin C was no better than a placebo in making people healthy, and eventually the medical establishment dismissed Pauling's claims as just another example of medical quackery.[74]

Linus Pauling was one of the most brilliant scientific minds in modern times, but it seems that he fell victim to a fallacy as old as logic itself. He took vitamin C and didn't get sick. When he did get sick, he took vitamin C and got better. It was only a short jump to conclude that taking vitamin C fends off illness when you're well and cures you when you're not.

The Latin name for this logical fallacy is *post hoc, ergo propter hoc*. Literally translated, the words mean "after this, therefore because of this." The error arises whenever we think something is caused by something else merely because the something else happened first. If you have ever known someone who wears a lucky pair of socks or rubs a charm for luck because once, after he or she wore those socks or rubbed that charm, good things followed, you've seen the *post hoc, ergo propter hoc* fallacy in action.

In its baldest form, the fallacy is easy to spot and poke fun at. A rooster crows at the break of dawn. Therefore, because one followed the other, the logic (or rather the illogic) would be, the sun rose *because* the rooster crowed simply because one followed the other. Without the intrepid rooster's daily intervention, the world would be doomed to darkness.

The *post hoc, ergo propter hoc* fallacy is at the root of superstitions of all kinds. Broken mirrors and black cats owe their bad reputations to misfortunes that followed close on their heels. In the *post hoc, ergo propter hoc* world there are no coincidences.

The *post hoc, ergo propter hoc* fallacy is powerful and persistent because true causes necessarily precede their true effects, so chronological sequence definitely matters. Only things that come earlier in time can be the causes of things that come later. The bleeding from a bloody nose could not possibly have caused the punch because the punch came first. Nevertheless, just because something happens earlier in time does not mean that it caused whatever happens to have come later.

Politicians love the *post hoc ergo, propter hoc* fallacy. In 1994, President Bill Clinton convinced Congress to enact a Community Oriented Policing Services program (with the well-conceived acronym COPS). Under the COPS program, the federal government would pay to put 100,000 new police officers on the streets of cities across the country.

By the time President Clinton left office in January 2001, the overall national crime rate declined for eight consecutive years and stood at the lowest level since 1973. President Clinton delighted in taking credit for this by attributing the reduction in crime to his COPS program.[75] The conclusion President Clinton wanted the public to draw was that, by putting extra police officers on the streets, his COPS program *caused* the drop in crime that took place in the 1990s. Without more information, however, that suggestion was just an appeal to the *post hoc, ergo propter hoc* fallacy. The COPS program happened. Crime fell. Therefore, the COPS program caused crime to fall. But did it?

Post hoc, ergo propter hoc thinking ignores all the other things that came before. The fallacy lies in not considering the possibility that one of these many other events might be the true cause.

In the case of the COPS program, in 2005, the federal Government Accountability Office (GAO) reviewed the impact that the additional police officers from the COPS program had on reducing crime rates. The GAO concluded that, while the extra police officers helped, they helped only a little. Between 1993 and 2000, the overall crime rate fell by 26 percent. According to the GAO, the COPS program was responsible for only 1.3 percentage points of that decline, an overall impact of about 5 percent.[76] Not bad, but not the kind of numbers that allows politicians to take significant credit.

What accounted for the rest of the change in the crime rate? The GAO identified the following as contributors: "federal law enforcement expenditures other than COPS grants, local economic conditions and changes in population composition, and changes in state-level policies and practices that could be correlated with crime, such as incarceration and sentencing policy."[77] While any reduction in crime is a good thing, as the GAO study shows, just because crime fell after the COPS program went into effect doesn't mean that the one is necessarily the cause of the other (or at least not the sole cause, or even in this case, the main cause).

The suggestive power of a sequence of events plays a large role in the legal system. Over and over, two events are put together in sequence, with the subtle or not-so-subtle suggestion that the one that came first was the cause of the one that came later.

Take, for example, a typical claim of whistleblower retaliation. Under standard whistleblower retaliation laws, a person who makes a good faith report that someone else in his or her organization is breaking the law is legally protected from being fired because he or she made the report. Then this happens: Suzanne works as an executive assistant for the company's chief financial officer (CFO). The CFO and Suzanne have had a rocky relationship for some time. The CFO thinks Suzanne's work is sloppy and frequently makes her stay late to fix reports that Suzanne has prepared. For her part, Suzanne thinks the CFO is unreasonably demanding and uncaring about her life outside of work.

One day, Suzanne reports to the company's internal audit team that she thinks the CFO is embezzling money. The auditors review the books and determine that Suzanne has misinterpreted the company's ledgers, and the CFO is cleared of all charges. One month later, the CFO fires Suzanne. Suzanne brings a lawsuit and claims that she was illegally fired because she blew the whistle on her boss. You're the jury. Did the CFO break the law by illegally retaliating against Suzanne when he fired her?

In this very common scenario, the power of the sequence is almost irresistible. Suzanne blew the whistle on her boss. One month later, her boss fired her. Case closed. Right? Maybe, but not necessarily. Those aren't the only two events that happened in this story. A different telling of the same events might go something like: Suzanne turned in reports that were substandard and had to be re-done. One month later, she was fired. Is the case still closed?

Both events—the whistleblowing and the preparing of poor reports—occurred before Suzanne was fired. Which one was the true cause? And as we think about that question, we should also consider the possibilities that both were partial causes or that neither is the true cause and something else happened which we don't know about that caused Suzanne to lose her job.

As a matter of logic, timing alone does not answer the question of whether one thing caused another. Correlation is not causation, as many have observed.[78] Nevertheless, the appeal of the *post hoc, ergo propter hoc* fallacy is strong. Being able to leverage its power is a significant advantage in a dispute and countering its pull an equally significant challenge.

Predicting the Future After It Has Already Happened

In the fall of 1968, Prosenjit Poddar, a graduate student at the University of California, Berkeley, started taking a folk dancing class to meet new people. There he met Tatiana Tarasoff, a good-looking young woman with long, dark hair and an engaging smile. Poddar immediately took a fancy to Tarasoff. They saw each other regularly at the dancing class, struck up a friendship, and on New Year's Eve, they briefly kissed.

Poddar was excited at this budding romance, but when he let Tarasoff know how he felt about her, she told him that she was very sorry, but she just wasn't interested. Poddar was devastated. Over time, he grew angry and resentful. He neglected his studies and his health. He began to stalk her and brood over the possibility of revenge.

In the summer of 1969, Poddar began seeing a therapist to help him work out his issues. In the course of his therapy sessions, Poddar confided that he was so angry that he wanted to kill Tarasoff. The therapist diagnosed Poddar as suffering from paranoid schizophrenia. Worried that Poddar could be serious about killing Tarasoff, the therapist notified the Berkeley campus police, who briefly detained Poddar, but Poddar seemed calm and rational, so the police let him go after he promised that he would stay away from Tarasoff. By the fall, Poddar stopped seeing his therapist and returned to his normal life at the university.

Then tragedy struck. On October 27, 1969, Poddar brutally stabbed Tatiana Tarasoff to death.

Tarasoff's parents were devastated by the loss of their daughter and felt that the therapist bore a share of the blame. The therapist, they argued, had known that Poddar was dangerous. He had diagnosed Poddar with a delusional disorder, heard Poddar fantasize about killing their daughter, had grown concerned enough to notify the police, but had never once reached out to Tarasoff herself to let her know that her life was in mortal peril.

Should the therapist have seen this coming?

The California Supreme Court considered the Tarasoff family's legal claims against the therapist and ultimately concluded that, "[w]hen a therapist determines, or pursuant to the standards of his profession should determine, that his patient presents a serious danger of violence to another, he incurs an obligation to use reasonable care to protect the intended victim against such danger."[79]

The legal standard announced by the California Supreme Court depends on figuring out whether the therapist knew, or should have known, that his patient was a "serious danger"— *before* the patient actually does something dangerous. Is it really possible for a therapist (or anyone else) to know in advance that another person is going to snap and start committing acts of violence? Or is this the kind of prediction that can only be made reliably in the clear light of hindsight?

Hindsight bias is the tendency of people to judge an event as more predictable and more likely after it has occurred.[80] Niels Bohr famously quipped that predictions are very difficult, especially about the future.[81] It is one thing to be certain that something would happen—that a sports team would win or that one political candidate would be elected or that a certain stock would go up or down—*after* it has happened. It is quite another to be certain that something will happen in advance. Hindsight bias is the feeling that we guessed, or would have guessed, the future, but only after the event has already come to pass.

In the *Tarasoff* case, the therapist argued that it was unfair to expect him to warn potential targets of violence because it was impossible to know which patients would actually become violent. The therapist raised the specter that judges and juries fueled with hindsight bias would punish therapists every time the unthinkable came to pass, even if no one could have predicted it.

The court recognized the problem, but minimized its significance:

> Within the broad range of reasonable practice
> and treatment in which professional opinion
> and judgment may differ, the therapist is free to
> exercise his or her own best judgment without

liability; proof, aided by hindsight, that he or she judged wrongly is insufficient to establish negligence.[82]

In other words, the court says hindsight doesn't count. What the court doesn't explain is how to keep hindsight from influencing our judgments. How can we be sure that our feelings about whether the therapist weighed the risks correctly are not influenced by the fact that we know that the risk, however remote, did in fact come to pass?

Imagine that you are a juror, and the parents of a murdered child relate the agony of losing their beloved daughter to a deranged lunatic who was under the clinical care of the mental health professional sitting in the defendant's chair. The parents and their attorney claim that the therapist should have seen the warning signs that his patient would snap and go on a bloody binge of violence that would end in their daughter's death. They point to the killer's journals that are filled with violent fantasies, the descriptions of dreams of death and destruction that he recounted, his delusions of grandeur, and his desire for a dramatic end to his pain and suffering. Combine all that with his fixation, anger, and resentment at the woman who became his victim, and you have a powerful case that justice requires some kind of compensation.

The therapist responds that many patients have exactly the same symptoms and never carry out their violent fantasies. He had no way of knowing that this patient would be the one who would cross the terrible line between fantasy and murder.

From the jury box, would knowing that the patient committed the murder—something that was only a possibility at the time the therapist saw the patient, but tragically became a grim reality—influence your decision about whether the therapist should have foreseen the tragedy that was to come?

Two psychologists, Susan and Gary LaBine, set out to test whether the power of hindsight made people more likely to believe that therapists should be able to predict a patient's turn to real, not merely imagined, violence.[83] The LaBines asked three groups of people to rate the likelihood that a person seeing a therapist would become violent.

The first group was given a bare description of the patient. The second was given the same description, but this group was also told that ultimately, the patient never acted on his fantasies of aggression. The third was given the same description, but this group was told that the patient ultimately became violent. Which group do you think was most likely to conclude that the therapist should have been able to foresee that the patient would become violent?

If you guessed the third group, congratulations. The third group, knowing that the patient did in fact become violent, were fifty percent more likely than the other two groups to believe that the violence was foreseeable and the therapist's failure to warn was unreasonable. When it came to deciding whether the therapist was "negligent" (the legal standard for making the therapist pay damages to the parents), the third group who was told that the patient turned violent was three times more likely to hold the therapist responsible than the groups who did not have the benefit of that hindsight knowledge.

Psychologist Baruch Fischoff was one of the earliest researchers to document the power of hindsight bias. In his study, Fischoff asked people to estimate the probability of who would win an obscure war that took place more than 150 years ago. Participants were given a description of the opposing sides and a summary of the strengths and weaknesses of their respective armies. Some people in the study were told what actually had happened. Others were left in the dark about how the battle had played out historically. The people who were told the actual outcome estimated the probability of that outcome between 6 and 44 percent higher than people who did not know the history.[84]

A different study tried to measure the effect of the hindsight bias by giving mock jurors identical accounts of how the city of Duluth, Minnesota, wrestled with the question of whether to hire—at considerable expense—a full-time bridge monitor to protect against the relatively remote risk that debris might get caught on the bridge, block the free flow of water, and cause a flood. In the scenario, the city debated the pros and cons, weighed the risk, and ultimately decided to take a chance and not hire the bridge operator.

Half the jurors were told only the facts that the city considered in its deliberations in coming to its decision not to hire the bridge monitor. The other half was told the same information, but was given the additional fact that because there was no bridge monitor, the serious accident that the city had considered to be a remote risk had indeed come to pass.

Among the jurors who were told only what the city knew at the time, more than 76 percent found that the city's decision was reasonable (i.e., not negligent). Only 24 percent thought the city had made a mistake.

Among the jurors who were also told that a serious accident had occurred, the result was very different. For those jurors who had the benefit of hindsight, more than twice as many (57 percent to be exact) thought that the city was negligent for not hiring the bridge monitor. The knowledge that something went wrong radically changed what people thought about the reasonableness of the city's actions.[85]

The hindsight bias is so common and easy to demonstrate, countless studies have illustrated its effects.[86] Suffice it to say, the pull of hindsight is strong.

The legal system is particularly vulnerable to the distortions of the hindsight bias. If risks don't materialize and no one is hurt, there are no lawsuits. Lawsuits are only brought *after* something has gone wrong. However unlikely or unforeseeable the turn of events that brought about the lawsuit might have been, the danger is that judges and juries reviewing the case will think that the event was more likely and more foreseeable than if they did not know about the bad outcome. This is bad news for those who try to provide mental health care for deeply troubled patients. When things go wrong, they are vulnerable to accusations that they failed to take enough precautions.

It takes a lot of work to convince people that a bad outcome that has already occurred was not preordained. While there is no magic inoculation against hindsight bias, jury experts recommend a number of techniques to limit its influence on decisions.[87] One tactic is to caution explicitly against being a Monday-morning quarterback. The phrase "Monday-morning quarterback" is common and familiar enough to resonate with many people and make them think about the perspective of a person making a decision in the face of uncertain outcomes. Another approach is to encourage a focus on the information that was available at the time the decision was made, and not the information that only became apparent after things went wrong. A related technique is to ask jurors to imagine all the possible outcomes, not just the one that happened, to dispel the sense of inevitability that comes from knowing the end of the story.

Hindsight is twenty-twenty. The satirical magazine *The Onion* nailed it with the headline: "Winning Lottery Numbers So Obvious in Hindsight." ("That 58 at the beginning? Talk about a gimme.")[88] While often amusing, hindsight bias is no joke. It can heavily influence who wins and who loses a legal dispute. Most actions entail some degree of risk, and some fraction of people will roll snake eyes. When the unlucky number comes up, and the lawsuit inevitably follows, skeptical jurors and judges under the influence of hindsight will require strong convincing that what actually happened was not completely foreseeable.

The Pull of Anchors

Anchoring is the tendency to be unduly influenced by the first information we encounter. Researchers have delighted in demonstrating that anchoring affects people even when the initial information is obviously and clearly irrelevant.

Daniel Kahneman and Amos Tversky, pioneers in the field of behavioral economics, ran an experiment where they spun a wheel and then asked university students questions about the percentage of African nations in the United Nations. Obviously, the number on the wheel had no bearing on the percentage of African nations in the United Nations. Nevertheless, the students consistently guessed higher if the wheel landed on a high number and lower if the wheel came up with a low one.[89]

Dan Ariely, a professor of management at MIT, conducted another well-known demonstration of the power of anchoring. Ariely "asked students to write down the last two digits of their

Social Security numbers, and then submit bids on such items as bottles of wine and chocolate. The half of the group with higher two-digit numbers bid between 60 percent and 120 percent more on the items."[90] Social security numbers and the value of wine and chocolate have no obvious connection, and yet the data suggested that just thinking about a higher number led to higher bids.

Anchoring is well known to advertisers and marketers. One common trick among retailers is to mark up a product and then offer a substantial discount in a "sale." The ultimate price is the same, but consumers think that they are getting a good deal. J.C. Penney got some bad press when employees publicly complained that the retail store had simply doubled all of its prices before declaring a 50-percent-off sale.[91] The retail giant defended its actions by saying that its "promotional pricing model" was "employed often in the retail industry."[92]

Anchoring works because, as Professor Ariely puts it, "People don't know how much something is worth to them."[93] It is easier to start from a reference point and adjust a valuation up or down than to determine a fair value working from a blank slate.

Anchoring is particularly important in law because, in many cases, the legal system is called upon to place monetary values on things that have no obvious market prices. For example, a woman is hit by a car and paralyzed from the waist down. How do we place a value on losing the ability to walk? In a lawsuit, both sides might try to make reasonable guesses, but anchoring very much favors the plaintiff.

Because plaintiffs typically go first in a trial, plaintiffs benefit from presenting the initial information that serves as an anchor for the rest of the case. In making their pitches for compensation, plaintiffs essentially have no upper limit in what they might claim for damages. In contrast, defendants are stuck with zero as the lowest number they can propose.

For example, the plaintiff who has lost the ability to walk might ask for $10 million. Even if the plaintiff believes that she is unlikely to receive that entire amount, the anchoring effect works in the plaintiff's favor by inflating the award that a judge or jury considers appropriate.

Arguing the defendant's position is more complicated. If the defendant is contesting liability, the defendant may not want to acknowledge that any damages are appropriate. If the defendant does put out a number to serve as a reference point to counter the plaintiff's inflated figure, the defendant has to be careful not to seem callous or uncaring, so offering zero damages often isn't a viable strategy. If the defendant goes ahead and ventures a number, the danger is that the jury will see the defendant's number as a floor for the damages, and maybe even decide to "split the difference" with the plaintiff's number, which can result in a verdict much higher than the defendant would like to see.

Researchers have found that the more money plaintiffs ask for, the more money juries award them.[94] In one eye-opening study, mock jurors watched a reenactment of a trial

> where the defendant was sued for causing the deaths of two children in an auto accident. Some jurors saw the plaintiff's lawyer request $2 million in damages; the other group saw the lawyer request $20 million. The jurors in the first group made average awards of just over $1 million, while the average award from the second set of jurors was just over $9 million.[95]

In other words, in a case where the only difference in the presentation of evidence was that the plaintiff asked for ten times as much money, mock jurors rewarded the aggressive ask and gave nine times as much money than they awarded in response to the more modest demand.

Anchoring plays an important role anytime we try to place a value on something that does not have a clear and obvious market price. Our minds strike out for some point of reference. One hopes that reference points will have some roots in reason and rationality, but as the saying goes, "any port in a storm." Strategic use of anchors can give a powerful edge to a claim, and so anchors need to be carefully identified, examined, and questioned.

A MEASURE OF DOUBT

We all rely on other people for information about the world, and so the problem of proof is particularly bedeviling. Although it often makes no difference whether what we're told or what we believe is true, when disputes arise, the exact facts make all the difference in the world. Never is this more true than when we're locked in a lawsuit with another person.

The legal mind approaches every account about the past with a large dollop of caution and a dash of outright skepticism. As we've seen, people lie. Even when people are not lying, what they tell you is often wrong. Our memories are horribly inaccurate. The worst part is that people often don't even know they have misremembered something, and in fact, they can be utterly convinced that their false and mistaken memory is correct, even in the face of irrefutable evidence to the contrary. The legal mind, therefore, distrusts unaided memory and searches for independent confirmation of events.

Complicating our weak memories is our sketchy perception of events. Sometimes, we see only what we expect to see and miss things that common sense says should be blindingly obvious—like kissing a chimp or overlooking a gorilla on a basketball court. Common sense is wrong. The legal mind knows that our eyes deceive us, and study after study, and a string of exonerations, demonstrate that eyewitness testimony is some of the most unreliable evidence available.

The problem of proof is not just a problem for the legal system. The problem arises any time someone tells us a story and again when we try to convince another person that what we know is true. Just as we can't always rely on what other people say they know, other people can't always rely upon what we say we know either. When knowing the truth really matters, the problem of proof teaches us always to reserve a measure of doubt for all claims and assertions about the past—including our own.

2

The Problem of Rules

For every complex problem, there is an answer that is clear, simple, and wrong.
–H.L. Mencken

COMPLICATED LAWS FOR A COMPLICATED WORLD

The law is a system of rules, no different than the system of rules for baseball or poker or Monopoly. Like the rules of games, the rules of law are arbitrary in the sense that they are made up by people and could be (and in fact have been) very different than they are now. What distinguishes laws from other rules, policies, and guidelines is that laws are backed up by the coercive power of the state. If you break enough laws for long enough, at the end of the legal road you will find officers with guns waiting to enforce the rules. The law is serious business.

Every year, the U.S. Congress, state legislatures, county boards, and city councils convene to discuss, debate, and enact new laws. The 2009 edition of the Code of Federal Regulations alone encompassed 163,333 pages in 226 individual books.[96] And those are just *federal* regulations.

So why are there so many laws and why are they so complicated?

About two hundred and twenty-five years ago, in 1787, leaders from across the newly free American states gathered in Philadelphia, huddled for three months in a hot and humid room about the size of a basketball court, and emerged with the Constitution of the United States, a four-page document that has organized this country ever since. Yet the America of the late eighteenth century was a very different place than the America of the early twenty-first century.

At the time the Constitution was written, the population of the United States was only about 3.9 million people.[97] Today, more than 315 million people live in America, and the number is growing every day.[98] For white Americans in 1790, the average age of the population at the time was a youthful 16.[99] In 2010, the median age for all Americans more than doubled to 37.2 years, and the population continues to get older.[100]

At the time of the framing of the Constitution, America was mostly an agrarian economy. Over 90 percent of Americans lived on farms at the end of the eighteenth century.[101] By 1991, fewer than 2 percent of Americans lived on farms, and the census bureau concluded that there were too few American farmers to bother counting.[102] In eighteenth century America, many of the men (no women were invited to participate) who wrote the Constitution owned slaves. Over the intervening centuries, this agrarian, slave-owning society evolved into an urban, multi-cultural, information-based society that is America in the twenty-first century. The country changed, and the laws have had to keep up.

The short answer to the question about why the laws are complicated is, well, our world is complicated. For some small societies in the distant past, a legal code as simple as the Ten Commandments might have been sufficient to keep harmony among the people. But even the books of the Torah are strewn with commands and rules from the practical to the esoteric to the bizarre.[103]

Much of the complexity of modern life is hidden from us, or if not exactly hidden, the complexity is not in the forefront of our minds. In a famous essay entitled "I, Pencil," economist and philosopher Leonard E. Read illustrated the profound complexity of the modern world by making the case that no single person on the face of the Earth has the knowledge, skill, and ability needed to make something as commonplace and seemingly simple as a pencil.[104]

To create a pencil, Read argued, the contributions of countless people are required, each of whom has at best only a dim appreciation for the tasks that others in the chain must perform. Loggers cut the trees, truckers transport the logs, and millers cut them up. Graphite must be mined from the earth, transported by ship, mixed with clay and other materials, and molded into shape. The lacquer for the pencil's exterior starts from castor beans and must be precisely prepared according to ancient formulas. All of the elements must be combined, assembled, packaged, transported, and eventually sold. The same story could be told about the pencil's eraser and the metal band that holds eraser and wood together.

But the complexity does not stop there. Each step in this long and complex chain requires a chain of its own that needed to be accomplished first. Cutting logs requires tools, which themselves have a chain of production, and truckers need trucks and roads, which also need to be built, and the same with miners and shippers and growers and so on. Yet, notwithstanding this enormous expenditure of effort, the price for the final product is pennies.

The complexity of the modern world has been a long time in the making. Roving bands of tightly knit hunter-gatherers connected by kinship gave way to farmers who mostly grew and ate their own food who in turn have given way to our modern industrial world where most of us know next to nothing about the creation of most of the goods and services that we consume and rely upon.

In developed countries, we live in a world where we hardly know our neighbors, let alone the people who produce, transport, and distribute the innumerable things upon which our lives depend, like food, water, electricity, and fuel, to name a few essentials among countless others. Yet we want to be assured that our food will be safe, our medicines will help us and not harm us, our wages will be paid, our property secured, and our families protected from threats of all kinds. In our anonymous world, we have substituted the flexible bonds of trust that come from family and close friendships for the rigid order offered by law.

This shift from kinship to law has expanded our horizons. With the security the law provides, we can do business with total strangers, people we've never met before, and many of whom we will never meet at all at any time. We trust that these unknown strangers working outside of our view will do their duties or face the consequences of the law.

The complexity of the law, then, is not a defect. By mirroring the complexity of our society and economy, the law allows commerce to flourish. The law's complexity permits each of us to contribute an infinitesimal portion of knowledge, skill, and work, and reap enormous benefits—from air travel to heart transplants to the simple pencil—none of which any one person could produce without the security of the law invisibly threading together all the people and relationships needed to bring them into being. The law binds us together, and thereby frees us to do things that we could never imagine accomplishing alone.

BRIGHT LINES AND STANDARDS

It is the beginning of the school year, and your teenage daughter is feeling a budding sense of independence, but she's a good kid and wants to act responsibly, so she takes the initiative and approaches you about the rules for going out with her friends during the next year.

You trust your daughter and want her to have a good time with her friends. At the same time, you also want her to be safe and rested for all of the other things she needs to do, like schoolwork, sports, music, and afterschool jobs. And you know, perhaps from experience, that the teenage mind is not always the keenest at making sound decisions. As you think about what would make a sensible curfew, you consider two possible rules: (a) don't stay out too late, or (b) make sure you're home by eleven. Which one is better?

Both rules have strengths and weaknesses. If you tell your daughter not to stay out "too late", you are not committed to a specific time and retain some flexibility in applying the rule. "Too late" could mean different things depending on the night of the week (Friday night versus Wednesday), what might be happening the next day (an early morning soccer game versus a lazy morning of sleeping in), or other circumstances that might change how late is too late (prom night versus the first night of a motorcycle gang convention that has rolled into town).

On the other hand, what you think is "too late" might not match up very well with what your daughter considers to be too late. If you and your daughter interpret the rule differently, you might argue, and who needs that?

The alternative is to lay down a definitive time for her curfew that doesn't change. The advantage of a fixed rule is that there is little chance for dispute. The hour is an objective reference point. Either the clock has struck eleven by the time she comes home or it hasn't. This clarity comes at the price of inflexibility. There may be occasions when you feel that relaxing the curfew would be appropriate. But once you start making exceptions, then you are right back to where you started, arguing over the curfew, and the clear rule is no longer quite so clear.

Rules can either be **standards** or **bright lines**. Standards are general descriptions but without precise directives. Bright lines are precise rules, clear but inflexible. A speed limit (do not drive above 65 mph) is a bright line. A prohibition against "reckless driving" is a standard.

Standards and bright lines are both commonly used in the legal system. The Sherman Antitrust Act of 1890 is an example of a standard. The Sherman Act prohibits "[e]very contract, combination, ... or conspiracy, in restraint of trade or commerce."[105] The statute does not attempt to define the precise conduct that constitutes a "restraint of trade or commerce." To apply the rule, courts must exercise their judgment to determine whether a particular course of conduct is or is not a prohibited restraint.

In contrast, the rule of civil procedure that an appellant must file an appeal within 30 days of the entry of judgment in the trial court is a bright line.[106] Try to file your appeal on the 31st day, and you will lose the case. The law prohibits driving with a blood alcohol level greater than .08. If your blood alcohol level is .079, you're fine. If it is .081, you've committed a crime.[107]

Standards create a degree of uncertainty. If you are a business, the antitrust statute does not give you clear guidance on whether the deal you are contemplating will be considered an illegal "restraint" or not. If you choose to go forward and are later challenged in court, you won't know for sure if you violated the law until the judge tells you whether you won or lost the case.

At the same time, standards allow the rule to fit circumstances that can be hard to anticipate. It would be difficult indeed, if not impossible, to write a law that prohibited every "restraint of trade or commerce" that the ingenuity of the human mind could devise for all types of agreements across all possible industries. The generality of the standard allows a court to examine specific, concrete actions and measure them against the policies and purposes of the rule to sort the legitimate from the illegitimate.

Applying standards requires judgment. Any exercise of judgment, however, will be prone to error precisely because human beings are weighing circumstances that don't always point in the same direction. They are not simply applying fixed algorithms to known, measured quantities. These errors can be the products of ignorance, misunderstanding, or mistake. They can also be the products of bias, prejudice, or even malice. The same flexibility that allows rules to be tailored to a situation also allows abuse when winners and losers are chosen for arbitrary or unfair reasons.

Bright lines are the opposite of standards. Bright lines are clear, and therefore, resist idiosyncratic applications. Either your car was traveling at a speed greater than 65 miles per hour or it wasn't. The certainty of the rule helps you know in advance what conduct will get you in trouble and allows you to modify your behavior to stay within its bounds. If you break the rule, you will know it.

Bright lines eliminate much of the judgment from judging. Faced with a fixed, inflexible speed limit, courts cannot easily take into account factors that might suggest the rule wasn't intended to apply to a particular situation. A fixed speed limit is blind to whether you are rushing your pregnant, laboring wife to the hospital (although police officers will often give a pass if they sympathize with the reason for the excessive speed, albeit introducing an element of idiosyncrasy and potential bias into the bright line). All the bright line rule knows is the number on your speedometer. The bright line's world is black and white.

Both standards and bright lines have their place. Standards are most useful when the variation in possible conduct is too great to catalogue. Conspiracies to restrain trade are one example. Schemes to defraud stock buyers are another example.[108] Closer to home, resolving custody disputes based on the "best interests of the child" is another.

A standard allows you to put off into the future a final decision on what is allowed and what isn't until you have more information about the precise facts and circumstances of a particular case. Lawmakers might not be able to articulate in the abstract exactly what "unfair competition" is, but by leaving the rule as an undefined standard, the courts can identify and punish it when they see it.

In contrast, when the conduct falls within a common, predictable, and knowable range, bright lines are often better rules. The amount of pollution a factory can spew into the environment is an example of where a bright line works well.

The conduct can be easily measured and does not vary much from one factory to the next. Bright line rules cut down on disputes and protect against arbitrary decisions that go beyond the intentions of the original rule.

In many cases, choosing between the flexibility of a standard and the clarity of a bright line isn't easy—as parents and teenage children the world over can attest.

THE LAWS OF OUR FATHERS

Quick trivia: Which country has the oldest written Constitution that is still in effect today? The answer is counterintuitive for a country that prides itself on its youth. It is none other than the United States of America.

Written in the summer of 1787 and ratified by the states in 1789, except for twenty-seven amendments, the U.S. Constitution has remained fixed for the last 225 years. We Americans are so used to the enduring permanence of our Constitution, that this enormous passage of time often goes unnoticed. Not everyone, however, agrees that a constitution should last so long.

Thomas Jefferson, author of the Declaration of Independence, third president of the United States, revolutionary, statesman, and scholar, argued, "Every constitution, then, and every law, naturally expires at the end of nineteen years. If it be enforced longer, it is an act of force, and not of right."[109] In Jefferson's view, the Constitution should be re-written every twenty years so that no generation is shackled to the rules of their parents and grandparents, let alone their ancestors ten generations back.

Underlying Jefferson's radical suggestion (he was a revolutionary, after all) is the observation that legal rules are captured in written words that remain immutable and unchanging even as years roll into decades and decades roll into centuries.

The modern American legal system responds to the immutability of the written word in several ways. Of course, laws can be and are changed, even the venerable U.S. Constitution. After the long and bloody Civil War, for example, in 1865 the U.S. Constitution was amended to prohibit slavery, where before the Constitution permitted it. In the case of the Constitution, changing the words is extremely challenging because of the onerous amendment process that the Constitution requires.[110] But with ordinary statutes and laws, the legislative body (Congress for the federal government and state legislatures for the states) can revise rules that seem outdated. Nevertheless, nothing like Jefferson's nineteen-year expiration date compels lawmakers to update old rules.

Another response to old rules is infusing them with new meaning. When old rules must be applied to new situations, new interpretations can be given to the old words. Sometimes, it is argued that these meanings were there all along and their significance has only recently been appreciated. Other times, it is argued that the meanings are indeed new but should be embraced anyway because they represent what the words mean in a contemporary world and not in a world that long ago faded into the past. This way words from centuries past are molded to fit contemporary times, technology, culture, and values.

In the end, laws must be applied by the living to the living and for the living. The world as we know it today would be barely recognizable to a citizen of a century ago and would appear as fantastical as a fairy tale to the denizens of the late eighteenth century when the United States began as an independent nation. The laws must keep up with the times. This means new laws must be written, and old laws must be interpreted and re-interpreted. This constant process of renewal and growth, building upon what has come before contributes to the law's complexity.

Not everyone agrees, of course, with giving new meanings to old words. This school of thought holds that a word's meaning should be fixed at the time it is set to paper. This method of understanding rules works best when that original meaning is known. As rules become more ancient, discerning the original understanding of a word becomes more challenging. Think about how difficult it is to define words like "liberty" or "freedom of speech" or "due process", and then consider how much more difficult it is to understand what those words meant to the elite class of men at the end of the eighteenth century who wrote the Constitution, let alone how those eighteenth-century definitions should be applied to a twenty-first-century world they never imagined.

As time passes, words become more slippery and become more likely to suffer from the ambiguity of language.

THE AMBIGUITY OF LANGUAGE

In Lewis Carroll's *Through the Looking Glass*, the classic sequel to *Alice in Wonderland*, young Alice meets Humpty Dumpty sitting precariously on a wall. At one point in their conversation, Alice tells Humpty that she did not understand what he meant when he used a certain word. Humpty replies contemptuously, "Of course you don't—till I tell you." Humpty, it turns out, uses words to mean what he wants them to mean, and not what everyone else thinks the words mean.

"'When I use a word,' Humpty Dumpty said, in a rather scornful tone, 'it means just what I choose it to mean—neither more nor less.'"

Confused, Alice innocently asks Humpty "whether you can make words mean so many different things," to which Humpty replies with the superiority of an egg perched imperiously on a wall, "The question is ... which is to be master—that's all."[111]

As Humpty Dumpty demonstrates to a befuddled Alice, words can mean different things to different people. Just because two people use the same word, that doesn't mean that they truly share a common understanding.

Human language is plagued by imprecision, but most of the time we don't notice. Take the following, seemingly simple sentence: "John is tall." Any three-year-old has the vocabulary to produce and understand these words, but do we truly understand what these words really mean?

As an experiment, close your eyes and try to imagine John standing at his full height. Visualize the soles of his feet, the length of his legs, the straightness of his spine, the height of his head, and the cut of his hair. Once you have as clear a picture as you can muster, ask yourself this question: How tall is John?

You don't know? Of course, you couldn't know because the simple declaration that John is "tall" does not specify an exact height. Yet the sentence seemed to make sense when we read it, so some meaning was conveyed, but what was that meaning? There are many possibilities. Here are a few:

• John is taller than 98 percent of all men, so maybe he stands six feet, six inches or taller.[112]

• John is taller than the average man, so maybe John is just taller than 5 feet, 8 inches (1.72 meters),[113] but how much taller is unknown.

• John is taller than I am.

Now, what if I told you John's height is four feet tall? You might cry foul and argue that if John is only four feet tall, then he is not tall at all and the original declaration was false. But what if I told you John was only four years old? Then John would be enormous—for his age.

A word like "tall" only has meaning compared to some point of reference. The trouble with the word is that the speaker and the listener may not have the same point of reference, which can lead to misunderstanding. A misunderstanding is especially likely if two people have significant financial incentives to embrace different meanings of the same word.[114]

Human language is riddled with imprecise words, like "tall." Arguably, outside the precision of mathematics and quantitative measurements, all words are imprecise, which makes it extremely difficult to write with a clarity that can be understood by all people in all situations without further elaboration or clarification.

The meaning of words can be thought of as something like the concentric circles of a target. At the center is the bull's-eye, the core meaning of the word. As you move farther from that central core, the meaning becomes less clear. Certainly, a person who stands seven feet qualifies as "tall." High noon qualifies as "daytime." We usually use words with their core meanings in mind, but those are the simple cases. The legal mind looks at the outer reaches of a word's possible meanings. It is at these edges where disputes will arise over where exactly the line should be drawn between tall and short, night and day, and a hit and a miss.

Especially when people's financial interests are at stake, different people will interpret the same word radically differently. In the midst of the American Civil War, President Abraham Lincoln observed, "The world has never had a good definition of liberty."[115] As the South fought for slavery and the North fought against it, Lincoln pointed out, "we all declare for liberty; but in using the same word we do not all mean the same thing." For the South, liberty meant the right to hold men, women, and children in bondage because of the color of their skin. For the North, liberty meant each person should be free. The meaning of liberty was very much a matter of perspective. As Lincoln vividly put it:

> The shepherd drives the wolf from the sheep's throat, for which the sheep thanks the shepherd as a liberator, while the wolf denounces him for the same act as the destroyer of liberty, especially as the sheep was a black one. Plainly the sheep and the wolf are not agreed upon a definition of the word liberty.

Since laws are written in words, the unavoidable uncertainty inherent in language means disagreements are inevitable. As a first line of defense, the legal mind will deploy more words in legal documents than in normal language to try to reduce uncertainty through greater exposition. This is why contracts and other legal documents are so long and wordy. Nevertheless, even in the most detailed documents, ambiguities almost always persist.

Consider this classic example of ambiguity in action.[116] The central city park of Ruleville is a place frequented by families with young children who go there in search of fresh air, peace, and quiet, but their outings are spoiled by the thrum and stench of cars rolling through the park. One day a young child chasing after a ball is nearly killed when he runs into the road and a car just misses him. The community's outrage flares. Letters are sent, telephone calls made, editorials written. Responding to the growing clamor of complaints, the city council passes an ordinance banning all "vehicles" in the park. Champagne flows freely in Ruleville that night as the good citizens celebrate a victory for clean air, for children's safety, and for friends and families taking well-deserved refuge from the city streets and cars.

The next day, as the buzz of celebration wears off, one family sets off to the park to take advantage of the new peace and quiet, when things begin to go wrong. A police officer approaches and pulls out a ticket book. The family protests that they've done nothing wrong. The officer calmly reminds them that vehicles are strictly prohibited in the park. Baffled by this response, the family objects that they don't have any vehicles. The officer politely shakes his head and starts ticking off citations.

He points at the family's baby stroller. "Four wheels. Transporting a person. Looks like a vehicle to me," the officer says coolly. Next, he points to the remote control car in the hands of their young son. "Motorized. Four wheels. That's a car, and cars are clearly vehicles." He nods at their teenager with his skateboard and the parents with their bicycles. "Vehicle, vehicle, vehicle," says the officer, writing quickly. He leaves the family in stunned silence holding a costly ticket in utter disbelief.

Is the officer right to issue a citation to this family or is he wrong? It all depends on what you think the word "vehicle" means in the city ordinance. This is precisely the kind of legal question that courts are often called upon to decide. In the next section, we'll see how.

RESOLVING AMBIGUITIES

We left off with an officious officer handing out tickets to a poor family in Ruleville's central park. Their stroller, toy car, skateboard, and bicycles, according to the officer, were all vehicles banned by the city ordinance that prohibited vehicles in the park. Was the officer right or wrong to issue the tickets? The answer to that question depends on what the ordinance means when it uses the word "vehicle."

The first stop in figuring out what words mean is the words themselves. If the meaning of the words is clear and obvious—"plain" is the preferred descriptor in the legal trade—then that is the meaning that should be used. Unfortunately, the meaning of a word is not plain nearly as often as one might think. Even native speakers of a language can struggle with defining words with precision, even ones that they use every day.

Dictionaries were created to address this very problem, and sometimes a reference to a dictionary or two will settle doubts about what a word means. But dictionaries are often of limited help. For example, one dictionary definition of "vehicle" is "a means of carrying or transporting something."[117] Certainly, a car would meet the dictionary definition, but what about a baby stroller? Isn't a stroller a "means of carrying or transporting something," specifically a baby? What about a toy remote-controlled car? It doesn't seem to carry anything, but the remote-controlled car can travel under its own power, and cars are vehicles, so isn't the toy car just a vehicle that also happens to be a toy?

At this point, you might be thinking that this semantic argument is ridiculous, that the meaning of the word "vehicle" is obvious, and this kind of detailed parsing of words and definitions is just lawyers trying to make the law seem more complicated and mysterious than it needs to be. And yet, what is obvious to one person isn't always obvious to another, especially when the meaning of the word will determine who wins a dispute.

A striking example was the California Supreme Court's decision in the case of *Harris v. City of Santa Monica*.[118] California law prohibits employers from taking an employment action against a person "because of" the person's race, sex, disability, sexual orientation, or other protected characteristic. The question for California's high court was what do the words "because of" mean. The phrase "because of" clearly means that one thing must cause the other, but how much causing is enough? The court considered three possible interpretations:

• "Because of" could mean that an employer's consideration of a protected characteristic must be *necessary* to its decision to take the employment action at issue. In other words, the employer would not have taken the action *but for* the protected characteristic.

• "Because of" could mean that the protected characteristic was a substantial factor in the decision. In other words, the employer might have had multiple reasons for the employment action, but a significant reason was the employee's protected characteristic.

• "Because of" could mean that the protected characteristic was a motivating factor in the decision. In other words, if the employee's protected characteristic played any role in the employer's decision, that is enough to meet the definition.

Dictionary definitions would allow any of the three possible interpretations, but the law can only mean one of them. Because the words "because of" could have more than one meaning, dictionaries, while a useful place to start, were not able to provide a definitive definition in the *Harris* case. Ultimately, in *Harris* the California Supreme Court took the middle course and adopted the substantial-motivating-factor test for employment discrimination lawsuits. But how can the court reach a decision like that when it couldn't just look up the answer in a dictionary?

If dictionaries aren't the final word on what a word or phrase means in a particular context, courts must look to other sources. Returning to our hypothetical ban on vehicles in the park, one source of information about what the city council meant when it used the word "vehicles" is the city council itself.

Before a law is passed, a legislative body like the city council invariably does some preliminary work. For example, the city council might hold a public hearing about the problems with vehicles in the park. Records of those hearings could be consulted to glean insight into which kinds of vehicles were sources of concern (cars, in this hypothetical case) and which kind of vehicles, such as baby strollers, weren't.

In addition to the hearings, a committee or some other official body might prepare a report about a proposed law with explanations about why the law is needed and what it hopes to achieve. Politicians love to hear themselves talk, and so there may well be records of debates on the law in the legislative body that reveal what supporters and opponents thought the law would do. These statements also shed light on the law's intended purpose.

Proposed laws are also frequently amended as they make their way through the law-making process. These changes can sometimes yield insights into what the goal of the law is. For example, if the proposed ban originally referred to motor vehicles, but then the language was amended to remove the word "motor," the elimination of the requirement that the law apply only to "motor" vehicles might suggest that non-motorized vehicles, like bicycles and skateboards, were intended to be included within the ban. (But then again, it might not. Such is the ambiguity of language.)

The sum total of all the records of the body that enacted a law is referred to as the **legislative history**, and like any inquiry into history, this evidence can be equally, if not more, ambiguous than the words and their dictionary definitions. Different lawmakers will have different purposes. Their statements will not all be consistent, nor will their reasons for voting for or against a law. Especially in the case of laws that are older, the legislative history may be completely silent because the situation that has come up under the law was never contemplated in the first place.

For example, the U.S. Supreme Court looked at the question of whether a state could prohibit minors from buying violent video games without their parents' consent.[119] One of the legal questions was whether the First Amendment's protection of freedom of speech included depictions of graphic violence in video games marketed to kids.

At the oral argument in the case, commenting on a question posed by a colleague, Justice Samuel Alito quipped, "What Justice Scalia wants to know is what James Madison [the author of the First Amendment] thought about video games."[120] The remark drew laughs in the courtroom—(I know, there's a reason why judges keep their day jobs)—because as visionary as James Madison was, it is perfectly obvious that from where he sat at the end of the eighteenth century the idea of a video game never once remotely entered his consciousness.

If the plain meaning and the legislative history do not establish a definitive interpretation of an ambiguous word or phrase, courts will consider the effects of different interpretations and try to pick the interpretation that seems most reasonable and sensible to the judges doing the picking. For example, like many states concerned about drivers distracted by talking on cell phones, California passed a law that prohibited the use of a cell phone while driving unless the phone was being used in a hands-free manner. One unlucky motorist picked up his cell phone while stopped at a red light just at the moment that a police officer pulled up next to him and saw him holding the phone in his hand. The driver dropped the phone, the light turned green, and the driver put his car in motion, only to be immediately pulled over by the officer, who promptly wrote him a ticket.

The driver objected to the ticket. He argued that the law prohibited using a cell phone while driving, but he wasn't *driving* when he used his phone. He was at a full and complete stop. The legal question the court had to decide was whether the phrase "while driving," as used in that particular statute, included waiting at a stoplight or whether driving required a car to be in motion.

The court that addressed the question looked at the plain meaning, the legislative history, and prior cases interpreting the word "driving" in other statutes. But to clinch its analysis the court considered what the practical effects would be if it accepted the driver's argument that talking on cell phones was permitted so long as the driver only used the phone while stopped.

The clear purpose of the law was to reduce accidents resulting from drivers distracted by their phones. Even when stopped at a red light, a driver could be distracted and cause an accident. Moreover, allowing drivers to talk while at red lights could lead to clear-cut violations of the law. If drivers could use their phones at red lights, then they would have to cut off conversations the moment the light turned green, and as a practical matter, that would be awkward, which would mean in many cases conversations would continue even after the car had started moving again, which would clearly violate the law. These practical considerations are frequently called **public policy** considerations, and in this case, the public policy helped lead the court to reject the driver's argument and rule that a motorist is still driving even when at a complete stop at a red light (at least for purposes of the cell phone law).[121]

In summary, three main tools assist courts in resolving the ambiguities that are often inevitably embedded in rules.
- The plain meaning of the words themselves
- The legislative history of the rule
- Public policy considerations of different interpretations

Inevitably, the clarifications from the courts create ambiguities of their own, which in turn require more discussion and refinement. Lawyers love to argue, and the slippery nature of language provides a fertile field for disputes over meanings, which the courts resolve as best they can within the limits of language itself.

AMBIGUITY IS NOT ALWAYS BAD

Ambiguity can tie us in knots trying to figure out what *exactly* words mean, but ambiguity also has its advantages. Ambiguity allows flexibility so that rules can be tailored to fit our intuitions of justice for individual situations.

We may all agree that a bright line rule about the speed of cars on the public roads is a good thing so drivers will know with numerical exactitude just how fast they can permissibly go. Yet even for this brightest of bright line rules, our intuitions of justice might reach out for exceptions. For example, should the joyrider racing on the streets be treated the same as the mother rushing her bleeding child to the hospital? While we may have no sympathy for the joyrider putting other motorists in danger by disregarding limits on her speed, the mother seems not only justified, but commanded by a moral duty to break the speed limit if it means saving her daughter's life.

Flexibility has its own problems because even in cases that at first may appear clear-cut, our intuition is not always a reliable guide. While we may agree that breaking the speed limit may be justified to save a child's life, this exception itself has limits. Would we agree that the mother is justified in stealing medicine from a pharmacy? What about stealing medicine from a neighbor? If we're comfortable with stealing medicine, what about stealing an organ, for example by tricking the surgeons by impersonating the expected recipient?

Maybe we're comfortable with the breaking of minor laws like speed limits, but not major ones like laws against theft. Yet one person's minor law is another person's major one, so the distinction between minor and major laws is a difficult principle to apply in practice.

Allowing our moral intuitions to dictate exceptions is dangerous because it permits each person to set the law for him or herself. Rules might have exceptions, but they should apply equally to all, not just when it's convenient. Finding the right balance between general rules and exceptions to those rules is not easy. Courts routinely wrestle with situations that don't quite fit the main paradigm for a particular rule, and in those cases, a little ambiguity helps.

Ambiguity makes room for flexibility in decision-making that allows us (or more precisely the judges who decide legal cases) to exercise some discretion—judgment—in how and when to apply a rule and when to make an exception. With discretion, however, comes the ability to do good and the possibility to do bad. In the words of Stan Lee, telling the tale about the origins of his reluctant superhero Spider-Man, "with great power there must also come—great responsibility!"[122]

Part Two

Evidence and Precedent

IN THE YEAR 1215, a cataclysmic event rocked the legal system in all of Europe, sending shock waves that still reverberate to this day, nine centuries later.

It started on April 19, 1213, when Pope Innocent III, the spiritual leader of Europe, issued a papal bull convening the Fourth Council of the Lateran.[123] Church leaders from throughout Europe travelled to Rome to consider a host of questions of faith, politics, and power. The council commenced on November 11, 1215 with seventy-one patriarchs and metropolitan bishops, four hundred and twelve bishops, nine hundred abbots and priors, and representatives of monarchs and royalty.[124] In other words, this was a big deal.

The council considered issues as diverse as the doctrine of transubstantiation, the proper dress for Jews and Muslims, and who should serve as the Holy Roman Emperor. The gathered religious leaders also took up a vital question of law: how to determine whether a person was guilty or innocent of a crime.

The thirteenth century in Europe was a religious age. The people saw God taking an active role in all aspects of human affairs, from selecting their rulers to passing judgment on their individual failings. The judgment of the Lord could be terrible and severe, but no one questioned its justice. For these devout people, the surest way to learn whether a person deserved punishment was to put the question directly to God.

Despite his keen involvement in human affairs, God would not answer questions directly, so indirect methods were required to discover the Lord's judgment. The solution they devised was simple and relatively quick: **the trial by ordeal.**

The trial by ordeal—also known at the time as trial by judgment—involved burning a hot iron into the hand of the accused or plunging the accused's hand into a pot of boiling water up to the wrist (the original trial by fire). The hand would be bandaged up and three days later examined by the local priest in front of the entire community.

The idea was that God would work a miracle to save the innocent. If the hand healed and was free of infection, it was a sign that God had pronounced the accused innocent. If the hand did not heal, God himself had passed the judgment of guilt.[125]

The trial by ordeal was an elegant solution to the problem of proof and the problem of rules for a time and place that believed that divine power knew all and was ready and willing to share that information at the drop of a hand into a boiling pot. The determination of a person's guilt or innocence was not left to the vagaries of human testimony, with its tendency toward lies, forgetting, and mistake. Technical questions of law did not require nuanced and uncertain debate. God resolved all questions of fact and law when the bandaged hand was exposed for all to see.

Not just anyone could invoke God's assistance, however. To be sure that the result was truly endorsed by divine power, trial by ordeal required the involvement of priests, a service the clergy happily provided. The justice system was simple to administer and provided clear, if not always accurate, results.

(But then, what system devised by human beings produces no errors?)

Despite the occasional critic who argued that a person's life should hang on surer proofs than the healing powers of his or her hand, things were going smoothly until the Fourth Lateran Council pulled the rug out from this carefully crafted judicial system. The council's Canon 18 decreed that "Neither shall anyone in judicial tests or ordeals by hot or cold water or hot iron bestow any blessing."[126]

In other words, the Fourth Lateran Council put priests out of the trial by ordeal business. By forbidding the participation of clergy in trials by ordeal, the practice lost the imprimatur of the Church and by extension the approval of God. Without God, the ordeal was just another barbaric practice that returned random results. And so, the practice of determining guilt or innocence by burning people's hands, which had ably served for so long, suddenly, on a single day, lost its legitimacy.

Without God to decide the winners and losers in legal disputes, a new system was needed, and so it was that the legal system turned to evidence and proofs produced by human beings, with all the flaws, errors, and uncertainties that entails. Over time, the legal system we know today evolved from the big bang of the Fourth Lateran Council. In England, trial by jury was given room to grow and evolve. Professional judges began to replace local nobles and priests, and a common law began to develop. Complicated proofs and legal arguments became a permanent feature of the legal system. The problem of proof and the problem of law went from being a matter of divine concern to an all-too-human responsibility.

3

Proving What You Know

The most incomprehensible thing about the world is that it is at all comprehensible.

−Albert Einstein

CONVINCING OTHERS

You have a story to tell, and you want people to believe you. To succeed, you need to convince them that you are not lying, your original perception was not distorted, and your memory has not failed. If these obstacles weren't formidable enough, if you're locked in a dispute, your version of events must compete with a contradictory version offered by your adversary. The challenge is to convince other people—people who have no reason to believe you or give you the benefit of the doubt—that you're telling the truth.

For most of our daily discussions and debates with family, friends, and co-workers, we start with a reservoir of trust and general credence. In legal disputes, suspicion is the starting point.

Everyone who is charged with a crime learns very quickly that the protest "I didn't do it!" does little to convince anyone. The guilty are just as likely to claim innocence as the innocent. From the point of view of a neutral third-party, the true denials of the innocent are indistinguishable from the false denials of the guilty.

There is no magic formula for persuading another person that you are telling the truth, but the legal system's centuries of experience dealing with conflicting stories can help. The keys to convincing others are a coherent story that makes sense and doesn't contradict itself and corroboration from trustworthy sources. Trustworthiness is measured by the extent to which decision-makers find evidence to be unbiased, disinterested, and accurate.

This formula seems simple, but in practice, assembling persuasive proofs into a coherent whole presents a profound challenge.

PLAUSIBILITY

By 1970, the era of Beatlemania was over. The Beatles had broken up the year before, and as a new decade began each of the Fab Four were trying their hand at solo careers. In November, it was George Harrison's turn. For years, Harrison had lived in shadow of his band mates John Lennon and Paul McCartney who together redefined songwriting for popular music. Bursting from years of pent-up songwriting frustration, for his solo debut Harrison released a triple-album called *All Things Must Pass*. One song off the album became an instant and major hit.

In January 1971, Harrison released "My Sweet Lord" as a single, and by the end of the month the song was sitting at number one on the music charts. With its open references to wanting to see and be with God, "My Sweet Lord" was a daring expression of religious faith and longing. The song broke from standard pop music formulas of broken hearts and wished-for romance by laying bare some of Harrison's most personal thoughts and feelings. The former Beatle must have been nervous about how the public would receive music that was so different than most of what dominated the airwaves of the time. He didn't have to worry long. The record flew off the shelves. The immediate and widespread success must have had Harrison feeling on top of the world, sweet vindication for a songwriting talent that had been mostly overlooked and overshadowed. The happy feeling did not last long.

Within a month of releasing his chart-topping hit, Harrison was slapped with a copyright infringement lawsuit. The lawsuit claimed that Harrison had copied the music and the melody for "My Sweet Lord" from another band that, in 1963, had found pop chart success with a song called "He's So Fine." Played together, the echoes of the earlier song in Harrison's were unmistakable.

In his defense, Harrison claimed that he wasn't "consciously aware of the similarity" when he wrote his song, but on February 23, 1976, the copyright claims against him went to trial, and when the verdict came in, Harrison lost. The court sympathized with Harrison, generously finding that Harrison had "subconsciously" plagiarized the earlier song, but that sympathy didn't stop the court from ordering Harrison to pay $1,599,987 in damages—the lion's share of royalties from his single and from the triple-album it appeared on.

At the end of the day, Harrison's protestations of innocence simply weren't plausible. Even former band mate John Lennon publicly doubted Harrison's claim that he didn't copy the earlier song, saying, "He must have known, you know. He's smarter than that." Harrison himself, confronted with the undeniable similarities between the two tunes, later asked himself, "Why didn't I realize it?" He had no answer.[127]

George Harrison was a member of the most successful rock music band of the prior decade. He had written hit songs that had become instant classics, like "Something" and "Here Comes the Sun." If anyone was entitled to the benefit of the doubt when it came to writing pop music, it was George Harrison. Yet Harrison couldn't get a court to believe his protestations that he didn't copy "He's So Fine" when he wrote "My Sweet Lord." His problem was that his denial simply wasn't *plausible*.

We have all had the experience of watching a movie or reading a book and getting to a point in the story that makes us sit back and groan, "That never would have happened in real life." Mark Twain once remarked, "Truth is stranger than fiction, but it is because Fiction is obliged to stick to possibilities. Truth isn't."[128] While the world will take strange and inexplicable turns, the strange and unusual are not good starting places for persuasion.

We all have an inherent sense of what is plausible and what is not. Our intuitions about how the world works spring from our experiences, and when we hear an account that runs against the grain of our understanding of the world, our instinct is to reject it. The first element of a persuasive story is that it have the ring of plausibility.

Excuses like "the dog ate my homework" are disbelieved because they seem unlikely. The modern equivalent is "my hard drive crashed." Hard drives crash all the time (just like dogs chew things up all the time). One study estimated that over 20 percent of consumer hard drives fail within the first four years of use (you are backing up your data, right?).[129] Even so, it is hard to believe that a generally reliable piece of equipment would fail just as a crucial piece of information stored on that equipment became important in a dispute. The failure seems just too convenient, even if that's exactly what happened. On its face, it *seems* more plausible that the person in the dispute deliberately destroyed the hard drive to gain some perceived advantage.

Stories that start from an implausible place ("You're never going to believe this, but...") engender immediate and deep skepticism that requires proportionally great corroboration if that skepticism is to be overcome. As Carl Sagan was fond of saying when publicly doubting the claims of religion and the paranormal, "Extraordinary claims require extraordinary proof."[130]

When George Harrison said he didn't copy "He's So Fine," his story wasn't plausible. It is entirely possible that two musicians working independently within the conventions of a certain style and using typical chord progressions and melodies might each come up with songs that are substantially similar, and for all we know, that is what happened when Harrison sat down and wrote "My Sweet Lord," jamming with his guitar and thinking about God. It's just that when two pieces of music are very similar, it's much more plausible that copying was involved. Harrison's story just didn't make sense, so he lost. A plausible story wins out over an implausible one almost every time.

Our assumptions about how other people act play a big role in whether we find a person's story to be plausible. While it may not be fair, if a woman claims to be the victim of rape, she is more likely to be believed if she cries or shows despair when she tells her story.[131] Meeting expectations—whether fair or unfair—increases the believability of a person's story.

One of these assumptions about human nature is that people will act in their own self-interest, even if that means that they might break a few rules in the process, especially if they think there's a fair chance that they won't get caught. We expect people to cheat and lie if it benefits them.

By the same token, judges and juries tend to be dubious of claims that a person acted selflessly or out of pure altruism. Judges and juries like to understand people's motives, and explanations are more plausible if it is clear what was in it for them.

A corollary to the assumption that people will act in their self-interest is that if someone says or does something that seems obviously not in his or her own self-interest, then we are very likely to assume that it is true.[132]

Consider a case where a person sues a company for a defective product, say a toaster that shorted out and caused a fire. The plaintiff says that the wiring was shoddy. If the toaster manufacturer admits that it did not inspect the toasters for defects before shipping them, then chances are high that the statement will be accepted as a fact, much more so than if the same company claimed that it did inspect the product. The statement that damages the manufacturer's interests is more readily believed than the one that advances its interests because people presume that the company wouldn't have said such a damaging thing if it weren't true.

Plausibility is the first step to believability, and sadly, the most plausible explanations tend to be the ones that put human character into the worst light.

CONSISTENCY

While plausibility opens the door to persuasion, consistency is the key to credibility. Nothing says liar quicker than changes in a person's story.

If you tell your doctor that you've had back pain for years, but then testify that you were in perfect health until the auto accident, judges and juries will sense a sneak. If you tell your boss that you are going to your mother's funeral and then later ask for time off to visit her in the hospital, don't expect your employer to bother with fact-checking your stories. They can't both be true, so your credibility is shot.

Inconsistency with your own story isn't the only possible pitfall. For many events, more than one person was there. If other people remember things differently than you do, that also spells potential trouble.

You might be safe if only your litigation opponents, with their own vested interests in the outcome of the dispute, contest your story. Their disagreement might be discounted because of their bias in the outcome of the dispute.

If, however, people who have no stake in the outcome disagree with you, then you're in trouble. Inconsistency with third-party testimony will not necessarily mark you as a liar in the same way that inconsistency with your own prior stories does, but as between you and people with no interest in the dispute, the disinterested witnesses are much more likely to be believed. At the very least, the discrepancy between your version and the recollections of disinterested witnesses will need a very good explanation.

Finally, inconsistency can arise not only with people but also with written records. The power of writing has been revered from its invention, and in disputes, if there is a written account of events, deviations from the written record will be highly suspect.

Inconsistency, of course, is not all downside. It is also opportunity. Often it is difficult to tell liars apart from truth-tellers. Inconsistency in other people's stories is an opportunity to damage their credibility and cast doubt on everything they say. Being attuned to inconsistency—both in your own stories and those of your opponents—provides a major advantage in persuading other people.

Savvy litigants are highly alert to inconsistencies and spend much of their time trying to stamp it out in their own stories and search it out in the stories of their opponents.

DOCUMENTS RULE

Lying is really easy. Try it now and see. Repeat after me: I won the Congressional Medal of Honor. I am a Nobel Laureate. I can travel back in time. False words roll off the tongue as easily as true ones.

Some lies, however, are harder to maintain than others. If I said I could dunk a basketball, you could expose the falsehood simply by handing me a ball in front of a hoop and saying jump. A lie about the past is harder to detect. If I told you I could dunk a basketball in high school, confirming or refuting the assertion requires more legwork. For questions about the past, documents often play the critical role.

The Rotunda for the Charters of Freedom is a majestic, circular chamber in the National Archives in Washington, D.C. with marble floors, painted ceilings, and exquisite artwork. Within its walls reside the foundational documents of the United States: the Declaration of Independence and the U.S. Constitution. Together, those two documents represent the radical new beginning that was the American Revolution and the establishment of government of the people, by the people, and for the people.

Both documents were drafted and committed to parchment at the end of the eighteenth century in a world that can seem unimaginably strange and distant from our perch in the twenty-first century. Despite that distance in time, millions of people visit the National Archives every year to look upon the famous and historic words of the Declaration of Independence and the Constitution. These are the same pages and the same ink signed by the greatest luminaries in the revolutionary pantheon: John Adams and Thomas Jefferson for the Declaration, Alexander Hamilton, James Madison, and George Washington for the Constitution.

The powerful words of these documents resonate through the centuries to this very day. The Declaration and the Constitution marked the radical and astonishing birth of a world where freedom and democracy were, for the first time in human history, real and enduring possibilities, a bolt of lightning that would streak across a planet shrouded everywhere else in the darkness of tyranny. And it is the miracle of writing, unchanging black marks ticked across an ancient page, that lets modern people, centuries later, experience for themselves the words of these two famous documents. If ever a question were raised about what those documents said, all doubts could be dispelled and all debates settled by a simple trip to the National Archives where anyone could personally and directly examine and inspect the original pages themselves.

Documents are special because they have a permanence that our personal memories do not. The words of the Declaration and the Constitution today are the same as they were centuries ago when the ink was fresh on their pages. In contrast, our recollection of those words is hazy and ephemeral at best. Don't take my word for it. See the contrast yourself. Read out loud the preamble to the Constitution (it's worth it just to hear its inspiring words):

We the People of the United States, in Order to form a more perfect Union, establish Justice, insure domestic Tranquility, provide for the common Defence, promote the general Welfare, and secure the Blessings of Liberty to ourselves and our Posterity, do ordain and establish this Constitution for the United States of America.

Finished? Now close your eyes and try to repeat the words you just read. Were you able to perfectly recite the words you read only a moment before? If not, you're not alone. As we've seen, human memory is fragile and fleeting. Now look again at the passage. The words are unchanged. You can read them as many times as you like. They will always be the same.

This quality of permanence gives documents a special place of power in questions of proof. Assuming a document is authentic and unaltered, you can be confident that the words you read today are the same as they were when the document was first created, whether that was last week, last month, last year, or last century.

Documents can be virtually anything—letters, memos, contracts, correspondence, emails, text messages, Facebook posts, diaries, notes, computer metadata, spreadsheets, ledgers, account statements, and more or less anything else you can think of that is readable in any way, with or without assistance. Documents are crucial to the litigation process, and in big cases, lawyers spend more time arguing over, gathering, and analyzing documents than they do in any other activity, with the possible exception of the trial itself.

Documents hold a special sway over judges and jurors. The age-old advice to anyone concerned about later disputes is to "get it in writing." The conventional wisdom has it exactly right, but because of their extreme importance, it is worth pausing to appreciate the qualities that make scraps of writing such useful and convincing sources of proof.

Documents, as already discussed, are unchanging (set aside the possibility of forgery for the moment). This permanence protects documents from the vicissitudes of human memory. Not only are documents immune from the danger of forgetting, once committed to tangible form, documents have no intrinsic bias. Unlike testimony, documents do not alter themselves to suit the convenience of current circumstances. They are incapable of lying to help themselves out of a jam or to gain an advantage.

Imagine the following situation. You get a call from the school nurse. Your nine-year old son has had an accident, possibly broken his arm, and you are needed right away. As you rush for your car, you tell your boss about the family emergency and apologize for leaving early. Your boss is understanding, and you feel bad because a deadline looms, and your boss will have to pick up the work that you're leaving unfinished. But family comes first.

Out of breath and fighting back panic, you burst into the nurse's office, calling for your son. But he's not there. Terror runs through your gut like a lance in your stomach. You start to babble questions, but the nurse calms you down. It was a false alarm. The injury was superficial; there was blood but no real damage, and after a few moments to catch his breath and a lollipop, your son is back in his classroom, safe and sound. She apologizes for the panicked telephone call.

Relieved, you thank the nurse and then decide to share your good news with your social network on-line. You dash off a quick message. "Big scare today. Nurse called and said kid was seriously hurt. Rushed to school, but turned out everything was fine. I've never been so happy to hear a false alarm." You hit post and leave the school.

Your son is fine, but your heart is still racing, so you decide that you need a moment to catch your breath and maybe a little something stronger than a lollipop to settle your nerves. You stop by a restaurant and order food and a cold drink. It's late by the time you're finished, too late to get anything useful done at work, so you run an errand or two, and later that evening you take your son out to a special dinner just to appreciate how nice it is when everything turns out okay.

The next day, you return to work to find your boss, arms crossed, head cocked, eyes narrowed. She's clearly mad. She had to work late into the night finishing the report—the one you were supposed to do, but didn't. You apologize and tell her that if it hadn't been for your son's injury, you wouldn't have left her in the lurch. Now her narrow eyes narrow even more until they are just two horizontal slits.

She says, "But he wasn't hurt."

For a moment you're confused. The call from the nurse, you begin, but are cut off by a sharp shake of your boss's head. At this point, you want to protest, maybe even exaggerate a little, anything to put an end to this grilling, but before you can come up with something to say, your boss produces a print-out of your social network post and points to the words "false alarm."

The bottom falls out of your stomach. Those aren't the words you would choose now to explain to your boss why you didn't return to work yesterday, but there they are, an indictment in black and white.

Documents have no desires to achieve, no embarrassments to conceal, no secrets to keep, and no lawsuits to win or lose. As inanimate objects, documents are more trustworthy than the people who created them because inanimate words on a page do not know whether they are helpful or hurtful to a particular cause. All they can do is reveal their contents without regard for who benefits and who doesn't.

In many cases, like the ill-conceived social network post in our example, documents are prepared with no notion that a dispute might later arise that the documents would be called upon to settle. On the contrary, most documents are prepared to create a record where accuracy and preservation of information is the entire purpose for which the document was prepared. You want your bank statement to tally every penny in your name—until your spouse files for divorce and asks for half of everything you own, at which point you might prefer if the bank records were a little less exact.

Contrast the indifference of documents with human testimony. When motivated and given half a chance, people can and will lie. They will change their stories to suit the moment. They will shade their recollections, either intentionally with the purpose of deceiving or unconsciously to put themselves in a gentler light. Even the most honest of citizens will, because of our imperfect memories, alter details in their stories with each retelling.

Words on a page stay in place over time and over multiple readings. Documents inspected months or years later are identical to what they looked like the day they were created. They cannot bend to meet the perceived needs of the moment. They are what they were, and that is all they will be. Therein lies their strength.

Documents have another advantage over human memory. A recollection must be summoned at the time it is needed, which can often be years later. As we've seen, it's tough enough to remember things we've experienced only a few seconds ago. Memory stretched back over months or years is fraught with potential error.

In contrast, documents are generally prepared very close in time to the events that they are created to record. For example, the social media post in our example was created virtually simultaneously with the news from the nurse. Because the post was prepared so close in time to the news, it has a higher chance of accurately reflecting your state of mind at that moment in time than unassisted memory attempting to recall the event years, months, days, or even hours later.

Finally, a document is less susceptible to fabrication or alteration. While forgeries certainly exist, most people lack the skill to create a convincing copy. Getting all the details right and keeping the forgery consistent with all the other authentic documents floating around is a formidable challenge even for people practiced in the art of deception and is well beyond the reach of amateurs who decide to monkey with documents for the first time when a dispute has come upon them. In addition, in this digital age, it is a rare thing for a person to be in exclusive possession of the sole copy of a document. Duplicates invariably exist on hard drives and computer servers, where forensic techniques can reveal when, how, and by whom a particular electronic document has been changed or deleted.[133]

For these reasons, documents are highly valued as accurate, reliable, and trustworthy depictions of the true state of affairs. Nevertheless, documents have their shortcomings, which need to be appreciated to put their probative weight in proper perspective.

First, a document's accuracy is only as good as the person who prepared it. All of the same errors that creep into human thinking find their way into the documents we prepare. Our mistakes are not erased simply because we've committed them to writing. Nevertheless, for the reasons discussed above (preparation close in time to actual events, motivation for accuracy, lack of knowledge of dispute, immunity to change over time), documents—while certainly susceptible to error—are less prone to mistake.

Second, while contemporaneous documents normally are prepared for purposes other than litigation, that is not always the case. A person who anticipates a lawsuit might start "papering the file," that is, intentionally creating favorable records for the specific purpose of using them in a later dispute. When that happens, the documents lose their objectivity and begin to resemble slanted testimony.

That is not to say that documents prepared with the possibility of a dispute in mind are necessarily untrue, any more than a person's testimony is necessarily untrue merely because it is "self-serving." On the contrary, if a dispute is in the offing, it is prudent and wise to start keeping written records of important conversations and events so that what happens doesn't simply slip from your mind and memory. Nevertheless, notes prepared for use in a lawsuit are more suspect because the preparer has the opportunity to record the favorable and omit the unfavorable and even, for the most unscrupulous, just make things up.

Another shortcoming of documents is that their meaning can sometimes be unclear, ambiguous, and subject to multiple interpretations. For example, take Carl, a rookie supervisor who is anxious about steering far clear of any trouble in the workplace. Carl has decided that Cheryl may be ready for a promotion and wants to talk to her about the possibility of taking on greater responsibility. Carl sends Cheryl an email that reads, "Cheryl, please come to my office. I have something important to tell you. I think you'll like it."

This seems harmless enough. Yet what does this email look like if Cheryl files a sexual harassment lawsuit against Carl and claims that Carl propositioned her in his office?

As Cheryl tells the story, the "something important" in the email was Carl's attraction to her, and the "it" Carl thought she would like was his proposal for an illicit, workplace affair. Carl, of course, denies everything and protests that his meaning was completely innocent, but who is to say for sure?

The words of the email are perfectly preserved and beyond debate, but the meaning of those words can be hotly contested, and the document alone is not sufficient to resolve the potential dispute. Something that can seem clear enough to you when you write it can be given a decidedly different spin by a determined adversary.

Even in contracts, legal documents prepared for the explicit purpose of recording the details of an agreement between two people, ambiguities can creep in that create room for arguments. Some contractual terms are inherently ambiguous. For example, one person might promise another to use "best efforts" to ship a product by a certain date, but the phrase "best efforts" has no fixed meaning.

This ambiguity is not a defect, but rather precisely the reason the phrase is used. The ambiguity relieves the parties from having to spell out every detail of every act that each expects the other to perform to carry out the contract. It is a standard, not a bright line.

Yet the ambiguity creates room for disagreement. If one person claims that the other person's efforts were not their "best," answering that challenge requires examining what someone did and comparing it with what they could have done. In those cases where vague words are used on purpose, the contract serves only as the starting point of the inquiry, not the end.

In other cases, words can seem to have precise meanings, yet still be susceptible to more than one interpretation. If I promise to sell you a ton of steel, a dispute could arise over whether the agreed upon amount was a metric ton or a standard ton. If we agree that I am entitled to a schedule extension "in the event of a strike," a dispute could arise whether the extension is due if in a labor dispute my business is hit with a sickout but not a formal strike.

In ordinary conversation, uncertainties like these would be cleared up with a quick explanation, but when words are fixed on a page, there is no way to add or subtract from what is written. After a dispute has arisen, clarifications come in the form of contentious arguments over what should be added and what should be subtracted.

Words can be slippery things, but they are the tools we have to communicate with each other. Documents solve some of the problems of shifting meanings and recollections, but not all of them. No form of evidence is perfect, but despite their limitations, documents are a solid foundation for building a case and are usually the first sources the legal mind turns to when trying to figure out what really happened.

A STORY ONLY A MOTHER COULD LOVE

We expect mothers to love their children. In most cases, that's a wonderful thing. In legal settings, if your mother is your only witness, it's deadly.

Your mother's testimony may be accurate, balanced, and true, but it's an uphill battle persuading anyone to believe it.

Most people will believe, based on their experiences with devoted mothers whose love for their children blinds them to their offsprings' shortcomings and failings, that a mother's testimony is untrustworthy because mothers are likely to be willing to lie for their children.

Your own testimony suffers from the same defect. You may be as honest as the day is long, but in a dispute, your account of events will be viewed with suspicion because of your obvious self-interest in the outcome.

Put yourself in the position of a judge or jury. Two people come to you with wildly different accounts of the same conversation. The first is a young graduate student working in the laboratory of a senior research scientist at a prestigious university. She is smart, ambitious, and attractive. She says that the head of her laboratory, the professor who is supposed to be her mentor and guide as she develops her own career, told her that if she wanted his support she would have to sleep with him.

The second is a respected, middle-aged professor, nationally recognized for his accomplishments, with no hint of misconduct anywhere in his thirty-year career at the university. He says that the graduate student came into his office, closed the door, and told him that she was attracted to older men and invited him to have an affair. He refused, of course. She became angry, shouted that he would be sorry, and stormed out, slamming the door behind her.

Two people. Two stories. Who do you believe?

The stories are irreconcilable and, ultimately, unresolvable, without more evidence. The professor has an obvious motive to lie. If he propositioned his graduate student, he would be guilty of sexual harassment. He could lose his career, his marriage, everything he ever worked for. His self-serving denial of the accusation must be heavily discounted. The guilty, after all, are just as likely to claim innocence as the guiltless.

The graduate student also has a motive to lie. If the professor's story is true, her advances were spurned and her accusations are cold revenge. If her story is believed, she may also be able to cash in through a legal settlement. Her story puts her in a favorable light and is as self-serving as the professor's.

In fact, calling the testimony of parties to a dispute self-serving is almost a tautology. Did you rob a bank today? No? That's just what we would expect a guilty bank robber to say, isn't it? Did you hit anyone with your car, cheat on your taxes, or leave a stingy tip for the server at a restaurant? No? Your denials are self-serving—but they also could be perfectly true. Nevertheless, the whiff of self-interest taints testimony offered in one's own defense, and those wise in the ways of the law take precautions against being in situations where their only evidence is their own word.

Bias is the enemy of believability. That's why your own and your mother's efforts at corroboration are likely to fail to persuade. The testimony of a random person who chances to be walking down the street at the time of a car accident will be, in nearly all cases, much more convincing about the color of a streetlight than the testimony of either of the drivers, even though drivers, presumably, have the best views.

A random person has no apparent reason to favor one side or the other in a dispute, while the drivers are presumed to be ready to say whatever most suits their interests. With no motive to shade the truth in favor of one side or another, uninvolved bystanders are assumed to tell only the honest truth. If bias is the great enemy of believability, cool disinterest is its closest friend.

Questions of bias inevitably arise if people are connected by family, sex, or money. Blood is thicker than water, the saying goes, and so it is generally assumed that it is only natural for people to be willing to stretch the truth, if not outright lie, to benefit their relatives.

Romantic relationships carry that same assumption, often with even greater force than relatives. All is fair in love and war, and truth is too often one of the first casualties.

Of all the sources of potential bias, it is possible that none is more potent than cold, hard cash. Upton Sinclair famously wrote, "It is difficult to get a man to understand something, when his salary depends on his not understanding it."[134] The typical lawsuit is a fight over money, so people are motivated to remember only favorable events, stretch the truth, and lie outright. You may have never told a lie in your whole life, but enough of your fellow travelers in this world have, and so it's hard to believe someone who has something to gain or lose by saying something is or is not so.

Since evidence that comes from an independent source will be given significantly more weight, third parties with no financial or familial ties to one side or the other are valued prizes in pursuit of winning a dispute.

THE FACTS INSIDE OUR HEADS

Actions speak louder than words, or so we are told, but we judge people not just by their actions, but also by the reasons for those actions. Was the push a bump or a shove? Was the comment a joke or serious criticism? Was your birthday forgotten or are you being snubbed? Frequently, the defining quality of an action is the intention behind it.

People's intentions are locked in their heads, so direct observation of what they are thinking isn't possible. Most of the time, we can make our own judgments and choose to believe whatever we want to believe, and that is the end of it. On the strength of our own personal assessments, we can break off friendships, take our business elsewhere, or refuse to deal with another person, unrestrained by whether we are right or wrong or whether other people agree or disagree with our decisions.

When a dispute spills over to the legal arena, our private judgments don't matter, or at least they don't matter very much. What determines the outcomes of disputes are the judgments of impartial third parties—judges and juries, typically—who have no reason to accept our judgments without concrete evidence.

In the law governing employers and employees, the employers' intentions often determine whether a given act is legal or illegal. The normal rule for employment in the United States is that the employee serves "at will," meaning that, absent a contract to the contrary, an employer can fire an employee at any time for any reason or for no reason at all. The rule works both ways, so an at-will employee can walk off the job at any time and for any reason, without consequence or penalty.[135] This general rule—that employment relationships can be terminated for any reason or for no reason—has numerous exceptions,[136] the most important of which are the statutory laws against discrimination in the workplace.

Under Title VII of the Civil Rights Act of 1964, it is illegal to discriminate against a person "because of such individual's race, color, religion, sex, or national origin."[137] In other words, it is perfectly fine for an employer to fire someone for no reason, but not for an improper reason such as the person's sex or race.

A typical legal claim under Title VII looks something like this. The employer fires the employee. The employee claims that he or she was fired because of his or her "race, color, religion, sex, or national origin." The employer denies that was the reason. The employee maintains that the employer's denial is a lie.[138]

The dispute is not about what happened. Everyone agrees that the employer fired the employee. The dispute is about *why* it happened. What was the employer's reason? Was it legitimate or illegal?

The conundrum for both the employer and the employee is to find a way to prove what was going on inside the employer's head at the time the employer made the decision to fire the employee. Obviously, this problem cannot be solved simply by asking employers whether they had an illegal motive when they let an employee go. Both innocent and guilty employers will say the same thing: of course, they did not discriminate. How can we tell the difference between the guilty and the innocent?

Because the thoughts in a person's head have no tangible manifestation, the proof must be indirect. The first piece of evidence of what someone is thinking is the person's own words. People are often not all that complicated. When they are thinking something, they say it or they write it, if not publicly, then in private where they think only themselves and their closest friends and associates will hear their intimate thoughts.

The simplest cases, then, are those where people disclose their biases, plans, or intentions. When people say things that put themselves in a bad light—a "statement against interest" in legal parlance—it is especially believable because, presumably, they would have no reason to make a statement that harms their own interests.

So if Sally Supervisor announces at a staff meeting that "there's too much testosterone in the office," Sally's words will come back to haunt her if she then fires Hapless Harry, and Harry responds with a lawsuit for sex discrimination. Sally may protest in her defense that her words were a "joke" or "taken out of context" or "misunderstood," but her denials and evasions will have to overcome the clear implication from her announcement that she is upset with having too many male employees. The natural inference will be that when she chose to fire Harry, his sex played a role, which is against the law.

Yet if someone is doing something wrong and the person knows it, if the person is thinking at all, he or she isn't likely to come out and say it in plain language. On the contrary, if the person is smart, he or she will say the opposite of what's meant and do the opposite of what's said.

So if Sally wants to thin the ranks of male employees, not only will she keep her plans to herself, but she might also publicly profess her commitment to gender equality. Words alone will usually not settle the question of Sally's true intentions.

If Sally selects poor Harry's job for the chopping block, her motives will also be measured by their consistency with the reasons Sally gives for laying Harry off. If Sally says she had to let Harry go because the firm is in financial trouble, but then she spends lavishly on a holiday party, the free-flowing money for a party calls into question the legitimacy of the claimed financial troubles and raises doubts about whether some other, more nefarious motive is at play. If Sally says Harry was performing badly by missing his sales targets, but Harry's numbers are better than other employees who got to keep their jobs, Sally will have some explaining to do. If Sally says that Harry had a habit of coming to work late, but others have a worse record of tardiness; if Sally says that Harry's position was no longer needed, but she fills the same position a month after letting Harry go; or if Sally says that Harry made an unforgivable mistake, but others have made the same mistake with no consequence, then Sally must either have a very good explanation for why she singled Harry out or risk a judgment that her stated reasons were pretexts to conceal the real motive for her actions.

Inconsistency is the crack through which light can worm its way into the inner recesses of people's true motives. If you're truly worried about money, you won't spend lavishly. If you're truly concerned about tardiness, you will punish everyone who shows up late. If a position truly adds no value, you won't hire a replacement to fill the job after you eliminate it. Although the employment-at-will doctrine clearly allows an employer to terminate an employee for "no reason," the reality is that people always have reasons, and more importantly, third parties who sit in judgment of the actions of others believe that there is always a reason. If a good reason can't be produced and supported, skeptical judges and juries may conclude that the real reason must have been a bad one. If the reasons for an action are legitimate, they will not be contradicted by other actions. If the stated reasons are contradicted by other actions, the logic goes, the true reasons must be illegitimate.

Timing will also play a role. Although the logic of *post hoc, ergo propter hoc* is a classic fallacy, the intuition that something that happens after is caused by what happened before is very powerful. And it is not always wrong.

If someone makes a complaint and then is fired soon afterwards, a natural inference will be that the complainant was fired *because* she complained. If someone who never has bought a stock in his life loads up on shares of an obscure company and days later the company's stock takes off because some regulatory approval is publicly announced, a strong inference will be that the novice investor was illegally tipped off. If a group of competitors all meet for lunch one day and a week later they all raise their prices at the same time, the inference will be that they formed an illegal conspiracy to fix prices and restrain trade. Although the inferences that come from suspicious timing are not conclusive, they raise questions that require very good explanations.

Our thoughts are uniquely our own. Sometimes this is helpful when we want to conceal something (whether for good purposes, like a surprise party or the fact that we've bought an engagement ring, or for bad, like cheating an elderly couple out of their life savings with a real estate scam). The impenetrability of our minds can also be frustrating when we want to convince others of our sincerity and have no concrete proofs to offer.

Despite their intangibility, our thoughts and intentions often leave discernible traces. Our words are one marker. Our deeds, especially our actions in analogous situations, are another. The timing of an action, especially an action that we could have taken at any time before but didn't, is another clue. Through these indirections, we come to conclusions about why a person did what he or she did.

MAKING YOUR CASE

The purpose of proof is persuading other people. If we want to convince others, it is imperative that we understand what other people find convincing.

Of all the evidence that can be produced, documents are by far the most compelling. Writing holds a special power over the mind. Seeing something in black and white is much more persuasive to most people than even the most heartfelt words uttered into ephemeral air.

What this means, then, is that as we approach disputes, we should arm ourselves with records to support our case. Documents signed or produced by the opposing party are particularly persuasive, but even documents we produce for ourselves—a memo to the file, a notation in a notebook, an entry in a diary or log—will often hold more weight than the same story supported only by our words. Producing a document can cut off a dispute at the pass, without the need for the laborious process of involving neutral third parties to adjudicate a resolution.

So get it in writing, and if it is not in writing, put it in writing.

Of course, documents are not the only proof, nor could they be. For all proof, clear, neutral, consistent, coherent corroboration is the key to a convincing case. If you are going into a contentious situation where you think recollections might differ after the fact, take someone along to serve as a witness, preferably someone who is not too obviously biased in your favor. Corroboration from a neutral source is the first place impartial judges look for a sign of what is true and what is not.

The knowledge inside our own heads can seem so obvious and convincing that it is tempting to think that no one could ever believe anything else. The legal mind knows that this is not true—far from it.

In a dispute, what you know or think you know becomes just one more piece of evidence to be weighed and considered against all the other evidence, including the testimony of your adversary. In most cases, your word will *not* be good enough all by itself.

Forewarned is forearmed, so when a fact makes a difference to something important, remember to keep written records and identify neutral witnesses. If anyone ever asks, you will definitely need them.

4

The Precedent Is Prologue

Wisdom too often never comes, and so one ought not to reject it merely because it comes too late.

—Felix Frankfurter

BECAUSE I SAID SO

"What's past is prologue," wrote Shakespeare in his play *The Tempest*. He was not talking about the legal system, but he easily could have been.

The cornerstone of the American legal system is the doctrine of *stare decisis*. *Stare decisis* is shorthand for the Latin phrase *stare decisis et non quieta movere*: "to stand by decisions and not disturb the undisturbed."[139] At its core, the doctrine of *stare decisis* directs courts and judges to apply the same rules and principles earlier courts and judges applied in earlier cases. Put another way, *stare decisis* dictates that similar cases should have similar outcomes.

Under the doctrine of *stare decisis*, a court is supposed to search for earlier cases similar to the one the court is trying to decide. If the court finds a similar case, then the court is supposed to identify the rules that led to the decision in the earlier case. Once those rules are identified, the court is supposed to make its judgment by applying those rules to the current case that the court is reviewing.

The earlier cases are called **precedents**. The rules contained in the precedents are called the **holdings** (or holding, if there is only one).

The doctrine of *stare decisis* is a conservative principle, not in the political sense but in the sense that it makes the legal system highly resistant to change. The legal system never approaches a new situation with a clean slate and fresh eyes. Instead, its gaze is always fixed firmly on the past. The legal system tries to fit novel cases into the molds of the precedents that have come before. The effort to squeeze the present into the patterns of the past has varying degrees of success.

The doctrine of *stare decisis* also discourages independent thinking. Judges are to follow the rules of the past as set out in the precedents. They are not supposed to question the wisdom of those rules. They are not supposed to experiment by testing out alternatives. Obedience to these prior rules is the principal value in a legal system built on following precedent.

Nevertheless, the doctrine of *stare decisis* is not, and in many cases simply cannot be, mechanically applied because of the critical requirement that *similar* cases must have similar outcomes. The most important legal question when a prior legal decision is offered as a binding precedent is whether the earlier case is truly similar to the current one. In making that determination, a judge must decide—must exercise *judgment*—about which qualities in the first case are the ones that matter and which qualities are merely accidental and irrelevant.

Sorting cases into the similar and dissimilar is where much of the action is for lawyers to argue and judges to judge. When a lawyer or a judge argues that a seemingly similar case is not truly similar because of some important difference, it is called

distinguishing the precedent. Once decided, every case can serve as a precedent for any another, and at the same time, every case can be distinguished from all other cases. The critical questions will be

- What are the similarities?
- What are the differences?
- Which similarities and which differences are the ones that really matter?

Figuring out which similarities and differences matter is no easy task. Law libraries are filled with pages and pages of books applying and distinguishing precedents.

The doctrine of *stare decisis* is the ultimate appeal to authority. The wisdom and rightness of the earlier decision is taken as a given merely because the earlier case was decided as it was. It is not that different than the classic reply of the exasperated parent at his wit's end to answer his child's constant barrage of "why" questions: "because I said so."

THE STING OF PRECEDENT

The full impact of the *stare decisis* doctrine is only apparent when the doctrine makes a judge do something different than he or she thinks is the right thing to do. Consider this example.

A hunter races through the forest. He has wounded a fox, but his quarry has not fallen. The hunter can see the fox's trail, but not the fox itself. He hurries so as not to lose his prize in the trees and undergrowth.

Meanwhile, another hunter wanders the same forest on the brink of despair. He has seen no game today, and hasn't for a long time. If he brings nothing home, his family will go hungry. He searches the bushes with the intensity of a man who knows that failure could mean disaster.

Suddenly, the second hunter's luck changes. A fox, bleeding and exhausted, bursts through the bushes and collapses right at his feet. The fox takes its last breath and expires right then and there. The hunter cannot believe his good fortune. He bends down and scoops up the fox, praising all that is good in the universe for sending him such unexpected fortune.

Before the second hunter can complete the thought, the first hunter bursts through the same bushes as the fox. He is breathing hard. His face and hands are bleeding from where the branches of the forest have cut him in the heat of his pursuit. He sees the second hunter holding his fox and stops short.

The first hunter regards the second, eyeing the fox in the other man's arms. The second returns the stare and squeezes the fox a little closer to his chest. A tense silence hangs in the air.

The first hunter speaks and explains how he had wounded the fox and had spent the better part of the day running the animal to ground. With as much calm as a man can muster seeing someone else holding his hard-won prize, he asks if he could kindly have his fox back.

The second hunter shakes his head. He is not about to let a late-coming interloper pry his prize from his hungry hands. The second hunter expresses his regrets but firmly maintains that he is the one who captured the fox, and so the fox belongs to him.

Naturally, this dispute winds up in court. If you were the judge, what would you do?

Do you give the fox to the first hunter who wounded the fox and chased him to the point of exhaustion and collapse? Or do you give the fox to the second hunter who had the good fortune to come upon the fox just as it was giving up its life, but who otherwise expended no effort other than bending down to pick the dead animal up?

In the case of *Pierson v. Post*,[140] a court confronted this question more than two hundred years ago. Good arguments exist for both hunters, and so it is not surprising that the court itself was divided over who had the better claim to the fox. In the end, the majority of the court sided with the second hunter. The fox was a wild animal, and the only way to gain ownership of a wild animal was to capture it. Wounding it and pursuing it to exhaustion were not enough.

Pierson v. Post is an important case in the development of the law of personal property, and so is worth knowing about for that reason, but we consider it here because the case is one where people can, and in fact did, disagree about the right result. When people disagree about what is a just rule, the doctrine of *stare decisis* plays its most important role.

Imagine for a moment that you are a judge who happens to disagree with the court's decision. In your opinion, the first hunter who had wounded and chased the fox had done all the work, and the law should reward and encourage that work by awarding the fox to the first hunter. The second hunter, in your view, is a meddler and a freeloader who interfered with a legitimate hunt and misappropriated a benefit that he did not earn. What the doctrine of *stare decisis* means is that your opinion doesn't matter.

When a second case arises, say with a deer instead of a fox, and one hunter has wounded, chased, and all but captured the game, when another hunter swoops in at the last minute and snatches the prize away, as a judge considering the question of who should get the deer, your views of who has the better claim do not (or at least, should not) come into play. Instead, you must apply the rule laid out in the precedent. In *Pierson v. Post*, the second hunter won the case. In this second case, the second hunter must win as well.

If you think the second hunter has the better claim and you would rule in the second hunter's favor on your own, the precedent doesn't force you to do anything. Precedent only exerts power over you if you disagree with the prior ruling. If unconstrained you would do something differently, the precedents and the doctrine of *stare decisis* stop you. You must obey the earlier decision, even though you disagree with it. Therein lies precedent's sting. Your personal view of the justice of the particular case must take a back seat to the application of a rule that some other person at some other time decided was the just result.

THE ODDITY OF PRECEDENT

Nowadays we are so used to a legal system built on precedent that it might seem the most natural thing in the world. Yet there is something strange about basing today's decisions on decisions that have been made in the past.

Outside of the legal system, precedent plays almost no role in our lives. Think about how you approach going out to dinner. If you return to the same restaurant you visited the week before, you will not feel compelled to order the same dish just because that is what you had the last time you dined there. We choose what to eat based on what strikes our fancy at the moment. If you choose to eat the same meal, it is because you want to, not because you feel an obligation to do so because that's what you ordered the first time.

Or even more to the point, if your friend goes to a restaurant, tells you she had the salmon and it was delicious, and recommends that you go to the restaurant too, you probably don't feel that you have to eat what your friend ate merely because your friend went there first. You will make your own decision based on what makes the most sense to you at the moment.

If you or your friend had salmon last week, there is no reason you can't choose a salad this week, and something completely different the next. While the past might help you make up your mind—if the salad was soaked in too much dressing last time, it might be wise to ask for the dressing on the side this time—the past is not the master of the present or the future. Every decision is made fresh based on the best wisdom you have at the time you make your decision.

Precedent plays virtually no role in our lives because, at every moment, we are trying to make the best decision we can with the information we have. If that means doing the same thing we did before, then that's great. If it means trying something different, that's great too. If we embrace patterns and habits, it is by choice, not by compulsion. Our present selves are not slaves to the past.

Our constant reevaluation of what to do seems like the most basic common sense. Why would you do something that seemed to you wrong or foolish just because you did it once before when you had less wisdom or knowledge about how things might work out? You wouldn't, and it would never occur to you to do so.

Yet the law works on the opposite principle. Obedience to the past is the principal command of *stare decisis*. The system of precedent is so ingrained in our legal system that this may seem as natural as spring following winter, but it is an oddity that is worth pausing over because it is a cornerstone of the legal system itself, and it has deep and lasting ramifications.

To justify forcing judges (and by extension the rest of us who must live under and abide by these judge-made rules) to do what has been done before rather than what they, in their own judgment, consider just, the doctrine of *stare decisis* must have some significant benefits, which we will examine next.

THE BENEFITS OF PRECEDENT

Imagine if you woke up one morning, and you had forgotten all of the rules of the road. Should you drive your car on the left- or right-hand side of the road? Does red on a traffic light mean stop or go? Do pedestrians have the right of way in a crosswalk, or are they supposed to wait for the cars to go by?

It's possible that with sufficient time and thought, you could puzzle out answers to some of these questions. It's safer for everyone if the cars wait for pedestrians to get out of the way. Others have no inherently right answer. Cars can drive on either the right or the left side of the road as long as everyone follows the same convention. There is nothing inherently special about the color red and the color green.

The first time a court must examine a legal question, it is like the amnesiac driver. The rule must be arrived at by reasoning from general principles or by analogy from comparable situations or by drawing upon practicalities informed by experience. This initial assessment of a legal question by a court is called a **case of first impression**, and it can be hard work.

Many legal rules are framed in vague terms, requiring people to act reasonably or avoid acting unfairly or deceptively. What is reasonable, unfair, and deceptive is a judgment call that heavily depends on the specific circumstances of a particular situation. Other times, legal rules seem perfectly clear but then become muddier when applied to situations not originally contemplated by the rule. When novel situations arise, some significant thinking is required to figure out the right rule.

The doctrine of *stare decisis* helps ease this burden by requiring judges to adopt whatever rule was identified in a binding precedent. The judge does not need to consider the rightness or wrongness of the rule, its wisdom or its folly. In fact, the judge is forbidden from considering those questions. Rather, the task of the judge is limited to determining whether the particular facts of the particular case fall within the class of cases where a pre-established rule applies. If the case falls within the scope of the rule, the rule is applied, and that is that. In this way, the doctrine of *stare decisis* promotes efficiency in judicial decision-making and conserves judicial resources.

The doctrine of *stare decisis* isn't efficient only for busy judges with large caseloads. *Stare decisis* helps people organize their affairs by allowing them to predict outcomes.

In rural areas where raising cattle is a way of life and cows will wander if not constrained, two different legal regimes are commonly used to handle the problem of one person's cows wandering onto another person's land.[141] In one regime, if your cow wanders over to your neighbor's land, you as the cow owner pay for any damage caused by the cow. Don't want to pay for your neighbor's trampled crops? Build a fence at the property line, and make sure that your cows don't cross it.

In a different legal regime, if your neighbor's cow wanders over to your land and eats your grass and drinks your water, you as the landowner bear the loss for any damages caused by the cows. You have no recourse against the cow owner. Don't want your neighbor's cows eating your grass and drinking your water? Build a fence at the property line and make sure your neighbor's cows don't cross it.

In the first system, the onus is on the cow owner to keep his cows fenced in. In the second system, the onus is on the neighbor to keep his neighbor's cows fenced out. There are arguments for and against both systems, but what is important is that once one regime is adopted by a court and locked into the legal system through the doctrine of *stare decisis*, everyone knows what they have to do.

In fence-in systems, cow-owners must build fences. In fence-out systems, neighbors must build fences. The legal rule chosen is less important than having a definitive rule that can be counted on to be consistently applied. If the rule is clear, the predictability produced by the doctrine of *stare decisis* allows and encourages people to organize their affairs to achieve the result that they want within the rule.

The doctrine of *stare decisis* also promotes fairness. While precisely defining what is fair is a task best left to philosophers, one element of fairness is that similar people who face similar situations should experience similar results. For particular cases, we can debate whether people are similar or whether situations are similar or whether results are similar (and, in fact, those are exactly the kinds of questions that the courts struggle with on a daily basis), but if my neighbor doesn't have to pay damages when his cow wanders onto my property, then I should not have to pay damages when my cow wanders onto his. The doctrine of *stare decisis* ensures that everyone who comes to court will have the same rules applied from the same binding precedents.

Finally, the consistent application of past rules to present cases creates a presumption against change in the legal system, which promotes stability in the law. Rather than veer off in new directions every time something novel arises, courts guided by *stare decisis* will look to connect the new with the old, the novel with the familiar, the unknown with well-worn paths. The value of stability can be hard to quantify, but it is anchored by the fact that people have more confidence in a system they understand, and people are more likely to understand the legal system if it doesn't change very often and when the changes that do occur are small and incremental. A stable legal system allows people to make plans and investments that will last many years, without fear that the rules of the game will suddenly, dramatically, and unexpectedly change.

In addition, a stable system is less likely to make a big mistake. Changes will not be dramatic, and so, while the ship of state might get dinged and scratched from time to time, it is unlikely to sink from the impact of a bad turn of the law.

In summary, the benefits of the doctrine of *stare decisis* are:

1. Efficiency
2. Predictability
3. Fairness, and
4. Stability

As Chief Justice John Roberts put it, *stare decisis* "promotes the evenhanded, predictable, and consistent development of legal principles, fosters reliance on judicial decisions, and contributes to the actual and perceived integrity of the judicial process."[142] These benefits have ensured that *stare decisis* remains a cornerstone of the legal system.

Nevertheless, *stare decisis* has its drawbacks and limitations.

WHY ARE COURTS MAKING LAW?

A staple of high school civics classes is the observation that the U.S. government is divided into three branches. The legislative branch (Congress) makes the laws; the executive branch (the president) carries out the laws; and the judicial branch (the courts) interprets and applies the laws. Yet when the courts make a ruling in a particular case and that ruling is applied to future cases (through the doctrine of *stare decisis*), the courts have for all practical purposes made a new law—a rule that must be followed and that will be enforced by the courts.

An argument can be made that, by making rules that apply to future cases, the courts usurp the authority of the legislative branch to make laws. The people do not (generally) elect judges, and (for the most part) judges are not subject to replacement through the electoral process. Much of the work of judging takes place in secret, within the confines of judges' chambers, and the number of judges involved in making a decision is quite small, ranging from one at a trial court to only nine at the U.S. Supreme Court. Case law, the argument goes, is therefore undemocratic.

The assertion by judges and the courts that they have the power to define the law through their decisions stretches back to the early days of the American republic.[143] In 1803, Chief Justice John Marshall, who would go on to become the longest serving chief justice of the U.S. Supreme Court and the most influential, famously wrote, in the landmark case of *Marbury v. Madison*, "It is emphatically the province and duty of the Judicial Department [*i.e.*, the courts] to say what the law is."[144]

The logic behind this claim of judicial power goes something like this.

In a legal case, it is not at all uncommon for both sides in the dispute to claim that the law is on their side. Especially for laws framed as standards rather than bright lines, the precise meaning of a particular rule can be hotly contested. One side will say that the other's conduct constitutes predatory pricing, and the other side will deny it. The outcome of the dispute turns on the *definition* of "predatory pricing." To resolve the conflict, the court must supply a definition (or interpret and apply the definition if the law already provides one). If the courts lacked the power to determine what the words in a rule meant, they would have no way of resolving the lawsuit.

Even obvious words require some minimal interpretation. If a contract calls for the delivery of ten cows and the promisor shows up with ten pigs, a judicial decision only makes sense if the court can say pigs are not cows.

Not all questions are that simple, and the hardest questions can sometimes seem impossible to answer. If a contract calls for delivery by the end of the day, when does the day end? Obviously, when the sun is high in the sky at noon, the day is not yet done, but where is its end exactly? Is it at five o'clock in the afternoon, a traditional time for businesses to close? Is it at sunset, when the sun dips behind the horizon? Is it after the last gleam of twilight has faded into the darkness of the night? Or is it at midnight when one day ends and the next one begins? All of these interpretations are plausible, and for a court to decide whether a contract was breached or not in a particular case, the court must pick one and apply it. As Chief Justice Marshall put it in *Marbury*, "Those who apply the rule to particular cases must, of necessity, expound and interpret that rule."[145]

One way to think about what it means to "expound and interpret" a rule is to think of judges as the great, human dictionaries of the law. Even if we have a general sense of what a word means, dictionaries are still helpful in pinning down precise meanings and distinguishing subtle nuances between different words. The necessity of interpreting the law means that judges must constantly be lumping one set of facts into one category and excluding that set of facts from another. By defining terms one case at a time, judges translate abstract legal rules into concrete actions and omissions.

Although case law resembles lawmaking in some ways, there are important differences. Judges and the judiciary do not operate without constraints. While the legislative branch can enact virtually any law of any kind that it deems appropriate (subject to a few limitations, like the U.S. Constitution), the courts do not have the same freedom of action. The courts may interpret laws but cannot create them out of whole cloth. A judicial interpretation must have its root in some other legal source, whether it be the Constitution, a statute, a regulation, or some prior precedent.

This requirement that the courts interpret, rather than create, rules is enforced by the practice that appellate courts must explain the reasons for their rulings in written opinions. The public can scrutinize the courts' written opinions. Judges who go beyond the bounds of judging can be criticized and shamed, and although it is not easy, the public holds the ultimate power to force unpopular rules to change by controlling the legislature at the ballot box.

PICKING PRECEDENTS

The doctrine of *stare decisis* seems simple enough: similar cases must have similar outcomes. A fair question is how do you know if two cases are similar?

In some sense, all cases are the same and all cases are different. All cases involve people, so in that sense they are the same. Every person is unique, so in that sense they are different. These similarities and differences aren't particularly illuminating. The trick is to pick out what matters and what doesn't.

Consider the case of a driver who runs a red light and hits a pedestrian. The court rules that the driver is liable for the pedestrian's injuries because the driver broke one of the rules of rules of road at the time of the accident. The red-light case becomes a precedent for future cases.

Future cases involving drivers running red lights and hitting pedestrians will rely on the red-light case as a binding precedent, but the red-light case can be understood as stating a larger principle that applies to more situations than just running red lights. The larger principle might be that drivers who break traffic laws will be held liable for injuries that result from their breaking the law. Understood this way, the rule in the red-light case can be applied to drivers running stop signs, exceeding the speed limit, and driving while under the influence of alcohol.

It would be entirely fair if you asked how do I know that the rule in the red-light case should apply to running stops signs, speeding, and drunk driving? The answer is I don't know. I can only guess.

Technically speaking, a case stands only for the question decided by that case on the facts presented, and so it is possible that there might be something special about running red lights that might not apply to other traffic violations. When the stop-sign, speeding, or drunk-driving cases come along, the lawyer defending the driver is free to argue that the red-light case does not apply because it is not truly similar.

If a lawyer makes this argument, the lawyer will need to come up with an argument that the other cases involving traffic violations are different or, to use the legal term, distinguishable. Are there any cases where a driver might be in violation of the traffic rules but *not* be automatically responsible for an accident?

Imagine if the driver is driving without a seat belt at the time of the accident. If the driver was doing everything else right—obeying all traffic signs, observing a safe speed, staying within lanes, etc.—would the mere fact that the driver wasn't wearing a seat belt at the time of the accident be enough all by itself to impose liability on the driver? What if the driver's car had an expired registration or if the driver's insurance had lapsed? Driving without a seat belt, current registration, or insurance are all violations of the vehicle code, but it seems odd to impose automatic liability for these technical violations if the driver was doing everything else right.

If failing to wear a seat belt doesn't create liability, then the rule can't be that *all* traffic violations automatically lead to liability. We can refine the rule of the red-light case to be that liability attaches only to traffic violations that contribute to causing the accident. But wait a minute. How can we tell the difference between traffic violations like running a red light that lead to liability and traffic violations like driving without a seat belt that don't? The distinction we drew between traffic violations that increase dangers to others and traffic violations that don't seems intuitively reasonable, but how do we *know* that this distinction is the right one?

This is where legal reasoning gets murky, and hand waving begins. Legal reasoning generally works by analogy. An analogy points to shared characteristics that make two different things similar. A house is like an apartment because they are both places where people live. In our example, when it comes to causing car accidents, running a stop sign is like running a red light, and it is not like driving without a seat belt. Running stop signs and red lights are analogous because they both involve failing to stop, and they both heighten the risk of injury to other people. Driving without a seat belt is not analogous to running a red light because it does not heighten the risk of injury to other people.

Analogies wield tremendous power in legal argument. The right analogy can win a case. One of the greatest challenges a judge faces in a legal dispute is defining a just rule. The two parties who are duking it out in court will almost always have very different ideas about what rules justice requires—usually, the rules most favorable to themselves.

Being able to draw a rule from an analogous case gives judges comfort that they are not just being bamboozled by one side or the other into adopting a rule that is unfair, illogical, or unworkable. The rules in the analogous cases pre-exist the litigants' dispute. While lawyers can argue for different interpretations of these pre-existing rules, the earlier cases are fixed. Knowing that a rule has worked successfully in another case increases confidence that the rule will work again.

Analogies are never perfect. A house may be like an apartment in that people live in both, but in other ways a house is not like an apartment. A house is a freestanding structure. An apartment is one unit within a building with many other units. When drawing an analogy, we must make a judgment about which characteristics matter.

If a case deals with standards of sanitation, the most important characteristic of houses and apartments might be that people live in both. If a case deals with whether elevators should be required, the most important characteristic might be that houses are single units while apartments are part of larger structures.

The question is how do we know when it is more important that both structures are homes for people and when it is more important that the two structures are constructed differently?

This is where the hand waving comes in. The purpose of analogies is to highlight what parts of a prior case are most relevant to a later case, but the analogy itself implies a judgment about what is relevant and what is not. And where does this judgment come from? One answer is experience and common sense, but another, perhaps more honest, answer is intuition and gut instinct. When reasoning is built on intuition and instinct, people can, and will, disagree.

The rarely acknowledged secret of judging is that judges are not precedent's prisoners. Judges pick and choose among precedents by deciding which features of a prior case are important and which features are not.

Despite its logical limitations, reasoning by analogy is the most common way of thinking about legal questions. The ability to think of convincing analogies is a valuable skill for anyone who is looking to win legal—and non-legal—arguments.

SAFETY VALVES: OVERRULING PRECEDENT

As important as the doctrine of *stare decisis* is for the administration of the American legal system, as the U.S. Supreme Court has noted, "the rule of stare decisis is not an inexorable command."[146] Sometimes, the first court to consider a question simply gets the answer wrong. In those cases, a court can overrule the precedent, declaring it null and void, and substituting a new rule in place of the old one.

The story of the most famous case of one court overruling a precedent begins in the last years of the nineteenth century when Homer Plessy, a shoemaker from New Orleans, took a ride on a train.

Plessy was the son of a carpenter and a seamstress of African and French descent, a creole in the racially charged nomenclature of the day. Plessy became involved in politics and planned a legal challenge to the Louisiana law that mandated that railroad companies maintain "equal but separate accommodations" for blacks and whites on trains. Under the law, the railroads either had to put blacks and whites into separate cars or install a partition if the train had only one car.

On June 7, 1892, Plessy bought a first class ticket on the East Louisiana Railroad and took a seat in the whites-only passenger car. A conductor approached Plessy and told him that he had to move. Plessy refused. An officer of the law was summoned, and Plessy was carried off to jail.[147]

When Plessy was brought to trial, in his defense he argued that the statute that required blacks to be separated from whites violated the Constitution. The judge rejected that argument. Plessy was convicted, and his case made its way to U.S. Supreme Court four years later.

In a seven to one decision, the Supreme Court rejected Plessy's plea for equality. In the Court's view, the Louisiana law did not stamp African-Americans with a "badge of inferiority" because on its face the law required that the accommodations be "equal" as well as "separate."[148]

By approving a legal requirement that separated blacks from whites, the Supreme Court provided the legal justification for an array of laws that prevented African-Americans from enjoying the same public accommodations as other Americans. Schools, buses, and even water fountains were segregated in a system that came to be known as the Jim Crow Laws.[149] The injustice of these laws was manifest at the time of the Plessy decision,[150] yet they persisted and grew with the blessing of America's highest court.

By the 1950s, largely due to the efforts of lawyers like Thurgood Marshall and organizations like the NAACP, the Jim Crow Laws faced an increasing number of legal challenges. The question of whether the Constitution permitted separate but (supposedly) equal accommodations arose again in a challenge to the practice in Kansas of requiring African-American children to attend different schools from other children in the landmark case of *Brown v. Board of Education of Topeka*.[151]

The question in *Brown* was identical in every material way to the question Homer Plessy raised half a century earlier. Both cases involved laws that required people to be separated based on the color of their skin. The only difference was *Plessy* involved trains and *Brown* involved schools. The doctrine of *stare decisis* dictated that the Supreme Court should follow the rule laid out in its earlier decision and find that the Constitution permitted sending children to different schools based on their race. But that's not what happened.

In *Brown*, the Supreme Court rejected its earlier ruling by focusing on the central role that public education plays in raising children, molding young citizens, and instilling the values of democratic government. Moreover, the Court relied upon recent scholarship in psychology that was not available at the time of its decision in Homer Plessy's case, which found that separating black children from white children inflicted significant harm by instilling the black children with a sense of inferiority and crippling their motivation to learn. By rejecting its earlier separate-but-equal rule, the Supreme Court started the slow process of dismantling the Jim Crow Laws and putting the country on the path towards racial equality and justice.

The story of *Brown* triumphing over segregation is one of the great achievements of the American legal system in the twentieth century, and it is not alone as an example where a rejection of precedent has become a fundamental part of the legal system. If the courts had refused to overrule precedents, "segregation would be legal, minimum wage laws would be unconstitutional, and the Government could wiretap ordinary criminal suspects without first obtaining warrants."[152] Overruling precedents is a safety valve in *stare decisis*, a means of avoiding the piling of error on top of error.

These celebrated departures from the strictures of *stare decisis* raise a question: how is a court to know when the doctrine of *stare decisis* should be set aside and a precedent overruled, and how is a court to know when it should abide by the precedent? The doctrine of *stare decisis* means little if its only effect is that courts should follow only the earlier decisions with which the courts already agree. If that were the case, then no rule would be necessary at all because people always do what they think right and best at the moment they make a decision (however mistaken their belief might happen to be). The force of *stare decisis* is only felt when a court is confronted with a precedent with which it disagrees, but the court must go ahead and apply the rule anyway.

If *stare decisis* is not an "inexorable command"—and long-standing practice demonstrates that it is not—then when is the command to be followed and when is it to be ignored? For good or ill, the courts have not established a clear and consistent set of criteria that defines when a precedent has outlived its usefulness and should be overruled. Nevertheless, the Supreme Court has offered some general guidance that might lead it to set aside one of its precedents.[153]

First, a court might ask whether "the rule has proven to be intolerable simply in defying practical workability." Second, a court might consider "whether the rule is subject to a kind of reliance that would lend a special hardship to the consequences of overruling and add inequity to the cost of repudiation." Third, a court might look at "whether related principles of law have so far developed as to have left the old rule no more than a remnant of abandoned doctrine." Finally, a court might weigh "whether facts have so changed, or come to be seen so differently, as to have robbed the old rule of significant application or justification."

These factors are by no means the only rationales advanced for overruling a precedent. The purpose of the doctrine of *stare decisis* is to ensure the rule of law and to avoid changes to rules based on the whims of judges or sympathy for or against a party or the desirability of a particular outcome for a particular case. So if fidelity to the precedent does more damage to the rule of law than departure from it, overruling may be appropriate. If the precedent itself departed from established law, then it may not be worthy of further

140

adherence. If the precedent has generated strong resistance by being hotly contested or having its underlying reasoning discredited, it may be time for the precedent to fall.

Although no fixed formula dictates when a precedent will be abandoned, the sentiment that undergirds a decision to depart from *stare decisis* and overrule a precedent is encapsulated in the observation of Chief Justice John Roberts that "*Stare decisis* is a doctrine of preservation, not transformation. It counsels deference to past mistakes, but provides no justification for making new ones."[154] Maybe simpler still would be the aphorism two wrongs don't make a right.

At this point, cynics might be tempted to say that *stare decisis* is a hoax. Judges follow precedents when they like and refuse to follow them when they don't, and all the reasons and rationales advanced for overruling a precedent are just made-up rationalizations to hide the fact that judges are just doing whatever they please. Chief Justice Charles Evans Hughes summarized this view when he said, "We are under a Constitution, but the Constitution is what the judges say it is."[155] In truth, in many cases it can certainly seem that judges start with results first and come up with reasons after. Nevertheless, it is an undeniable fact that courts regularly and routinely apply precedents without controversy or comment.

Just not every day.

LOOKING FORWARD AND BACK

The search for the right legal rule always begins with precedents if any exist. The pull of prior decisions exerts a gravitational force that draws today's decisions into the molds of the past.

Precedent is double-edged. It has the benefit of time-tested experience and saves time by economizing on the thought needed to render a decision. Yet when it comes to making a decision, saving time can be a false economy that leads us to repeat the mistakes of the past when we should be working on new solutions to old problems.

Nevertheless, precedent provides the safest ground upon which to base a decision, and so we should expect the people who are resolving our disputes to rely on precedent whenever it is available. Knowing this means that finding earlier examples immeasurably strengthens an argument—if not as a matter of logic, then as a matter of pure practicality. Even a single example can be foundation enough upon which to build a complex and novel argument.

In cases where the rules are not clear, the heavy work lies in distilling the essential sense of justice that motivated the earlier decisions and that might apply in the case at hand. This sense of justice is not a fixed star, but varies from person to person and situation to situation, and sometimes, different senses of justice will point in different directions.

The best arguments for adopting one legal rule over another are based, not on how the rule will benefit you, but on how the rule will benefit others as well. Although the legal system looks backward to precedents for the source of its rules, it is simultaneously striving to look forward, to make the world a better and more just place. The best arguments attend to both parts of the legal mind, the one that wants to honor the past and the one that wants to build a better future. The art of advocacy is getting the balance right.

Part Three

Trials and Appeals

EVERY LEGAL DECISION requires facts and laws. Determining what happened and the applicable rules are the two essential elements of legal thinking. We've already looked at some of the problems and solutions to proving facts and to figuring out laws. Now we'll look at the nuts and bolts of how the court system solves the problems of facts and laws.

Solving the problem of finding facts requires gathering and evaluating evidence, with all of the vagaries, uncertainties, and complexities of the whole messy universe of human endeavor. Witnesses must be found, their memories and perceptions tested, and differing accounts compared, contrasted, and reconciled. Documents must be collected, their contents reviewed, and their meanings interpreted. And all of this evidence must be distilled, packaged, and presented to a decision-maker empowered to say what happened and what didn't.

In contrast, finding laws is a much more bookish exercise. Laws are embodied in written rules—such as the Constitution, statutes, and administrative regulations—and reflected in judicial precedents. Laws have no separate existence outside of law libraries (or more commonly now, the Internet and the vast number of on-line resources about the law). Learning the law means lots and lots of reading.

The structure of the legal system reflects the different demands of these two types of searches by having two types of courts. **Trial courts** specialize in finding facts. **Appellate courts** specialize in finding laws. Each court employs radically different rules and procedures tailored to each one's specialized function.

While the differences are key to understanding the structure of the legal system, they are a matter of degree and should not be overly exaggerated. All legal decisions require both facts and law, so the distinction between trial courts and appellate courts is one of emphasis. In general, trial courts will take the law as given to them from the appellate courts and focus their energies on determining the facts underlying a dispute. Appellate courts, on the other hand, will generally take the facts as given to them from the trial courts and focus on figuring out the correct legal rules to apply to those facts.

In the chapters that follow, we will examine how the procedures of trial and appellate courts help each perform its primary functions in the legal system.

5

Trial Courts

Tell all the truth but tell it slant.
−Emily Dickinson

PLEADINGS

Two people come to you to settle an argument. What's the first thing you want to know? Chances are you'll want to know what they are arguing over and what their respective positions are. The legal system is no different.

To frame the boundaries of a legal dispute, the law requires the parties to a lawsuit to submit **pleadings**, formal documents that set forth their official positions with respect to the dispute.[156] The pleadings consist of two documents, the complaint and the answer.

Civil lawsuits begin with the plaintiff filing a **complaint**. The purpose of the complaint is to put the defendant and the court on notice of the nature of the legal controversy. A complaint has three parts: allegations, causes of actions, and prayers for relief.

The first part of a complaint sets out what happened that caused the plaintiff to bring a lawsuit against the defendant. These are the facts from the plaintiff's point of view. Because the purpose of the complaint is only to provide notice of the dispute, the complaint itself is not required to describe the evidence that the plaintiff will use to prove the facts in the complaint. Rather, the facts are merely asserted. Because the facts in a complaint are asserted without proof, they are called **allegations**. Much of the work of the trial court revolves around the plaintiff trying to prove the allegations and the defendant trying to refute them.

At the pleading stage, the plaintiff is not obligated to set out every single fact that supports his or her case. The plaintiff only has to set out enough facts to allow the defendant to understand the nature of the dispute, or in more legal parlance, to give the defendant adequate notice.

Although the allegations are merely the plaintiff's version of events, the allegations must be more than mere conclusions.[157] An allegation that "Joe stole my watch" is just a bare conclusion. The law will decide whether what Joe did was or was not "stealing." To make the allegation factual, the complaint should explain what Joe did by saying something like, "On August 13, Joe took Joan's watch from Joan's house without Joan's permission with the intent of keeping it for himself." That is an action. The legal consequences come next.

The second part of a complaint identifies the legal rules that the plaintiff believes entitles her to win the lawsuit. Most legal cases can be understood as either breaches of contracts or torts. In other words, the plaintiff claims that the defendant either failed to keep a promise or caused an injury in some wrongful way. The legal theories advanced by the plaintiff are often called **causes of action** or **claims for relief** or sometimes just claims.

The final part of a complaint is what the plaintiff wants. This part is called the **prayer for relief,** or prayer for short, and represents the remedy that the plaintiff wants the court to award for his or her injury. In general, there are three kinds of remedies that a plaintiff might ask for.

Money makes the world go round, and the legal world is no different. The most common remedy requested is money. In legal lingo, courts award **damages** to injured parties, but "damages" is just another way of saying money.

For some injuries, an award of damages is a perfect remedy. If you loan money to your ne'er-do-well brother and he doesn't pay you back, you can sue for damages in the form of the money you loaned but never received, plus interest for the time he had your money and you couldn't make use of it.

In other cases, money is manifestly inadequate but sometimes, all there is. If your child is run over by a drunk driver or dies on an operating table because of a medical mishap, the only true remedy would be to have your child back, alive and unharmed. But that remedy is beyond mortal power, and so the best recompense the law can offer is the cold comfort of damages. (Criminal charges might also be brought in these cases, but for now our focus is on the civil law. Criminal law will be briefly considered later.)

Although most litigants are happy to walk out of a courtroom with bags of money, sometimes people want action, not simply dollar bills. In those cases, people will sue for **injunctions**. An injunction is an order of the court directing a person to take an action or to refrain from taking an action.

The most famous case of a court issuing an injunction was *Brown v. Board of Education of Topeka*.[158] In *Brown*, the African-American children of Topeka, Kansas, represented by the National Association for the Advancement of Colored People (NAACP) and Thurgood Marshall, who would later go on to be solicitor general of the United States and an associate justice of the Supreme Court of the United States, challenged

Topeka's rule that prohibited African-American students from going to the same schools as white children. In that case, the children were not looking for money. They were looking for an order from the court directing the Board of Education to de-segregate the schools. And against all odds, they won.

Issuing an injunction is not something a court does lightly. Injunctions interfere with the liberty of individuals and can entangle courts in managing people's affairs for years to come. With a damages award, once the required amount of money changes hands, the case is over. Even if a judgment debtor refuses to pay a damages award, sheriffs can be sent to seize their assets, if there are any. Injunctions are much harder to enforce. For example, after *Brown*, the courts were involved for decades in the management of school districts throughout the country.

Because injunctions potentially demand extensive judicial resources, courts will only issue injunctions if damages are not adequate to compensate a plaintiff's injuries. In legal jargon, injunctions will issue only if there is "no adequate remedy at law."[159] So if someone smashes up your car, a court will not issue an injunction ordering the smasher to fix it. Rather, the court will make the smasher pay damages, and then you can use that money to fix your car. (Or not, since the award is money, you can do with it what you will.)

On the other hand, if you have lost your job for an illegal reason, a court can (and usually will) order your employer to hire you back. If you are in fear of a stalker, a court can order him to stay away from you. If your neighbor holds wild parties every night, a court can order her to refrain from making noise after a certain hour. In each of these cases, money does not adequately remedy the injury, so courts will issue injunctions.

The third remedy potentially sought in a lawsuit is **restitution**. Restitution is derived from the word "restore" and is a request that the court order the defendant to return property that the defendant illegally acquired or which it would be unjust for the defendant to retain.

Imagine that you own a very valuable painting painted by a famous painter, a Rembrandt, a Van Gogh, or a Picasso, for example. A shady art dealer approaches you and asks to buy your artistic treasure. The art dealer offers to pay you the full market value of the piece. He produces a stack of professional appraisals to demonstrate that his price is eminently fair and reasonable. It's a lot of cash, but you refuse without hesitation. For you, the painting is worth more than money. It's an heirloom and you want to keep it in the family (or if you're more altruistically minded, you want to hold it for a donation to your local museum).

So what does the art dealer do? Because he's shady, the art dealer breaks into your house in the dead of night and runs off with your painting. The next morning, you find the dealer and your painting in the dealer's art gallery. You demand the painting back, the dealer says, "Sue me," and so you do.

Your write up your complaint, with the allegations as described above, and assert a cause of action for conversion (the wrongful taking of another person's property—basically the civil law equivalent to theft). At the prayer for relief, however, you hesitate. If you ask for damages, what will happen? The court will determine the fair and reasonable value of the painting in dollars and award that exact amount to you. But then what? That was the same amount of the dealer's original offer, which you refused. If you pray for and are awarded damages, in essence you will have sold your painting for the fair market value, and that is not at all what you wanted to happen. Instead, you ask for restitution. In other words, you ask the court to return (restore) the painting to you because the painting is unique, and damages are not a fair approximation of the loss of the painting to you.

Restitution can be thought of as a species of injunction. An injunction is an order of the court compelling a person to do or refrain from doing some act. Restitution is an order of the court that compels a person to do a very particular act—that is, return property that has been wrongfully acquired.

As with injunctions, courts will only order restitution if damages are inadequate. In the usual case, property is all the same, so money is perfectly adequate compensation for its loss or damage. But in some cases, like the famous painter's painting, the property is unique, and there is no measure of the property's value other than the property itself. In those cases, restitution makes sense and is the right remedy to request.

The complaint, with its allegations, causes of action, and prayers for relief, frames the legal dispute from the plaintiff's perspective. Naturally, the defendant gets an equal opportunity to set out his or her position. The defendant's response to a complaint is called the **answer**.

Like a complaint, an answer has three parts. The first part is the defendant's response to the plaintiff's allegations. This response is referred to as the **denial** because it is where the defendant denies the facts that the plaintiff has alleged. Different jurisdictions handle denials differently, but in general the defendant simply denies the allegations one by one, or in some places all at once.

In a lawsuit the defendant does not have to prove anything because the plaintiff bears the burden of proof, so the defendant is not required to identify legal theories in the same way that the plaintiff must identify causes of action in the complaint. Nevertheless, for some legal defenses, the defendant bears the burden of proof, and consequently the defendant must identify them in his or her answer. These legal theories are called **affirmative defenses**.

Consider again our familiar example of Paul and Darryl. Paul comes out of a bar on a Saturday night and gets into a heated argument with Darryl. The confrontation culminates with Darryl punching Paul in the nose. Paul sues.

Paul's complaint has the typical three parts. His allegation is that Darryl punched him in the nose and injured him. His cause of action is battery, an unlawful touching of another person. His prayer is for damages for his medical expenses, the pain he suffered, and the emotional humiliation of getting punched in front of his friends.

In his answer, Darryl responds first by denying the main allegation. Darryl asserts that he did not hit Paul, but rather Paul tripped and injured his own nose when he fell.

Thus framed, the case seems straightforward. Either Darryl hit Paul or he didn't. If the evidence shows that Darryl hit Paul, Paul wins. Case closed. Or is it? Is there any way for someone who has hit another person to successfully defend a charge of battery? You've probably already guessed that the answer is yes.

In his answer, Darryl offers an additional argument. If (hypothetically speaking, of course) he did punch Paul in the nose, Darryl contends that he was acting in self-defense. In other words, if Darryl can show that Paul physically threatened him and that he used a reasonable amount of force to defend himself against that threat, Darryl should win the lawsuit, even though he punched Paul. Because Darryl has the burden of proving that Paul was threatening him and his use of force was reasonable, self-defense is an affirmative defense.

Probably the most common affirmative defense in civil cases is **the statute of limitations**. The purpose of a statute of limitations is to set a time limit for a plaintiff to bring a claim to court. The thinking is that very old claims are difficult to resolve fairly because evidence is lost. Documents are discarded; memories fade; and witnesses move on and can no longer be found. Contrary to its name, there is not just one statute of limitations, but rather, there are many different statutes setting out different amounts of time a plaintiff has to bring different claims.

The statute of limitations is an affirmative defense because, even if the plaintiff's allegations are all true and the defendant did violate the law and the plaintiff's legal rights, the plaintiff is still not entitled to relief if he or she waited too long to bring the lawsuit. The purpose of the statute of limitations is to ensure that plaintiffs bring their cases promptly or risk losing their claims altogether.

The final piece of a defendant's answer is a prayer for relief because the defendant, just as much as the plaintiff, wants something from the court. Mostly defendants want to win their cases and pay plaintiffs nothing, but in some cases, defendants will ask to have their attorney's fees reimbursed or some other remedy. The prayer for relief is the defendant's opportunity to spell out what he or she wants.

Together, the complaint and the answer frame the lawsuit. They set out the facts that are in dispute, the legal questions that must be answered, and the remedies that the respective parties desire. Once the positions of the parties are established in the pleadings, the action in the trial court really begins.

DISCOVERY

Trial courts are designed to figure out the facts—what really happened to the parties that brought them to court. Most of the work of figuring out the facts takes place outside of the courtroom in a process called **discovery**.

Discovery, as its name implies, involves discovering information. Mostly, discovery consists of the parties to a lawsuit exchanging information, but it also can involve gathering information from third parties, that is, people not directly involved in the lawsuit.

Discovery is not supposed to be a blind voyage of exploration. Discovery is circumscribed by the common-sense rule that the information sought must be "relevant" to the issues in the lawsuit (the issues framed by the pleadings). Because discovery occurs before all the facts are known, relevance at the discovery stage is broadly defined to include any information that "appears reasonably calculated to lead to the discovery of admissible evidence."[160] In other words, the information itself does not have to be relevant, but rather the information must reasonably appear to lead to evidence that would be relevant and admissible at trial.

For example, say a divorced dad goes to court to reduce the amount of child support he has to pay to his ex-wife and his children. The dad claims that he's broke. He's lost his job, and he has no savings. A relevant question would be what savings does the dad have. A question that is reasonably calculated to lead to the discovery of admissible evidence would be to ask for the names of all the banks or other financial institutions where the dad keeps any money. The names of the banks aren't directly relevant, but knowing the banks' names allows the ex-wife to find out directly from the banks how much money the divorced dad really has, and the amount of money the dad has in the bank is very relevant.

The facts that discovery seeks cannot be looked up in a library. They must be gathered from people who have pertinent knowledge or records. The law authorizes four primary ways for parties to a lawsuit to compel their opponents (and third parties) to provide evidence that will help resolve disputed facts: inspection requests, depositions, requests for admissions, and interrogatories. Let's examine each one in turn.

Requests to Inspect Documents and Things

As we've seen, when it comes to proof, documents rule. As a consequence of the power of written records, most discovery begins with a request to inspect documents in the other party's possession.

Documents can be anything written. They can be formal legal documents, like contracts or deeds or stock certificates or corporate bylaws. They can be any kind of correspondence, like letters, memos, notes, or emails. They can be business records, like hospital charts, bank statements, invoices, bills of lading, packing slips, and maintenance logs. They can be résumés or pay stubs. They can be journals or diaries. Anything written qualifies as a document that might be subject to inspection.

The great white whale of contemporary document discovery is email, also known as electronically stored information or simply ESI. According to a 2011 study, the amount of electronic information created and replicated in 2011 surpassed 1.8 zettabytes (1.8 trillion gigabytes).[161] And the pace of creation of electronic information is only accelerating. Text messages are the communication means of choice for many people, especially the young. According to one survey, 18- to 24- year-olds send and receive almost 130 text messages per day.[162] That number declines for older adults, but the bottom line remains: Because of the ubiquity of electronic gadgets, we are generating more documents more rapidly than at any time in history.

This massive reservoir of electronic information has spawned an entire industry dedicated to finding, searching, sorting, and producing electronic information in discovery. And the costs are not cheap. Some of the biggest, most complex, and most document-intensive cases are patent disputes. In a typical patent lawsuit, the fees, costs and expenses of litigating the claims alone typically run between two and a half and five million dollars.[163] Much of that cost is consumed by electronic discovery.[164]

In smaller cases, the costs of discovery can exceed the amount at stake in the lawsuit. Sensitive to the pressure that the cost of discovery can put on a litigant, in cases where the cost is particularly great and the probability of finding useful information is relatively low, some courts have ordered that the party making the request pay the costs of gathering and producing electronic and other documents.[165] Fee-shifting orders are still the exception and not the norm, so the cost of e-discovery remains a significant challenge, especially for corporations with dozens or hundreds or thousands of employees creating countless documents every second of every working day.

Every jurisdiction has its practices for how to format a request for documents, but as a legal matter, there is no special procedure for requesting documents from an opposing party in a lawsuit. All you have to do is ask for the documents in writing.

Sometimes, a party knows exactly what documents she is looking for from the other side. For example, you might want a copy of the manufacturer's warranty or a copy of the contract you signed.

Most of the time, one party doesn't know what documents the other side has. The discovery process is all about discovering what those documents are. So most discovery requests are framed in broad terms. Fishing expeditions (the preferred phrase in legal circles for wild-goose chases) are not allowed, but discovery requests invariably cast a wide net.

A typical document request will ask the opposing party to produce "all correspondence" that "refers or relates to" the issues in the case. The phrase "all correspondence" sweeps in letters and emails that the requestor is unaware of but are in the responding party's possession. The phrase "refers or relates to" attempts to capture any document that could have any bearing whatsoever in the lawsuit.

Document requests require a lot of trust and cooperation between parties who are otherwise at each other's throats fighting it out in the lawsuit. Because you don't know all the documents the other side has, you have no way to verify that the responding party has, in fact, given you *all* the documents that are potentially relevant.

Indeed, the other party has a huge incentive to withhold documents. They know that you only want the documents so that you can use the records against them in the lawsuit, and they have no interest in doing anything that helps you beat them. One reason document requests are so broadly worded is to cut off the responding party's natural inclination to read the requests narrowly so as not to have to turn over a document that might hurt their own case.

Of course, lawyers have an ethical and legal duty to respond to discovery requests in good faith and to turn over all responsive documents, whether for good or for ill. Yet, it is hard to avoid the suspicion that an opposing lawyer may be skirting his or her duty for a tactical advantage.

Some clients think to help themselves by destroying documents that they perceive as hurting their case. This is a bad idea. First, it can be hard to tell whether a document is really harmful. Documents that initially seem harmful might actually be helpful when more context becomes available.

Second, the risk of getting caught is high, and the penalties if you are caught can be severe. In many cases multiple copies of the document exist, so when the other copies are located, nothing has been gained, while questions about why you don't have the document might be raised. Especially with electronic records, computer forensic experts can often recover deleted files from storage devices and also pinpoint the date and time the record was deleted.

The destruction of records exposes the client to a huge risk of sanctions from the court for spoliation of evidence. Spoliation sanctions can include monetary fines, but that's only the beginning. A judge can instruct the jury that it should assume the destroyed evidence was damaging to the person who destroyed it. In egregious cases, a court could simply enter judgment for the opposing party. These consequences are severe.

All in all, it is best to play by the rules and produce documents when the law requires them to be produced. Clients, and sometimes lawyers, often underestimate the amount of room the ambiguity of language leaves for making arguments about what a document really means. In the hands of a skilled advocate, even a seemingly red-hot, killer document can often be turned around and recast in a more favorable light.

Lawsuits are complicated affairs, with lots of witnesses and lots of documents. Rarely will a case stand or fall entirely on the strength of a single bad document. It is almost impossible to fire up the shredders high enough—and in secret—to successfully destroy all copies of the bad documents, so it is better to play the hand with the documents as you find them.

In addition to documents, the law of discovery allows for the inspection of tangible things and even the inspection of places if they are relevant to the lawsuit. This could be a request to inspect a parcel of land that is in dispute or the remnants of a product that was allegedly defective or a computer hard drive that might have deleted, but still recoverable, bits and bytes hidden inside.

Inspection requests, especially requests for documents, are an incredibly powerful tool in the litigator's toolbox. They force the other side to disclose the records in their possession. By studying those records, you can learn what the opposing side knows and check their stories against their own records from an earlier time before the dispute created incentives to shade the truth. Documents are the first stop in the discovery process, but they are not the last.

Depositions

As important as they are, documents never tell the whole story on their own. To complete the picture of what happened in a particular case, the testimony of witnesses is required. Accordingly, in discovery, the law allows the parties to a lawsuit to take testimony under oath outside of court. This taking of testimony out of court is called a **deposition**.

Depositions have three critical features. First, the testimony is taken under oath. This means that witnesses (called **deponents**) swear to tell the truth, the whole truth, and nothing but the truth. This is the same oath that witnesses must take when they testify in court before a judge and a jury. In theory, witnesses who fail to tell the truth in a deposition can be criminally prosecuted for perjury, but in practice, perjury prosecutions for false testimony in civil cases are exceedingly rare. Nevertheless, deponents testifying in depositions have an obligation to be truthful that does not normally exist in ordinary conversation.[166]

Second, depositions take the form of questions and answers. The attorney taking the deposition asks the questions. The deponent (*i.e.*, the witness) answers them. This format allows the attorney posing the questions to follow up on statements made by the deponent to get more detail about a subject or to clarify the meaning of a word or phrase.

The questions are posed directly to the witness, and the answers come directly from the witness. This is important and unusual. For the most part, attorneys do the talking for their clients in a lawsuit, but not at a deposition. At a deposition, the witnesses must speak for themselves. The testimony is not mediated, filtered, or sanitized by the witness's attorney. It represents the witness's own thoughts and words. If the witness claims a fact to be true, the attorney asking the questions has an opportunity to confront the witness with contradictory evidence to demonstrate that the witness was either lying in the worst case or has a faulty memory in the best case.

The presentation of contradictory evidence is called **impeaching the witness**. Impeaching the witness is often a primary goal of the deposition because the witness's inconsistencies and misstatements and errors can be used at trial to undermine the witness's credibility.

Finally, depositions are taken in front of a stenographer (also called a court reporter) who transcribes everything that is said in the deposition. This transcription is the key to the power of the deposition. Words are wind; they vibrate in the air for a moment before vanishing without a trace. Because of the frailty of human memory, people can, and often do, argue about what exactly people said even moments after the words have left the speaker's mouth.

The stenographer eliminates those arguments. By making a transcript, oral testimony becomes a document and thereby takes on two of the most important properties of documents: permanence and immutability. The effect is almost magical. Spoken words become fixed. Disputes over what a person said are eliminated (although the possibility of disputes over the *meaning* of what was said remains). If witnesses change their story after a deposition, the transcript of the earlier testimony stands ready to call out the change and impeach the later testimony.

Of course, deposition transcripts also suffer from the same limitations of documents in general. In particular, the written words may require interpretation or additional context to appreciate their true meaning. Part of the art of lawyering is framing questions in depositions in such a way that the answers are clearly understandable not just when they are spoken aloud in the heat of conversation but also when read on a cold page.

In general, each side will only take the deposition of witnesses who are either aligned with the opposing party or who are neutral. It is very rare to take a deposition of your own client or your client's allies. The main purpose of discovery is to gather evidence to be presented at trial. You already know, or can find out any time you like, what your own client has to say. All you have to do is ask. Similarly, people who are aligned with your client (i.e., your client's employees or spouse or business partners, etc.) will, in most cases, also cooperate and tell you their stories. For people who are not aligned with your client or outright opposed, the deposition is the mechanism the legal system provides to compel them to disclose what they know.

Since most cases settle, depositions are often crucial moments, especially the depositions of the parties to the lawsuit and their main witnesses. The depositions reveal whether people will make good or bad witnesses. Their testimony is tested for logic (are the actions the deponent claims to have taken the kind of actions you would reasonably expect?), for internal consistency (are the deponent's claimed actions consistent with each other?), for external consistency (are the claimed actions consistent with other evidence, such as other deposition testimony or documents?), and for likability (does the deponent present him or herself in a credible, sympathetic manner or does he or she come off like a creep?). The performance of the key witnesses in depositions can dramatically swing the value of a case. A good, credible, consistent, sympathetic witness for the opposition is a frightening thing to face at trial.

Because of the importance of depositions, preparation is critical. Some parts of deposition preparation (or "depo prep" as lawyers like to call it) are obvious. Deposition testimony is given under oath, so deponents are advised to tell the truth. Nevertheless, to paraphrase Emily Dickinson, for most deponents the objective is to "tell all the truth but tell it slant."[167] When the deponent is a party to a lawsuit, he or she knows that the adversary's attorney's questions have the sole purpose of gathering information to use against him or her. While the oath requires that answers be truthful, it does not require that they be helpful.

A common instruction to deponents is to answer only the question asked. Do not volunteer additional information unless specifically required to answer the question. Short answers are better than longer ones, and the best answers of all are "yes," "no," and "I don't know."

For example, if someone asks, "Do you know what time it is?" most people, if they know, would volunteer the time, but the question technically asks only if you *know* the time—not what the time *is*. The technically correct answer to a question about whether you know something is either yes, you do, or no, you don't. The burden is on the questioning attorney to follow up if he or she wants to find out more.

Closely related to answering only the question asked is the common instruction not to speculate, but rather to limit answers to things you know from your own personal knowledge and not things you think or believe to be true. Many of our beliefs about the world are based on logic, experience, common sense, or what people or sources we consider reliable have told us. Those beliefs, however, are not the same thing as personal knowledge. If you did not personally see, hear, feel, taste, or smell something, then answering questions about it would be speculation.

For example, suppose your spouse leaves for work every day at eight in the morning and comes home promptly at six and has done so every working day for the past twenty years. In a deposition, you are asked where your spouse was at ten o'clock on a particular morning. The correct answer is you don't know. You did not personally see your spouse at work that day. You might reasonably *assume* that your spouse was at work, but you cannot testify to that fact because you did not directly observe it.

Cautiously narrow answers can be seen as evasive game-playing, calculated to mislead, or they can be understood as rigorously adhering to the requirement of answering the questions posed as truthfully and accurately as possible without giving a false impression of more knowledge or certainty than truly is warranted. Either way, because they are a fact of life in lawsuits, skilled lawyers must cut through circumscribed answers and pin down whatever personal knowledge the deponent does in fact have.

Continuing with the prior example of the spouse off at work, if this is an important issue, a lawyer could ask questions such as:

• "What was your spouse wearing? Are these the clothes that he or she normally wears when going to work?"

• "Did your spouse tell you anything about where he or she was going that morning? Did he or she say he was going to work?"

• "Do you have any reason to believe that your spouse did *not* go to work that day?"

These questions are only a start, but they are an effective beginning because they ask about things that the witness personally experienced, so the witness cannot avoid answering. The answers can be used to paint a picture about the spouse's patterns, actions, and expressed or presumed intentions so that a judge and jury can infer the spouse's whereabouts, using the same information that the witness would have used to form his or her own judgments.

A difficult decision in preparing for a deposition is how much to refresh a witness's recollection with documents. A common question at the beginning of depositions is whether the witness reviewed any documents to prepare for the deposition. If the witness answers affirmatively, the opposing lawyer is going to want to know what those documents were, which could disclose to the other side something about which documents its opponents consider most important.

Refreshing a witness's recollection in preparation for a deposition is not required. In a deposition, witnesses are only required to testify to the best of their recollection, so "I don't know" or "I don't recall" are perfectly acceptable answers. People's memories are naturally hazy and uneven in the best of circumstances. Recollections can be refreshed after the deposition, so the witness has a firm command of the facts and can deliver the story convincingly at trial.

But saving the best testimony for trial has its own risks. First, since most cases settle, if you've saved your best testimony, the settlement might not reflect the full value your testimony adds to the case. If you want to get the best deal, it pays to make sure that your opponent appreciates your full fighting strength.

Second, highly polished trial testimony might be met with significant skepticism if the deposition was riddled with I-don't-knows and I-don't-recalls. In a legal dispute, it is often the case that a handful of moments in time are pivotal. In the course of a busy life, however, those moments might not be obvious at the time and might easily pass by with no more attention than any of the other countless events that stream through our lives.

Nevertheless, there is a sense that people should remember important events, and so there is a certain expectation that people will remember events that are central to the issues in a lawsuit, even though their importance might only have been appreciated much later in time. Failing to have a firm recollection at a deposition can raise suspicions that a person only remembers what is helpful to his or her case. Reviewing documents can help sharpen hazy recollections and allow witnesses to give clearer and more confident testimony. Although this helps the other side, it can also help you by enhancing credibility and giving you an opportunity to put your story on the record.

Third, your deposition transcript can be shown to other witnesses to refresh—or influence, if you are of a more cynical bent—their recollections of events. If your testimony says only "I don't know," then that leaves other people to fill in the gaps with their own recollections, which may or may not be accurate. If instead your testimony has a clear articulation of what happened from your point of view, other people who might be uncertain of their own recollections might shy away from disagreeing with a confidently told account.

Preparing to take a deposition is every bit as important as preparing to give one. Taking a deposition is high stakes in litigation because a person can generally only be deposed once. If the attorney forgets to ask an important question, it is unlikely that he or she will get a second chance.

The attorney taking a deposition has several objectives. First, the attorney wants to figure out what the witness knows or doesn't know about the issues in dispute. This is discovery in the purest sense because the attorney is trying to discover the extent of the witness's knowledge.

Second, the attorney wants to pin the witness to a specific version of events. As a dispute develops, a witness can get a better and better sense of what testimony would be helpful and what testimony would be harmful. The deposition forces the witness to stake out a definitive position on the record, and that makes it difficult for the witness later to revise his or her account if subsequent developments make it inconvenient.

Finally, the attorney is looking for ways to test a witness's memory and credibility. Ultimately, the value of a witness's testimony is directly proportional to how much that witness is believed. Witnesses are believed or disbelieved for a host of reasons—some good, some bad. The moment that a witness is called to testify, the judge and the jury begin forming judgments about the witness's credibility. They observe how witnesses dress and how they carry themselves to the witness stand. There is a reason that police officers testify in full uniform. The clothes convey authority, and juries pick up on those cues.

Once the witness starts testifying, the witness's body language is closely observed as well.

- Does the witness sit up straight or slouch?
- Does the witness speak too quickly or too slowly?
- Does the witness take long pauses to answer questions?
- Does the witness squint or shift his or her eyes or body or sweat or tap his or her fingers or play with his or her hair?

The totality of how the witness presents himself or herself physically is commonly referred to as the witness's **demeanor**.

The witness's demeanor can, and often does, play a decisive role in whether a witness is believed or not, but there is some question about the accuracy of jurors who try to tell whether someone is lying by simply looking at the person. Many Americans say their greatest fear in life is public speaking—more than heights, insects, shots, and being trapped in small spaces (but behind snakes).[168] For most people, testifying—especially in court, under oath, in front of a crowded courtroom—is a once-in-a-lifetime experience. It should be no surprise, then, that many honest people would be nervous having to answer lots of questions in such an intimidating environment.

Moreover, as we've seen, the ability of ordinary people to figure out whether people are lying by observing their demeanor is notoriously weak.[169] Nevertheless, right or wrong, accurate or inaccurate, demeanor can heavily influence whether a witness is believed or not, and the deposition is an opportunity to see how opposing and friendly witnesses hold up to questioning. Strong witnesses increase the value of a case, while weak ones reduce it.

To put a witness's memory and credibility to the test, and to see how the witness reacts under stress, lawyers will often ask witnesses to give their recollections of events that are documented in other places. For example, the minutes of a meeting of a corporate board of directors will reflect who was present and who was absent and the agenda for the meeting. To gauge the sharpness of a witness's memory, a lawyer could ask the witness to recall who was at the meeting or what was discussed and use the meeting minutes as the measuring stick of the witness's accuracy and reliability.

Minor memory failures are small game. The real prize is if the witness says something crucial about the case that is demonstrably false. For example, in a race discrimination case, the lawyer for the plaintiff might ask the defendant if he ever used racial slurs to refer to people of another race. The defendant will know that admitting to using racial slurs will make him look like a racist and make it more likely that he will lose the lawsuit, so the defendant will have a strong impulse to deny it. If the defendant gives into that impulse and denies having ever used racial slurs, the plaintiff's lawyer (if he has the evidence) can exultantly produce an email sent by the defendant that contains the very racial slur the defendant has just denied ever using. Now, the defendant is not just a racist, but he is a liar as well, and the plaintiff's case just got a whole lot more valuable.

Preparation for the deposition requires careful review of documents and the testimony of other witnesses. The attorney who masters of all the evidence can spot when a witness deviates from established facts. Skillful questioners can maneuver witnesses into positions where the incentive to fudge the truth is so strong that witnesses give in to temptation, say something less than the whole truth, and then are brutally called out for lying.

A deposition is not like an ordinary conversation. The witness's words are frozen in a written transcript. Once spoken, the words are fixed. Clarifications, explanations, and amplifications can be offered, but the words themselves cannot be unsaid. Consequently, choosing words carefully is critical, both for questions and for answers. A successful deposition looks very different to the person taking the deposition than to the person giving the deposition. The one who emerges on the better side of the contest receives a significant boost in winning a dispute.

Requests for Admissions and Interrogatories

Document requests and depositions are the two discovery tools that are most likely to produce relevant, admissible evidence that will shed light on what really happened to the parties before they came to court. Two other discovery tools, while less useful, also are worthy of mention: requests for admissions and interrogatories.

A **request for admission** asks the opposing party to admit a fact is true. The responding party has two options: admit the fact or deny it. (Yes, the responding party can also object—this is law, after all, and objection is always possible—but objections need not detain us here.)

Before denying a fact, the responding party must conduct a reasonable inquiry. This means that a response cannot rely merely on the present recollection of the responder. Rather, a duty exists to examine reasonably available records.

Requests for admissions can be extremely powerful. If a fact is admitted, that fact is *conclusively established* for purposes of the lawsuit. In other words, no proof at trial is needed to show that the admitted fact is true, and the opposing party is not permitted to deny the truth of the fact at trial.

Because admissions are so powerful, no one wants to make one. Recognizing that parties have every incentive to deny everything, the law establishes a penalty for denying a fact that should have been admitted. If a party denies a fact, and the opposing party later proves that fact to be true at trial, the party that wrongfully denied it may have to pay the legal fees the opposing party incurred when it had to produce evidence to prove something that should have been admitted.

Requests for admissions are different from other discovery tools, which allow—and even encourage—broad questions to discover unknown facts. Requests for admissions are by their nature narrow and based on information you already know.

Imagine you were injured when a brick fell on your head as you were walking past a building that was under construction.

When you sue the construction company, you might make the following requests for admissions:

• Admit that you [i.e., the construction company] were engaging in construction activity at the building on the day of the injury.

• Admit that you failed to put up warning signs around the construction site.

• Admit that on the day of the injury you failed to put up a barrier to prevent pedestrians from using the sidewalk next to the building where construction was occurring.

Each of these requests for admissions helps establish the liability of the construction company. The first request, if admitted, establishes that the construction company was performing work on the building. The second tends to establish that the construction company failed to give adequate notice to passers-by of the dangers of the construction. The third tends to establish that the construction company failed to take a reasonable precaution (closing the sidewalk) that might have prevented the injury.

Yet to even form these requests, you must already have some very specific knowledge. You need to already know the name of the construction company, the absence of warning signs, and the failure to close the sidewalk.

Thus, a request for admission is not discovery in the truest sense of the word. A request for admission does not discover new information. Rather, it confirms what you already think you know.

Nevertheless, properly deployed, requests for admissions can play a very important role in a lawsuit. If you can get your opponent to admit a fact, that fact will *conclusively* be presumed to be true, and you are not required to prove that fact at trial. This can save a great deal of time and expense.

Some witnesses may no longer be required. Others may see their time on the witness stand reduced. With most lawyers billing by the hour, time saved translates directly into money saved.

In addition, requests for admissions can remove some of the uncertainty of trials. Because the admitted fact cannot be challenged, there is no concern that a witness might change her story or suffer a memory failure or simply leave a bad impression that causes the jury to dislike or disbelieve her.

Of course, a fact need only be admitted if it is true. Although the rules require that responses be in good faith, meaning that parties should admit the substance of a request if they can, in practice most litigants will deny a request if given half a chance. Thus, a request that the opposing party admit that she was driving 75 miles per hour at the time of the accident will be met with a denial if she was driving 76 or 74 miles per hour. The requested admission is technically wrong, so the denial is technically correct.

To avoid technically correct, but evasive or misleading denials, requests for admissions must be framed with great care. Ambiguities must be squeezed out because the opposing party, who knows that the admission will only be used against him or her in court, will seize upon any uncertainty to justify denying the request. The more precise the request, the more likely an admission will be required, but only if the request is precisely accurate. For that reason, requests for admissions will most usually be deployed toward the end of discovery, when the facts are better known, rather than at the very beginning.

Requests for admissions are very useful tools for narrowing the issues in a lawsuit to just the facts that are truly in dispute.

An **interrogatory** is a written question that the opposing party must answer in writing and under oath.[170]

171

Interrogatories have the distinct advantage that the person responding has an obligation to answer the questions with the information that is readily available, and not just based on what the person happens to recall at that particular moment, as happens in a deposition.

Interrogatories, however, suffer from a terrible drawback. Interrogatories are written questions that must be answered in writing, but who is it that writes the response? Is it the opposing party? Almost never. Litigants hire lawyers to do tasks like these, and the lawyers, acutely aware of what they need to say and what they need to avoid saying to win their cases, will frame their answers to load up on favorable claims and assertions, while actively minimizing disclosure of anything that could possibly hurt their cases.

Depositions cut through the evasions of opposing lawyers by posing questions directly to the people who have to answer without filtering their responses through their lawyers. While attorneys may try to coach deponents prior to the deposition, once the deposition starts, the witnesses are on their own. For interrogatories, the lawyer-coach can get in the game directly by writing the answers for the client and then just having the client verify the response. The possibility of catching a candid confession drops to just about zero.

In addition, while interrogatories may be used at trial, especially to impeach a witness who gives an answer that differs from the written interrogatory response, interrogatories, unlike requests for admissions, are generally not binding on a party, so a party is free to change her story at trial. In addition, interrogatory responses are often so verbose and opaque that it can be impossible to directly contrast a witness's oral statement at trial with the interrogatory response.

Interrogatories fall into two broad categories: identification interrogatories and contention interrogatories.[171] Identification interrogatories seek basic, factual information. A typical identification interrogatory might be to ask for the names and addresses of witnesses to the incident in question. Many identification interrogatories can be answered by producing records. For example, a question about how much money a company spent on delivery charges might be answered by producing the company's expense ledgers.

More controversial and more complicated are contention interrogatories. Contention interrogatories ask the opposing party to explain the factual and often the legal basis for their claims. For example, if a plaintiff sues a manufacturing company, alleging that the company's product (say a fire-walking pit) is defective because it is unreasonably dangerous, the defendant might serve the plaintiff with a contention interrogatory that looks something like the following: State all facts that support your contention that the product is unreasonably dangerous.

On the surface, the interrogatory is asking for facts. After all, it does begin with the words "state all facts." But really, this question is asking about the plaintiff's legal conclusion that the product is unreasonably dangerous, which in a products liability case is the ultimate fact that the plaintiff needs to prove. A complete answer to this question would require a summary of the prospective testimony of every witness and the contents of every pertinent record.

Preparing written answers with that level of detail is not feasible. So broadly worded questions are met with broadly worded answers. Lots of paper changes hands, but often not much information.

In the end, interrogatories are most likely to produce useful responses if they focus on simple and objective facts. If it is important to know the names of all the financial institutions where a business holds assets, an interrogatory is a good way to get the list.

Broad contention interrogatories, in contrast, while they are fun to write, rarely yield much that can be profitably used later in the case. Undoubtedly, contention interrogatories inflict costs and expenses on the opposing party by forcing her lawyer to stay up late writing vapid and meaningless responses, but lawyers skilled in obfuscation and protecting their cases can usually avoid any significant, self-inflicted wounds. If document requests and depositions are the razor-sharp saws in the discovery toolkit, interrogatories are the butter knife. Not totally useless, but close.

PRE-TRIAL MOTIONS

Lawsuits are long, expensive slogs. If a defendant can get out of a case early without having to go through all the work of discovery and trials, the defendant will stretch as far as possible to snatch that opportunity. Defendants have two main avenues to try to get a trial court to throw out a plaintiff's case without a trial: the motion to dismiss and the motion for summary judgment.

The Motion to Dismiss

The plaintiff's complaint sets out the plaintiff's allegations, legal theories, and remedies. Whether the allegations are true or not is a question that requires investigation into the real world, normally through the discovery process. Legal theories are different. Sometimes, you can tell right away that a legal theory simply isn't going to work.

A defendant files a **motion to dismiss** to challenge the legal sufficiency of the plaintiff's complaint.[172] Although different types of motions are possible, the most common is the motion to dismiss for **failure to state a claim**.[173] Since only the *legal* sufficiency of the complaint is under challenge in a motion to dismiss (as opposed to the complaint's *factual* sufficiency), a motion to dismiss accepts as true all of the factual allegations in the complaint. The allegations are considered true only for the purposes of resolving the motion. If the motion to dismiss is denied, the defendant can investigate the allegations in the discovery process and challenge the allegations at trial. By taking the allegations as true, the motion to dismiss zeroes in on whether the law supports the plaintiff's claims.

A motion to dismiss for failure to state a claim can attack a complaint in two different ways. The first type of attack challenges whether the cause of action alleged by the plaintiff is even a violation of the law at all under any circumstances.

Imagine you have gotten home from a relaxing day at the beach. Just as you're dusting the sand out of your toes, a process server appears at your door and hands you a complaint. An angry and distraught father is suing you for negligently letting his beloved daughter drown. According to the complaint, you were sitting on the beach when the plaintiff's daughter began to struggle in the water. You saw her distress, you were capable of coming to her aid, but you callously refused to act, and you let the waters drag her down.

Your first reaction is that you did nothing of the sort. The allegations are scurrilous lies. You are already angrily typing up your answer when you start thinking about the time and expense of discovery and then the even greater time and expense of going to court for a trial, and you start casting about for an easier way to get this frivolous lawsuit out of your life.

Having read this chapter, you hit upon the motion to dismiss. Even if you had sat on the beach and watched the plaintiff's daughter drown, as morally contemptible as that may be, did you have a *legal* duty to rescue the girl? In other words, even if the plaintiff's allegation that you failed to rescue his daughter were true, would that be a violation of the law?

A little research confirms that, in America (for the most part) there is no duty to rescue. That means, even if the allegations were true (they're not, but you assume their truth for the purposes of the motion), the plaintiff cannot win because the legal duty the plaintiff claims you violated does not exist. The motion to dismiss has just saved you a lot of time and headache by putting an end to the lawsuit before things really even got started.

The second type of attack a motion to dismiss can mount is a challenge to whether the facts as alleged in the complaint, assuming them all to be true, add up to a violation of law. Imagine that, tired of getting bossed around at a nine-to-five job, you decide to go into business for yourself. You love coffee, and there is always a long line outside a coffee shop in your neighborhood, so you decide to set up a coffee shop of your own across the street to see if you can capture some of the other coffee shop's business.

No sooner do you open your doors than a process server appears to hand you a complaint from the other coffee shop's owner. The complaint alleges that you are stealing her customers, and therefore, you are engaged in unfair competition. You do some quick research and learn that unfair competition is a valid cause of action and that it is defined as economic injury to a business through a deceptive or wrongful business practice.

You've just started a new business, and making a successful go of it will be tough enough without a protracted lawsuit draining your pocketbook. Again, the motion to dismiss is your ticket out of the lawsuit.

The only wrongful conduct alleged in the complaint is that you opened a competing business. In the motion to dismiss, you argue that opening a competing business is neither deceptive nor wrongful. On the contrary, free competition is the American way. If all goes as it should, the court should grant the motion because the allegation that you opened up a competing business does not meet the law's requirements for unfair competition.

From the defendant's point of view, the beauty of the motion to dismiss is that it can knock out a lawsuit before the much more expensive and time-consuming processes of discovery and trial. Motions to dismiss are also valuable for plaintiffs. If the plaintiff's case suffers from some fatal, legal defect apparent on the face of the complaint, it is better for the plaintiff to find that out before the plaintiff invests a lot of time, money, and energy pursuing a case that ultimately cannot be won.

The Motion for Summary Judgment

If the plaintiff has a well-pleaded complaint with valid legal theories and allegations that state the essential elements of the legal claims, an early victory for the defendant through a motion to dismiss will not be possible. For the defendant who would like to knock out the lawsuit before going through the expensive ordeal of a trial, all hope is not lost. If the defendant's case is very strong and the plaintiff's case is very weak, the defendant might be able to convince a court to throw out the case through a **motion for summary judgment**.

A motion for summary judgment asks the court to enter judgment without going through a trial. The summary part of the term refers to skipping the trial (like a summary execution of the plaintiff's case). The purpose of the trial is to resolve the parties' disputes about the facts of their case—in other words, figure out what really happened. If there is no real dispute to resolve about the facts, a trial serves no purpose. If all the facts are known and the legal rule can be determined, a legal judgment logically follows. Summary judgment is appropriate when only one reasonable result at trial is possible because the facts are not in dispute and all that is required is for the court to apply the law.

The legal standard for granting a motion for summary judgment holds that summary judgment is appropriate if (and only if) there is no *genuine* issue of *material* fact.[174] This is an important concept that is worth unpacking.

An issue is genuine if some evidence exists to support both sides of the disputed question. A fact is material if the fact could alter the outcome of the case.

Consider the following example. Paul says Darryl hit him, and Darryl says he never touched Paul. The issue in dispute is whether Darryl hit Paul or not. The issue is *genuine* because Paul's testimony ("Darryl hit me") is evidence that supports one side of the question, and Darryl's testimony ("No, I didn't") is evidence that supports the other. The fact is *material* because whether or not Darryl hit Paul will determine the outcome of the lawsuit. If Darryl did not, in fact, hit Paul, Paul must lose his lawsuit. In this example, because there is a genuine dispute about a material fact, summary judgment would *not* be appropriate.

Now consider the same case with slightly different evidence. If Paul's testimony were that *someone* hit him, and he *thinks* it was Darryl, but he isn't sure because he never saw who hit him, summary judgment would likely be appropriate. Darryl's testimony is evidence that he did not hit Paul, and Paul's testimony is that he doesn't know whether or not Darryl hit him. Now Darryl's side is the only one with any evidence. Since Paul doesn't have any evidence that Darryl hit him (only mere suspicion), there is only one reasonable result, and summary judgment should be entered for Darryl because there is no genuine issue of material fact.

It may be a little surprising that summary judgment is ever possible in any dispute. Why would anyone bring a case with *no evidence* to support the claims? While examples exist of people bringing lawsuits just to spite another person, that kind of vexatious conduct is not the norm. For the most part, litigants and their lawyers bring lawsuits to make money.

At the outset of a lawsuit, there can be a lot of unknowns. Even in the simple example of Paul and Darryl, if Paul suspects that Darryl hit him, Paul might bring the lawsuit even if he doesn't know for sure because a number of things could happen that would result in Paul getting paid for his trouble.

First, during discovery, Paul might discover evidence that Darryl was, in fact, the one who hit him. Darryl might admit to hitting Paul under cross-examination at his deposition. Paul might find someone else who was at the scene who could testify that Darryl hit him. Darryl might have sent an email or posted on Facebook that he hit Paul. If he doesn't bring his lawsuit, Paul may never find out whether evidence to confirm his suspicions is out there, and if he does find that evidence, then suddenly he has a very strong case.

Second, most lawsuits settle. There are many reasons for this, but the fact is that even frivolous cases have some value. Writing a motion for summary judgment costs money, and so a plaintiff can often get what is called a **nuisance value** settlement just to make the plaintiff go away.

So for many plaintiffs it's worth it to roll the dice on litigation in the hopes of finding favorable evidence or extracting some settlement. If a plaintiff overplays his hand, however, and pushes for too much money with a weak case, the defendant will take the trouble to write the motion for summary judgment, and if the plaintiff can't come up with some evidence to dispute the material facts, the plaintiff will walk away with nothing.

SETTLEMENT

Sometimes the facts are on your side and the law is on your side, and you still can't win—or at least it feels that way. Even with a winning case, you might be tempted to settle and walk away with less than you are due.

Most disputes are never brought to court, and of the few that do make it through the doors of the courthouse, the vast majority settle before they get to trial. For employment cases, almost 70 percent end in settlement.[175] For personal injury cases, the settlement rate is closer to 90 percent.[176] Overall, more than two out of three cases settle.[177] With that kind of settlement rate, litigation is often less about getting ready for your day in court and more about maneuvering to negotiate the best deal before getting out of the legal process.

People settle cases for many reasons. A big driver of settlement is the cost of litigation itself. Attorneys are expensive. In addition to paying for lawyers, clients are expected to pay for court fees, couriers, and copies. Every deposition your side takes means paying for a court reporter to prepare a transcript, not to mention your attorney's time to prepare for and appear at the deposition. If experts are needed (and they almost always are in modern litigation), clients have to pay for their services too, and experts frequently charge more per hour than lawyers. Add it all up, and the value of a case can be quickly drained by the fees and costs of prosecuting or defending it.

Lawsuits suck out your money, but they also suck up your time. Documents must be gathered, meetings must be attended, strategies must be developed, and decisions must be made. The time spent on the lawsuit is time not spent doing something more productive, like working on your business or your job, spending time with your family, contributing to your community, or simply relaxing and enjoying life.

In addition to costing money out of pocket and consuming time for day-to-day tasks, lawsuits also often impose significant mental costs. The anxiety that comes from worrying about the possibility of losing should not be discounted. Many sleepless nights can be lost to apprehension over an unfamiliar process with an inherently uncertain outcome.

Even for people who are not typically nervous, just thinking about the lawsuit can consume a disproportionate amount of a person's time and attention. It can be hard to stop thinking about a lawsuit. You might be on the floor playing with your kids when your mind wanders to a question you want asked in a deposition, an argument that should have been made in a brief, or just how angry you are that the other side is putting you through all of this. The stress and the distraction can be more costly than the attorneys' monthly bills.

Lawsuits can also bring unwanted publicity. For the most part, legal proceedings are matters of public record, so newspapers, bloggers, and busybodies can poke their noses into the details of a dispute and spread what they find far and wide. The most celebrated example involves the singer and actress Barbara Streisand.

Barbara Streisand owned a mansion on a high cliff in secluded Malibu, California, and she liked her privacy. Photographer Kenneth Adelman was working with the California Coastal Records Project on documenting erosion on the California coast by taking aerial photographs of the coastline. Adelman flew into Streisand's sights when he took a picture of Streisand's private estate.

Streisand was horrified that a picture of her precious home might be publicly available, so she sued. Her strategy backfired. Before her lawsuit, Adelman's previously obscure photo had been downloaded a mere seven times, two of which by Streisand's lawyers. After the lawsuit, more than fifty thousand people flocked to the California Coastal Records Project's website to see what all the fuss was about.

The Internet dubbed this ironic turn of events the Streisand Effect, which has come to describe any situation where taking action to keep something private only results in much more unwanted publicity than if the plaintiff had simply let well enough alone. Lawsuits frequently have an element of the Streisand Effect, which makes settlement an attractive alternative for the party who prefers to stay out of the press.

Even with strong cases, the pressure to settle can mount because there is always a risk of losing. Lawsuits and trials suffer many vagaries and uncertainties. Documents that are clear to you might seem ambiguous to a judge or jury. Testimony that you thought was rock solid might come out garbled or worse when delivered at a trial. Witnesses get cold feet or nervous. Memories fail and sometimes flip-flop. Sometimes honest people are simply disbelieved, even when they are telling the truth.

Even with the best evidence presented in a first-class way, in the end, decisions in legal cases are made by fallible people who make mistakes all the time. George Carlin once quipped, "Think of how dumb the average American is and then remember: half the people are dumber than that."[178] Entrusting an important decision to a random collection of strangers can seem highly unappealing when it's your life on the line.

On the opposite side of the spectrum, settlement usually makes sense in the cases where the outcome is a foregone conclusion. By the end of discovery in many cases, when all the documents have been exchanged, all the interrogatories answered, and all the depositions taken, a clear picture will emerge. In those cases where the facts are clear and the law is clear, both sides to the dispute can be reasonably sure of what the final outcome of the case is going to be when the dust settles and the trial is over. Settlement saves both sides the costs and trouble of traveling down the last stretch of road to a destination that is virtually predetermined. The savings from avoiding these litigation costs provide a fund that the parties can draw upon to quit the process early.

Other pressures to settle exist as well. In some cases, a defendant might be "judgment proof," meaning the defendant does not have any money with which to pay for damages. Nothing is gained by pursuing a judgment in court if the defendant can't pay it. In other cases, the amount at stake might not be high enough to justify the time and expense. If someone puts a small scratch on your car's paint, it is probably not worth it to go to court to obtain the nominal damages that could be recovered.

Many cases have insurance companies on one side or another or both. The presence of insurance changes the settlement dynamics. If you have insurance and face a lawsuit, you might be perfectly happy to settle for any amount that is within your insurance policy's limits because it will be the insurance company that pays and not you. Of course, the insurance company wants to pay as little as possible, but if insurance companies refuse a settlement offer that a court later deems was reasonable, the insurance company could be on the hook for double payments in a lawsuit claiming that the insurance company's decision not to settle was a "bad faith" breach of the insurance contract.

Courts like it when litigants settle. Every settlement represents a dispute that the courts do not need to resolve, freeing up their time for other cases. To promote settlements, courts frequently order the parties to a lawsuit to participate in **mediation**.

Mediation is an informal resolution process. The parties meet with a neutral facilitator (the mediator) who attempts to help the parties resolve their dispute. Mediations are strictly confidential. Nothing said in mediation is admissible in court.[179] Although a court might require litigants to participate in mediation, settlements are voluntary; no one is required to agree to anything at mediation. Mediation is an opportunity to get otherwise warring parties to talk.

Mediators have many techniques to encourage settlement. Generally, mediators will separate the parties. Seeing your adversary close-up can stir up emotions that make it harder to compromise. The mediator shuttles between the two camps, cajoling each side to compromise and conveying each side's settlement proposals and counter-proposals.

Having the mediator as an intermediary often helps people make and consider proposals that they might reject out of hand if they came directly from their opponents. A concession can be couched as the mediator's idea, so the person making it doesn't lose face and the person considering it doesn't look weak. In their separate rooms, the parties can vent their frustrations privately to the mediator, who can buffer the other side from passions that otherwise would get in the way of finding solutions to the dispute.

Mediators will push the parties toward compromise by pointing out weaknesses in their respective cases. Mediators will tell plaintiffs that if they gamble on a trial, they could walk away with nothing. At the same time, mediators will tell defendants that if they gamble on a trial, they could face crippling damages.

Normally, mediations begin in the morning and run until late in the day. The schedule is not accidental. In the morning, when everyone is fresh, litigants are ready for combat. They arrive expecting to insist that the opposing side meet their demands. By the end of the day, fatigue sets in, and fighting begins to lose its appeal. Everyone becomes tired, frustrated, and irritated. With spirits worn down, the parties often begin to see compromise as a good way to get everything over with.

Although mediations don't always result in settlements, they have a remarkably high success rate. One study of large construction disputes found that mediation led to full or partial settlements in nearly two thirds of cases.[180]

The lesson of mediation is that people often don't realize just how much they're willing to compromise. Only when they are tired and hungry and fed up do they start thinking that fighting might not really be worth it after all.

During the Presidency of John Adams in the late 1790s, French ships had a nasty habit of attacking American ships. President Adams sent a delegation to France to negotiate a stop to the attacks, but when the American diplomats arrived, a French minister demanded bribes as a prerequisite to opening negotiations. When word of the French minister's demands reached America, instant and widespread outrage flared among American leaders and the public at large. The incident became infamous as the XYZ Affair, named after the code names given to the corrupt French ministers. Americans united in their defiance against France under the slogan "Millions for defense, but not one cent for tribute."

This same sense that it is better to pay any price for honor motivates many a lawsuit. The costs in money, time, and distraction are disregarded, and instead the banner is raised that justice must be done. Only after the battle is joined is the full price of combat felt. As costs mount and victory remains elusive and uncertain, people begin to rethink whether perfect justice might not, in fact, have too high a price after all.

As for the XYZ affair, while Congress authorized money to build warships and armies, President Adams, recognizing that war with a major European power could spell disaster for the fledgling American republic, steered the country to a peaceful resolution, saving American lives and treasure, but costing him prestige in the eyes of a fevered public.

While in the heat of the moment it can seem that any price should be borne before an unjust payment is exacted, "any price" can be quite high. In a lawsuit, where the mental and monetary costs of vindication can sometimes dwarf the costs of a little ransom, settlement has a powerful pull that, ultimately, draws most people in.

Paying a few dollars for tribute doesn't seem so bad if it saves millions on defense.

TRIALS

The main event in the trial court is the trial, even though most cases never get there. Between settlements and pre-trial motions, most of the time the proverbial day in court never comes. Nevertheless, everything that happens in the trial court builds toward the trial.

The purpose of the trial is to resolve disputed issues of fact. If there are no disputed issues of fact, then a motion for summary judgment should dispose of the case. American trials are familiar staples of television, books, and movies, and they play a central role in the public's understanding of what justice at work looks like. Several key features of trials dictate how they work.

First, the distinction between facts and laws continues at trial. In general, the jury will be responsible for finding the facts, but sometimes the judge will play this role. Because of this specialized role, the jury is often called the trier of fact or the fact finder. The judge's role is to ensure that the trial proceeds in accordance with the rules for trials, and when the evidence has all been presented, the judge tells the trier of fact (*i.e.*, the jury) the laws that they need to apply to the facts.

Second, lawsuits are decided by people who know nothing about the people involved or the issues in dispute. The thinking is that the only way to ensure that the decision-maker is fair, impartial, and unbiased is to have someone who doesn't have any preconceived ideas that come from familiarity with the people or the issues. Interestingly, this reasoning is the exact opposite of the justification for juries when they were originally conceived in medieval England. At that time, jurors were *required* to be familiar with the parties and the facts, the thought being that only by knowing the people and something about what happened could the jury reach a correct result.[181]

Third, the responsibility for presenting the evidence that will form the basis of the decision falls to the parties to the lawsuit. In fact, jurors are forbidden from doing any independent research at all, and jury verdicts have been thrown out when it has come to light that jurors did something as simple, obvious, and seemingly innocuous as look up a word in a dictionary. The parties decide which witnesses to call, what questions to ask, and what documents to present. The judge has the power to exclude evidence, and sometimes will step in to ask a clarifying question or two, but the evidence that the jury hears is almost entirely decided by the litigants themselves.

Fourth, the presentation of evidence almost entirely takes the form of question and answer. A witness is called to testify, and the lawyers for each side lead the witness through his or her testimony by asking questions. Witnesses are not allowed to tell their story on their own without direction and unprompted by questions.

Fifth, for the most part, the parties' presentations of evidence takes place with no opportunity for feedback about what the jurors are thinking, what points the jurors think are important, or even whether the jurors are following and understanding the evidence. In fact, a standard admonition to jurors is that they are not to talk about a case with anyone, not even with other jurors, until all of the evidence has been submitted. The jurors are expected to sit silently and listen, but not form any opinions or reach any conclusions until all the evidence is in and they been instructed on the applicable law.[182]

These features of trials have significant ramifications on how litigants prepare and present their cases in court, which we will turn to in the following sections.

Voir Dire: Picking the Jury

The most important part of a decision-making process is the decision-maker. The decision-maker will bring his or her prejudices, biases, predispositions, and inclinations to bear in making up his or her mind. Both sides want those inherent, unavoidable, human tendencies to work in their favor. Only one (and possibly neither) will get their wish.

In jury trials, the decision-maker is the jury, and the first order of business is to select who will be on the jury. Picking a jury is tricky business. Jurors need to be impartial and free from prejudice for or against any party. Prospective jurors are drawn from the local community, typically selected at random from voter registration lists or driver's license records. They shuffle into the courthouse with varying levels of interest in being dragged away from their regular lives to do their civic duty.

The process of picking a jury is called **voir dire**. The term "voir dire" comes from the French words "to see" (voir) and "to say" (dire). Prospective jurors (also known as the **venire**) are brought up to a courtroom and asked to answer numerous questions about themselves. Jurors are frequently asked where they live, if they're married and have children, what their occupation is, and whether they've served on a jury before. Voir dire is the only point in the trial where the parties are allowed to pose questions directly to the prospective jurors.

The purpose of voir dire is to ensure that the jurors are impartial and unbiased and have no knowledge of the parties or the dispute. In the high-profile murder trial of George Zimmerman, who shot and killed an unarmed, African-American teenager claiming it was in self-defense, the media publicity around the case was so wild and pervasive that Zimmerman became a national figure familiar to almost everyone in the country. Zimmerman's lawyer alluded to the media frenzy by opening his case with a knock-knock joke. He said, "Knock, knock? Who's there? George Zimmerman. George Zimmerman, who? Congratulations, you're on the jury!"[183]

Putting aside the wisdom of starting a jury trial with a knock-knock joke (but hey, Zimmerman was acquitted, so maybe this is a case of you can't argue with success), after the prospective jurors have finished answering whatever questions the judge allows, prospective jurors can be removed from the pool in one of two ways. First, prospective jurors can be removed **for cause**. Good causes to remove a juror are things like:

• The juror knows the parties or the witnesses.

• The juror has a financial stake in the outcome (for example, by owning stock in a company that is a party to the lawsuit).

• The juror is unable to be fair and impartial (for example, because the juror or a close friend or relative has suffered a negative experience very similar to the issues in the trial).

• The juror is not able to take the time to serve (although this last excuse is looked upon with disfavor and skepticism by judges who are all too familiar with people who just want to get out of jury duty).

Prospective jurors can also be removed through a **peremptory challenge**. A peremptory challenge is when one of the parties removes a prospective juror from the jury pool without having to give a reason. Peremptory challenges are often exercised based on hunches and guesswork about what type of person would be most likely to favor the opponent's case, and so would be the kind of person you would not want sitting as a decision-maker.

The logic behind the peremptory challenge is that the lawyers from each side will remove from the pool the people who are most likely to be biased at both extremes. The plaintiff will remove defense-minded jurors, and the defendant will remove plaintiff-minded jurors. What will be left in the end, in theory, will be the people in the middle, with moderate views that do not skew dramatically in favor of one party or the other.

Although lawyers are not required to give a reason for using a peremptory challenge to remove a prospective juror from the jury pool, it is illegal to use peremptory challenges to remove people because of their race or gender. Even with the exclusion of those impermissible reasons, peremptory challenges are controversial because they allow parties to remove people based on prejudices and stereotypes. Engineers are too rule-bound. Soccer moms are too softhearted. People with children hold certain beliefs and people without hold other beliefs. None of these stereotypes is uniformly true, and critics of peremptory challenges argue that the courts should not indulge them by allowing litigants to deny people the chance to serve on a jury for such flimsy, arbitrary, and unfounded reasons.

Picking the jury is a high stakes moment in a trial. The jurors are the people who will be deciding the case, and like all people, they bring with them their experiences, biases, prejudices, and potential for error. The voir dire gives the parties a small glimpse into who are the people who will be deciding their fates.

Once the jurors are in place, the presentation of evidence begins.

Presenting the Evidence

At trial, the decision of what evidence to present and what not to present to the jury is left up to the parties themselves. This practice is so familiar that it might seem like no other system for fact-finding is possible, but outside of courtrooms, allowing adversaries to have complete control over the evidence in a dispute is very unusual.

In civilian life, if you want to get to the bottom of something, you investigate it yourself, or you hire an investigator to look into the matter for you. Investigators don't normally hold adversarial hearings. Instead, they interview each person who has relevant knowledge, usually in private and one at a time. Investigators take notes, gather documents, and assess credibility. They decide for themselves what's relevant and what's not, which leads to pursue and which to ignore, and what questions to ask and how to ask them.

Investigators absorb all of the information they have gathered and then they generally write up reports with their findings. In other words, in investigations, the decision-maker (*i.e.*, the investigator) is in control of what information is gathered and considered and, as such, is able to tailor the investigation to answer the questions that the decision-maker thinks are most important.

In American trials, the fact-finders do not have this same power. This means that sometimes they will be required to make decisions with unanswered questions weighing on their minds.

The benefit of a system that puts the burden on the parties to a dispute to gather, organize, and present all of the evidence is that the only work that the fact-finders have to do is listen. It's the difference between reading a book and writing one, watching a movie and making one. It would be impossible to run a jury system, with untrained people as jurors, if the jurors themselves were responsible for investigations. By relying on the litigants to gather and present all the evidence, the adversarial system allows the community, rather than just specialized professionals, to participate in the administration of justice.

No Feedback

In an adversarial process, the difficulty of educating the decision-maker is exponentially increased because there is no feedback from the jury (or, in general, the judge) about whether the evidence presented answers the questions that the decision-makers think are the most important to making a decision. A lawyer leading a witness through his testimony has no feedback about whether the jury understands the evidence.

If just telling someone something were enough to ensure that they actually understood what they were hearing, every student would get an A in math. But the reality is that many of us miss things and don't even know we have missed them. Most of us need things to be explained to us several times and in several ways before we really get them. Without practice, repetition, and feedback, we can't be sure that we've really grasped what we're being told.[184]

Since jurors start as essentially blank slates, they need to be educated about everything. By the time the trial starts, litigants typically have been working on a case for at least a year, and in bigger cases, sometimes two, three, or even more years. So the attorneys for each side know a lot, but the jurors know nothing, which means a lot of basic information needs to be communicated, and many questions need to be answered.

- Who are the parties?
- What is their relationship?
- What happened that brought them to court?
- When did it happen and why?
- Who are all the people giving testimony and what are their relationships?

In simple cases, this basic background can be covered quickly, but in complex ones, lots of time must be spent on this preliminary material before the main issue can be squarely faced.

When the presentation of evidence is over and the case is submitted to the jury for deliberation and decision, the parties have no chance to supplement the evidence to answer questions that might still be open in the jurors' minds. Because the parties don't get any feedback about what is working and what is not or what the jury considers important and what it doesn't, the pressure is on to put into evidence anything that might possibly help. This can lead to boring and excessive detail, which turns off the jury—not the desired effect.

Ideally, jurors listen attentively and patiently to all of the evidence from both sides before weighing the evidence and making up their minds. Research suggests that's not how jurors work in real life. In one experiment, mock jurors listened to an audiotaped reenactment of an actual murder trial and then reported how they would have voted and why. Most jurors didn't wait until all the evidence was in. Instead, most people immediately began constructing a story about what had happened and then, as evidence was presented during the mock trial, they tended to accept only the evidence that supported their preconceived version of events. Ironically, those who jumped to a conclusion the quickest were the most confident in the correctness of their decisions and were also most likely to support those decisions by voting for an extreme verdict.[185]

All of this conclusion jumping happens invisibly, without the knowledge of the litigants presenting the case.

Specialized Knowledge and Expert Witnesses

In modern litigation, almost every case requires at least some specialized knowledge, which the jury by design does not have. So the litigants must turn to expert witnesses for help.

An **expert witness** is a person who has "knowledge, skill, experience, training, or education" that will help the trier of fact understand the evidence and determine a fact that is at issue in a lawsuit.[186] An expert witness could be a ballistics expert who can tell whether a particular bullet came from a particular gun, a medical expert who can tell whether a surgeon made a mistake in surgery, an economist who can estimate how much money a company would have made if it had sold its products on time, or any of a host of other issues. Experts have become a fixture in modern litigation. Many cases turn on information that regular witnesses, who are limited by what they know from their own five senses, cannot provide.

Expert witnesses attempt to fill in gaps and do their best to educate juries about the applicable science. For many people, and hence for many jurors, science is not their strong suit, so absorbing technical evidence can be difficult, and the parties have to work extra hard to simplify the issues to an understandable level without talking down to the jurors who will be deciding the case. Lack of familiarity with specialized areas of knowledge increases the expert's power and influence over judges and juries. "Scientific proof may in some instances," observed the California Supreme Court, "assume a posture of mystic infallibility in the eyes of a jury."[187]

As we know, people disagree (which is why we have courts and lawsuits in the first place), and experts are no exception. Adversaries in litigation have every incentive to seek out experts who hold opinions favorable to their own positions. If a house is destroyed in a mudslide after a torrential rain, the plaintiff homeowner suing the defendant builder will find an expert to say (with the benefit of hindsight) that the construction was sitting on a muddy time bomb waiting to go off with the first heavy rainfall. At the same time, the defendant builder will find an expert who holds the view that no reasonable person could possibly have known that water was invisibly accumulating in the earth under the house in such a way that it would suddenly and without warning bring an entire hillside down.

Neither expert is necessarily lying. There are so many people with specialized knowledge in the world, and given the range of human opinion, with a little effort, someone with the requisite background, credentials, and expertise can generally be found who will support either side of a disputed question.[188]

Not only can the parties bias the presentation of expert testimony by seeking out experts who hold favorable opinions, the experts themselves can lose their objectivity and succumb, consciously or unconsciously, to the power of trying to win one for the team. This tendency to try to help your team win is sometimes called the allegiance effect.

One very telling study asked more than one hundred forensic psychologists and psychiatrists to review a criminal case file and render an opinion on how likely the criminal was to commit more crimes—a common question for judges who must decide criminal sentences. All of the psychologists and psychiatrists reviewed the same file, but half were told that they were working for the prosecution and half were told that they were working for the defense. Working from identical files, the psychologists and psychiatrists that were working for the prosecution returned significantly higher risk scores than those who were working for the defense. Just knowing which side they were working for subtly but significantly influenced the experts' opinions.[189]

In adversarial hearings, dueling experts can be highly misleading. It's entirely possible that one expert represents a decidedly minority view, while the other represents the vast majority of learned professionals in the field. Nevertheless, what the jury sees is one person with fancy credentials disagreeing with another person with fancy credentials. It can seem that the weight of the science rests equally on both sides, when really the consensus tips heavily one way.

In addition, experts can just be flat-out wrong. In the 1990s, women who had silicone breast implants brought a series of class-action lawsuits against Dow Corning, the implant's manufacturer. The women claimed that the implants had caused a wide variety of illnesses, including lupus, rheumatoid arthritis, and various neurological problems. Before the tidal wave was over, more than 500,000 women had joined the various lawsuits against the implant manufacturer.

On the strength of expert witnesses who supported the women's claims, Dow Corning lost multi-million dollar judgments,[190] and ultimately Dow Corning had to file for bankruptcy. Years later, several scientific studies concluded that there was no link between Dow Corning's implants and the diseases for which it had been held liable.[191] Expert testimony brought down Dow Corning, but only later did the science catch up with the lawsuits and showed that what the experts had thought and the juries found just wasn't true.[192]

Direct Examination

Although cross-examination is often held up as the centerpiece of the American trial, **direct examination** is the bread and butter. Direct examination is when one side asks questions of its own witnesses. Direct examination lacks the flashy fireworks of cross-examination, but it is here, through friendly, prepared witnesses, that lawyers build the bulk of their cases.

Before trial, lawyers will spend an extensive amount of time preparing their witnesses to testify. The witnesses will be walked through their prior deposition testimony and sworn statements and asked to recall the events so that their memories are fresh. In the direct examination, the witnesses are asked to tell what happened from their point of view. The goal is to have the witnesses tell their story in the clearest, most convincing way possible.

To help ensure that witnesses testify about their own thoughts and experiences and that they do not merely parrot back whatever their lawyer wants them to say, **leading**

questions are not allowed in a direct examination. A leading question is one that suggests the answer to the witness. "What time was it that the meeting took place?" is not a leading question because it doesn't suggest the time. "Isn't it true that the meeting took place at two p.m.?" is a leading question because the question has embedded in it the answer that the lawyer is looking for.

Litigants often say that they just want to have their day in court to tell their story. The direct examination is their chance. When they're done, they must face the cross-examination.

Cross-Examination

The centerpiece of the presentation of evidence—and one of the hallmarks of the American legal system—is **cross-examination**. Cross-examination is when an attorney poses questions to a witness friendly to the opposing side. "Cross-examination," wrote John Wigmore, one of the great writers about evidence, "is the greatest legal engine ever invented for the discovery of truth."[193]

Cross-examination allows one side to test the truthfulness of a witness's testimony by rigorous questioning. Cross-examinations tend to attack a witness's credibility through some combination of six different tactics:

Direct Contradiction. A witness can be confronted with documents that are inconsistent with his or her testimony or asked to explain why his or her account differs from accounts of the same incident from unbiased sources. If a witness testified differently in his or her deposition, the contradiction can be pointed out to suggest fabrication or forgetfulness or both.

Inconsistent Action. If a witness makes a claim, a common cross-examination technique is to ask why the witness didn't take other actions that common sense suggests would be consistent with the claim. If your house is on fire, you call the fire department. If someone didn't, or if he or she waited for a long time before making the call, then on cross-examination the inconsistent action will look like the person wanted the house to burn to collect the insurance money.

Evidence of Bias. Witnesses who are friendly to one side usually have a reason to be friendly. They are relatives, friends, or business associates, and these relationships are obvious sources of bias. Cross-examination will attempt to expose these biases and suggest that they may have influenced the witnesses' testimony.

Forgetfulness. The fragility of human memory pervades every aspect of the legal system, and cross-examination is no exception. The ability of witnesses to recall important details of events that occurred in the past can be challenged by showing inconsistencies in their recollections and contemporaneous documents and the witness's own prior statements. The number of things the witness doesn't remember can be exposed with the suggestion that what is remembered is too spotty to be trusted or believed.

Perception. Witnesses can only testify to what they saw, heard, touched, smelled or tasted, or what the witnesses thought they saw, heard, touched, smelled or tasted. A witness's perception, however, could be wrong. The gun shot the witness heard might have been a car backfiring or even a balloon popping. The knife he saw in the defendant's hand might have been a cell phone glinting in the moonlight. Distance, darkness, and speed all impede, and potentially distort, perception, and all are fodder for cross-examination.

Lack of Qualification/Shaky Methodology (for expert witnesses). The authority of expert witnesses stems directly from their skills, knowledge, and experience. If an expert witness does not have the right qualifications, his or her opinion should be discounted, if not dismissed outright or excluded from the trial altogether. Cross-examination can elicit information about lack of formal training or pertinent experience that damages the expert witness's credibility as an expert.

Since expert witnesses do not testify about what they directly experienced, their opinions are only as good as the methods they use to arrive at them. Faulty methods lead to faulty conclusions, or more colloquially, garbage in, garbage out.

While the purpose of cross-examination is to challenge the testimony of opposing witnesses, cross-examination should not be rude or obnoxious. The theatrics common in movies and television rarely have any place in a courtroom. Judges won't permit it, and juries won't tolerate it. Nothing wins sympathy for a witness faster than being badgered by an overbearing lawyer. The art of cross-examination is undermining the witness's testimony without alienating the judge and the jury. It's a delicate balance.

From the moment the opposing lawyer stands to cross-examine a witness, the jury's natural sympathy will be with the witness. The lawyer is a hired gun and a trained professional. The witness, in most cases, is an ordinary citizen, just like the jurors watching the trial. A professional boxer wins no fans by beating up an untrained innocent, and so a lawyer must tread carefully, attacking a witness only if the witness has already lost the respect of the jury by appearing to lie, evade, or mislead.

For this reason, not all witnesses are subjected to the full cross-examination treatment. Many witnesses are third parties whose testimony cannot reasonably be doubted or called into question. They are honest people giving their honest recollections to the best of their abilities. They might be wrong. They might have forgotten important details or misperceived critical events, but they are not liars. In some cases, cross-examination can draw out some helpful points from these generally neutral witnesses. In other cases, these witnesses might not be cross-examined at all. They have told the truth from their perspective. The only way to contradict them is with more compelling evidence to the contrary, so nothing is gained by attacking these witnesses' stories directly.

When all the questions have been asked and answered, and all the documents that are admissible have been admitted into evidence, the presentation of the evidence comes to a close. All of the facts are before the jury (or the judge, if the judge is the decision-maker), and the time has come to supply the missing ingredient of law to the soup.

The Burden of Proof: How Much Proof Is Enough?

The purpose of evidence is to convince another person. As conspiracy theorists throughout the world amply demonstrate, for some people no amount of evidence is enough to dispel all doubts. Before a case goes to a jury for final decision, two critical questions are *how much* proof is enough to consider a fact established and *who* has the responsibility of producing that evidence. The answer to these questions is what the law calls the **burden of proof**.

The *who* question is usually fairly straightforward. The person who claims that a fact is true (usually) has the burden (*i.e.*, the obligation) to prove the fact. Generally that means that the plaintiff must prove the allegations in the complaint. The defendant does not have to prove anything. If the plaintiff offers no evidence, then the defendant should win the case even if the defendant merely meets the plaintiff's silence with silence of her own. By the same token, the defendant will have the burden of producing evidence to prove the facts necessary to support her affirmative defenses.

To take a concrete example, if you bring a battery claim, as the plaintiff you must prove that the defendant hit you by producing evidence that you were in fact hit. In a battery case, that evidence could be as simple as your own sworn testimony. In fact, in many assault cases, in particular sexual assaults involving acquaintances (date rapes), the only evidence is often the victim's own testimony, but testimony is evidence. Whether a person's uncorroborated testimony is enough to win a case is answered by the second half of the burden of proof.

The *amount* of proof that must be produced depends on the type of case. For civil suits (private disputes), the standard of proof is the **preponderance of the evidence**. The preponderance of the evidence is evidence that persuades the trier of fact (*i.e.*, the jury or the judge) that the fact is "more likely to be true than not true."[194] While the law does not attempt to quantify the amount of proof that proves that a fact is "more likely to be true than not true," a common way of understanding the preponderance of the evidence is to say the test is met if the chance of the fact being true is more than fifty percent.

For criminal cases, the standard of proof is higher. To convict a person of a crime, the prosecution must prove that the defendant is guilty **beyond a reasonable doubt**. "Proof beyond a reasonable doubt is proof that leaves the trier of fact with an abiding conviction that the charge is true. The evidence need not eliminate all possible doubt because everything in life is open to some possible or imaginary doubt."[195] The law doesn't attempt to quantify proof beyond a reasonable doubt either. Nevertheless, many people would say proof beyond a reasonable doubt exists if the chance of the fact being true is more than ninety or ninety-five percent.[196]

Using numerical percentages for understanding the preponderance of the evidence and proof beyond a reasonable doubt is somewhat arbitrary and not officially approved by the courts. Even so, they provide a way of thinking about these vital, highly abstract concepts that the law does not (because it cannot) make precise. The numerical percentages highlight that under both standards of proof, absolute certainty is not required. Even under the more stringent beyond-a-reasonable-doubt standard, the possibility of being wrong hovers around 1 in 20 or 1 in 10.

With tens of thousands of criminal cases every year, error rates of 5 to 10 percent mean that many people will be convicted of crimes they did not commit. The alternative, however, is a system that requires perfect or near-perfect certainty. Such a high standard of proof would mean that innocent people would be very unlikely to suffer a wrongful conviction, but it would also mean that many people who are all but certainly guilty would escape punishment. Not only does this deny justice to the victims, but it also means that the rest of the community is exposed to increased risk from an offender who is free and at-large instead of safely behind bars.

The same risks of errors are present in civil cases, but they are even larger because the standard of proof is lower. The plaintiff's and the defendant's versions of events could be supported with evidence that is virtually equal, but if one has the smallest edge over the other, one wins and the other loses.

This lower burden of proof for civil cases reflects the legal system's judgment that less is at stake in civil disputes and it is better to tolerate a greater chance of error to promote final decisions. In theory, a mistake in a civil case has less impact because it does not result in the loss of a person's life or liberty—usually just the person's money. On the other hand, civil judgments can have such ruinous financial consequences that some people, if given the choice, would rather spend a little time in jail rather than deal with the consequences of bankruptcy.

The balance between wrongful convictions and wrongful acquittals is an uneasy one, but lines must be drawn for business to get done. In a system that must resolve disputes, draws are not possible. Because of our limited and imperfect ability to reconstruct the past, some amount of error is inevitable. The different standards for burden of proof reflect one place to draw the line between caution and action.

The Burden of Proof and the Trial of the Century

Burden of proof is a dry and arcane topic, but differences between the two standards of proof often decide whether a legal case is won or lost. They also help explain one of the most vexing legal cases at the end of the twentieth century.

Orenthal James Simpson (O.J., to the public) was a Heisman-trophy-winning running back who had a storied career in the National Football League (NFL). Simpson was the first NFL player to rush for more than 2,000 yards in a season and the only player ever to accomplish that feat in a 14-game season. After Simpson retired from professional football, he went on to have a successful career in television broadcasting and as an actor in movies. Simpson was inducted into the Pro Football Hall of Fame in 1985 and still holds the record for yards rushed per game in a single season. But the reason he's remembered (at least in this book) is because of how his experience illustrates the importance of the burden of proof.

On June 12, 1994, Nicole Brown, Simpson's ex-wife, and her friend Ronald Goldman were brutally slashed to death outside of Nicole's upscale Brentwood condominium. Suspicion quickly focused on Simpson as her ex-husband. On June 17, Simpson was to turn himself in to the police. In a bizarre, riveting scene, Simpson fled in a white Ford Bronco sport utility vehicle and proceeded to lead the Los Angeles Police Department on a slow-speed chase across Los Angeles for two hours. The spectacle was broadcast all over the country as twenty police cars and nearly as many helicopters followed the white Bronco over highways and down side streets at an almost comical 35 m.p.h. Eventually, Simpson gave up and turned himself in. Once in custody, Simpson pled not guilty to the murder charges and was held for trial.

The murder trial—billed as the trial of the century—began on January 24, 1995. Although Simpson had his sympathizers, many people thought he was plainly guilty. The trial did not go smoothly for the prosecution, and on October 3, 1995, at 10:00 a.m., the jury returned its verdict: Simpson was not guilty. For some, the verdict was vindication, for others, an outrage. But then this most unusual case took another unusual twist.

Unhappy with the result of the criminal case and convinced that Simpson had gotten away with murder, the parents of the murdered Ron Goldman brought a civil suit for wrongful death against Simpson, alleging that Simpson caused the death of their son, either intentionally or negligently, and damaged the parents financially as their son's survivors.[197]

The wrongful death lawsuit took many people by surprise because a criminal jury had just found Simpson *not* guilty of killing Ron Goldman. Even more people were surprised when the civil jury in the wrongful death case returned a verdict finding that Simpson had killed Ron Goldman and awarded the Goldman family more than $30 million in damages.

For some, the contradictory verdicts in Simpson's criminal and civil cases demonstrated that the legal system was basically a crapshoot, delivering random decisions with no rhyme or reason. The two verdicts, however, can be understood as the logical consequence of two trials with two different burdens of proof.

Imagining the two trials as a football game can help illuminate this point. In the criminal murder trial, the prosecutors had to establish Simpson's guilt beyond a reasonable doubt. In football terms, the prosecution had to receive the kick-off and avoid every tackle to run the ball all the way back to the opposing end zone for a touchdown.

In the civil wrongful death trial, the plaintiffs only had to establish Simpson's liability by a preponderance of the evidence, meaning that the evidence only had to show Simpson's guilt was more likely to be true than not true. In other words, the plaintiffs only had to receive the ball and run it across the fifty-yard line to win.

Without sitting through both trials and hearing all the evidence the two juries heard, we can only speculate about the amount of evidence against Simpson, but it is possible that the amount of evidence against Simpson was more than enough to get across the fifty-yard line, but not quite enough to get the ball all the way into the end zone. If it were the case that the evidence was such that Simpson's guilt was more likely to be true than not true, but was not so certain as to be beyond a reasonable doubt, both verdicts would be legally correct and entirely consistent.

As Simpson's case illustrates, the burden of proof can make a big difference in the outcome of real cases. The two standards reflect different levels of certainty. While often criminal and civil cases will be equally clear cut and the results will be the same, in the close cases, with highly contested facts, criminal and civil trial results will sometimes diverge—thanks to the different burdens of proof.

Closing Arguments, Jury Instructions, and Judgments

The evidence is in, but before the case can be decided, the second ingredient to a legal decision—the law—needs to be added into the mix. Trial court judges are responsible for determining what legal rules are applicable for a particular case. After the close of evidence, the judge prepares a summary of all of the applicable rules in what are called the **jury instructions**.

Typically, the judge will go over the jury instructions with the litigants and their lawyers, so everyone knows what rules the jury will be expected to apply. Then the lawyers get one last chance to persuade the jury that their side should win the case. This last chance to argue to the jury is called the **closing argument** or the **summation**. In the closing argument, the lawyers for each side go over the evidence presented and make their best pitches that the facts and the law are on their client's side.

When the lawyers have said their peace, it is the judge's turn to tell the jury what laws they must apply to the facts that the jury believes to be true. To make sure that the jurors have heard the rules at least once, the judge will *read* all of the jury instructions out loud to the jurors. Reading the jury instructions can take an hour or two in simple cases and several hours in complex cases. The jury is expected to listen attentively to this reading of the law and then remember and apply these rules to the evidence presented in the trial in making a decision in a case.

Nowadays, jurors will typically be given a copy of the jury instructions to refer to during their deliberations. Nevertheless, a group of non-experts must figure out how to apply the law they've heard exactly one time. It's no wonder litigants are scared of juries.

Jurors sometimes get a bad reputation for being particularly wild and unpredictable, but having judges decide cases without juries would not necessarily be better. A couple of studies have asked judges whether they agreed or disagreed with the verdicts returned by juries in trials over which the judges presided. The judges agreed with the juries around eighty percent of the time.[198] Of course, just because judges and juries agree doesn't necessarily mean that they are *right*. It just means that in the majority of cases, there isn't much difference between having a case heard by a judge or a jury.

On the other hand, if these studies are correct, twenty percent of the time there is a difference between what a jury does and what a judge would do. In those cases, it's impossible to say whether it is the jury or the judge who has reached the wrong conclusion, but this discrepancy suggests that in many cases reasonable minds can disagree on the outcome. If the difference in opinions is taken as an error rate, the idea that one out of five cases is erroneously decided is downright terrifying.

After the judge has read the jury instructions, the jury retires from the court to a nearby room and begins deliberations. Normally, jurors will be given a form to fill out to record their decisions.

The number of jurors can vary, but in all cases jurors are expected to discuss with each other the evidence they heard and make a decision collectively. In criminal cases, the jurors must all agree on the outcome. In civil cases, in some jurisdictions jurors do not all need to agree. In California, for example, in civil cases normally there will be twelve jurors, but only nine of the twelve must be in agreement for the jury to reach a final decision.

When the jury has reached a decision, the jurors let the court know, and when the judge, attorneys, and parties are assembled, they return to the courtroom to deliver their decision, which is called the **verdict**. The clerk of the court reads the verdict aloud, and if everything is in order, the judge thanks and discharges the jury.

Of course, things do not always go so smoothly. If the jurors cannot agree on a verdict, it is a **hung jury**, and the judge must declare a mistrial. Neither side wins in a mistrial. The factual disputes that underlie the lawsuit are left unresolved, and the case must be set for another trial in front of another jury, at which point the litigants and all of the witnesses must repeat the trial from scratch.

If the jury delivers a verdict, the jury goes home, but the trial court proceedings are not quite over. After the verdict is in, the lawyers have a last opportunity to make arguments that some error occurred in the trial and so the judge should reject or modify the jury's decision by making what is called a **post-trial motion**.

Jury verdicts are generally the final word, but not always. A veteran, Mississippi trial lawyer once told me the following story, which has the ring of a tall tale, but still makes a point.

After a long and hard-fought trial in a big case against a pharmaceutical company accused of selling a dangerous drug, the jury returned to the courtroom with its verdict. The foreperson handed the verdict form to the clerk, who handed it to the judge. The judge started by reading the jury's answer to the question of liability. According to the jury, the defendant pharmaceutical company had indeed sold a dangerous and harmful drug.

Next, the judge turned to the question of the damages the pharmaceutical company should pay the injured plaintiff. The judge paused, removed his glasses, gave them a good cleaning, and then looked at the verdict form again. For damages, the jury awarded the plaintiff one hundred *billion* dollars, more than twice the wealth of the richest person in the world.

The judge looked at the jury in disbelief and asked, "Did you mean one hundred *billion* dollars or one hundred *million* dollars?"

The foreperson shrugged his shoulders and replied, "One hundred million, one hundred billion—it's all the same to us."

That drew a laugh in the courtroom, but also a sigh of relief from the defendant. The defendant filed a post-trial motion asking that the jury's verdict be set aside because the jury did not compute damages based on evidence, but rather came up with an arbitrary number. The judge reluctantly had to agree.

The judge will accept or reject the parties' post-trial motions, and then when all the arguments have been resolved, the judge enters a final **judgment**. The judgment represents the final decision of the trial court, and with it, at long last, the trial court proceedings are over.

Even though the trial court proceedings may have ended, the lawsuit is not necessarily over because of the chance to appeal.

6

Appellate Courts

Everything that needs to be said has already been said. But since no one was listening, everything must be said again.

—André Gide

ERRORS OF LAW

Hands shaking and short of breath, a lawyer fresh from the courtroom frantically tries to make his fingers work to dial his client's number on the telephone. The jury has just returned its verdict in a hotly contested case. This is the call the client has been anxiously waiting for. The client's future depends on the jury's decision.

"What happened?" demands the client, desperate to know if the news is good or bad.

The lawyer draws a deep breath and solemnly intones, "Justice was done."

The client instantly responds, "Appeal!"

If a case goes all the way to the end of the trial court process, there will be a winner and a loser, and at least one party will be unhappy with the result. Sometimes, both parties will be unhappy. Luckily or unluckily, these unhappy people have the opportunity to spend a little more time and money in court by filing an appeal. An appeal asks another court to review the work of the trial court and correct any errors that the trial court may have committed.

Appellate courts are not in the business of reconstructing all of the work done in the trial court. The parties and the legal system have already invested a significant amount of time and money gathering and presenting evidence to reach a decision in the trial court. Absent unusual circumstances, an appellate court will not revisit all of that work.

Appellate courts perform a fundamentally different function than trial courts. While both courts combine facts and laws to form legal judgments, the trial courts focus on finding the facts, taking the law as given, while the appellate courts focus on defining the law, taking the facts as given. Accordingly, appellate courts will typically accept as true the facts of a case as determined by the trial courts and limit their review of the decisions of trial courts to searching for **errors of law**.

A trial court commits an error of law when it misstates or misapplies a legal rule. Errors of law are different from factual errors. A factual error is a mistake about what really happened in a particular case. If the trial court concluded that Johnny didn't hit Fred, when in reality Johnny did in fact hit Fred, that would be an error of fact, a question that appellate courts will generally not review.

If the trial court correctly found that Johnny hit Fred, but concluded that hitting didn't violate any laws, that would be an error of law. Hitting another person (absent some affirmative defense) is a wrongful act. If the trial court thought otherwise, the trial court was wrong about the law, and the appellate court's job is to correct that error of law.

Errors of law can crop up at almost every stage of the trial court process because every legal decision involves some combination of facts and law.

If a defendant challenges a plaintiff's complaint in a motion to dismiss, the trial judge can make an error of law in determining whether the allegations in the complaint adequately support a valid legal theory.

If a defendant files a motion for summary judgment, the trial court could incorrectly conclude that there is no genuine issue of material fact or apply the law incorrectly to facts even if they are undisputed.

And at trial, the trial judge must decide what evidence to allow and what evidence to exclude and must give the all-important jury instructions that summarize the law that the jury is required to apply.

Because the appellate court's focus is on errors of law committed by the trial court, several consequences follow. First, appellate courts will not re-try the case. The court will not hear witnesses or consider new documents. With few exceptions, appellate courts accept the facts of a case as the trial court finds them. In an appeal, parties may not submit new evidence to supplement or contradict the evidence that was presented to the trial court. The trial court is the fact-finder, not the appellate court.

Second, legal arguments that were not raised before the trial court generally may not be raised in the appeal. With the exception of egregious and obvious mistakes (known as **plain error**), the appellate court is looking for mistakes that the trial court made, but a trial court makes its rulings in reaction to the arguments raised by the parties before it. The trial court cannot be faulted for not considering a legal argument that the parties failed to make.

Accordingly, appellate courts limit their reviews to the **record** in the trial court. The record consists broadly of all the evidence and argument that was presented, or was attempted to be presented, to the trial court, including pleadings, motions, testimony, and documents admitted or refused to be admitted into evidence. The record is critical; appellate courts will not consider evidence or arguments that are not contained in the record.

This is the reason for the common phrase "I want to say something for the record." In normal conversation, the phrase makes little sense because there is no record. It's just people talking. In contrast, in court the failure to express a point and get it noted on the official record precludes its consideration later. Saying things for the record in the trial court is critical if the party wants to preserve the issue for later review by the appellate court.

The record provides the appellate court with its source for the facts of the case and the legal arguments that are in play in a dispute. Limiting appellate arguments to facts and arguments presented in the trial court and preserved in the record encourages litigants to make their best cases to the trial court. The trial court is not just a preliminary stop on the way to the more definitive appellate court. The trial court's specialized function of finding facts is every bit as important as the appellate function of determining the law. The trial court has the benefit of seeing the demeanor of witnesses and hearing their testimony live and in person. By not reviewing the factual findings of trial courts, appellate courts respect the special strength of the trial courts in figuring out who is telling the truth and who is not.

By limiting review to the record, appellate courts encourage the parties to make their best pitches to the trial courts and limit any incentive to hold back important arguments to gain some tactical advantage. If the trial court has all the facts and has heard all of the parties' arguments, the trial court is most likely to reach a correct result. If the trial court's action is correct, then appeals are less likely, saving the appellate courts time and resources, and saving the parties the trouble of having to repeat the trial to fix a mistake.

If litigants thought that they could slip in new evidence or arguments after the trial was over, they might try to game the system by holding back evidence to drag out the process or run up their opponent's expenses before snatching victory away on the appeal. Or they might hold back the evidence in the hopes that unveiling it later would give them a second shot if they lost their case the first time.

Forcing parties to prosecute their appeals based on the record as presented to the trial court eliminates those kinds of shenanigans.

MAKING LAW

While one is the standard number of judges for a trial court, appellate courts always work in groups. Typically, three judges will hear an appeal, but more can be involved in certain circumstances, and for the U.S. Supreme Court, the highest appellate court in the land, nine judges sit in review.

Appellate courts work by majority vote. Obviously, if all of the judges agree, their decision is unanimous. If disagreement exists and the appellate court consists of three judges, two will form the **majority** and one will be the **dissent**. In appellate courts, majority rules, so a dissenting judge may express his or her disagreement but cannot change the outcome.

By tradition, appellate courts communicate their decisions in writing. The decisions are called **judicial opinions** or just opinions because they express the opinion of the majority of the judges about the law.

Judges have a lot of flexibility in how they come to their decisions. They will hear the parties' arguments as presented in written briefs and at a hearing, but they can also accept arguments submitted by people who have an interest in the outcome. In cases that involve hot-button issues like gun rights, abortion, or the death penalty, many people will submit briefs to the appellate court for the judges' consideration. Non-litigants who submit briefs to courts are known as **amici curiae**, Latin for "friend of the court."

In addition, judges are permitted to conduct their own research into the issues. In their opinions, judges will sometimes cite social science studies, legal journals, and even Wikipedia.[199] The freedom judges have to consult any source they find informative contrasts sharply with the strict constraints put on jurors who can see their decisions overturned if they conduct any independent research, even using such innocuous sources as dictionaries. When judges base decisions on independent research, the facts they rely upon are not tested by the adversarial process—raising the distinct possibility that those facts could be wrong.

For example, in *Muller v. Oregon*, the U.S. Supreme Court had to decide whether a law limiting the work hours for women working in factories and laundries violated the freedom of women and employers to enter into contracts.[200] The Supreme Court decided that women's working hours could be limited by statute because of the Court's personal understanding of biology, physiology, and history. Pay particular attention to the Court's use of the words "obvious," "history," and "impossible."

"That woman's physical structure and the performance of maternal functions place her at a disadvantage in the struggle for subsistence," wrote the Court, "is obvious."[201] In the view of these early twentieth century judges, "history discloses the fact that woman has always been dependent upon man....It is impossible to close one's eyes to the fact that she still looks to her brother and depends upon him."[202]

Judges are no different than the rest of us, and we all must make decisions based on our best understanding of the way the world works. This usually serves us well, but sometimes what we think is true just isn't—a possibility that all of us, judges included, should always remember to consider.[203]

In making their decisions, judges are supposed to follow the law. This means obeying the Constitution and statutes passed by Congress (or the state legislatures for state laws). It also means applying binding precedents as dictated by the doctrine of *stare decisis*. Not all judicial decisions, however, count as binding precedents under *stare decisis*. First, only appellate court decisions count. Trial courts specialize in facts, and while there are many learned trial judges who write with great wisdom about the law and who may exert great influence as a result, their decisions are not *binding* on appellate courts.

Second, there are many different appellate courts, and only decisions from an appellate court in the same jurisdiction count. An appellate court in California cannot bind an appellate court in Virginia. They are not in the same jurisdiction. While one court can certainly influence the other, their decisions are not precedents for each other.

Third, even among appellate courts there is a hierarchy of authority. Most states and the federal court system are organized into three tiers. At the entry level sit the trial courts. At the second rung are intermediate appellate courts. Finally, at the top of the heap are the supreme courts, one for each state and one for the federal government.

Appellate courts are only bound by the decisions of other appellate courts of equal or higher rank in their jurisdiction. Since appellate courts in different jurisdictions are free to disagree with each other, inevitably disagreements happen. If two appellate courts reach contrary conclusions—which happens from time to time in close cases—the law becomes muddled. In the federal system, a division among appellate courts is called a **circuit split** (federal, intermediate appellate courts are called circuit courts).

Especially in the federal court system, a circuit split presents a deep problem for the legal system because it means that the same law in one part of the country means one thing, and in another part of the country it means another. One of the primary functions of the U.S. Supreme Court is to resolve circuit splits by issuing a definitive statement of the law in the contested area that will be applied uniformly throughout the country.

Over time, through the resolution of individual cases, the appellate courts define the laws that govern us.

Part Four

Consent and Duty

THE LAW RECOGNIZES only injuries that violate one or more of the law's rules. These rules can come from many different sources. The Constitution, statutes, administrative agency regulations, and case law (precedents) are the most common sources. The specifics of the law's rules fill vast libraries. The quantity and complexity of laws are such that no human being knows all the rules. Nevertheless, out of this thicket of multiplicity, some themes and principles emerge. To a large extent, the rules that regulate our private conduct can be understood with two general concepts: contracts and torts.

Contracts are private agreements. In essence, two people by their agreement create a private law between them, and if one breaks a promise, the law will enforce that private agreement. The source of the legal duty in a contract is the person's consent. While some limits to consent exist, in general people can agree to any rules that are not otherwise prohibited by law. In other words, private parties, through their personal consent, can create legal duties to each other, which are enforceable in courts.

Torts are legal injuries caused by wrongful or blameworthy acts. Torts do not arise from private agreement. Rather, the duty to refrain from committing torts—that is, from wrongfully injuring others—is imposed by the law regardless of whether a particular individual consents or not. This logic is reflected in the famous maxim that your freedom to swing your arm ends at the tip of my nose.[204] One person may think it is perfectly acceptable to throw a punch to settle a score or avenge an insult, but the law does not.

Most legal injuries can be broadly understood as either breaches of contract—that is, violations of private rules that a person voluntarily consented to—or a tort—that is, violations of the duty to avoid wrongful conduct that injures others. Understanding the logic of contracts and the logic of torts is the key to understanding how the legal mind thinks about people and their relationships.

7

Promises: The Law of Contracts

An ounce of performance is worth pounds of promises.

–Mae West

THE CHAINS THAT FREE US

If you're anything like most people, you like to keep your options open. Generally, this is a good strategy because something that seems like a good idea now might seem very different later when the time comes to actually do it. As useful as it is, keeping options open doesn't come without cost.

For example, say your friend is moving out of her apartment, and she needs help carrying her things to the truck she is going to rent for the day. She has couches and box springs and a television set that all require muscle to get to the curb. She asks you if you would be willing to pitch in. You shrug your shoulders nonchalantly and tell her that you'll swing by if nothing else comes up. You're happy to help, but you want to keep your options open.

Your friend frowns and then abruptly tells you not to bother. If she can't count on you to show up, then she will have to find someone else who can make a commitment. You successfully avoided tying yourself down, but you also let down a friend.

Maybe before going down this selfish road, you break your general rule about keeping your options open and tell your friend that you will definitely be there. Her face lights up, and she says in a thankful voice, "Promise?"

Taking a deep breath, you nod and say the words that kill options but save friendships, "I promise."

And then things go wrong—or maybe right, depending on your perspective. That cute girl you're interested in asks if you'd like to grab a bite. Your boss tells you that the promotion you've been hoping for is yours, but she needs you to meet the company CEO. Your agent has gotten your band an audition with a music industry executive. And all of these events have to happen on the same day you promised to help your friend move. What do you do?

You flake, of course. You go out on the date, meet your boss's boss, and play your heart out for the music industry executive, leaving your friend in the lurch with an apartment full of heavy objects and an empty, rented pick-up truck waiting to be filled. Now what?

In this case, your excuses are good and your friend may be the understanding type, but the next time you give your word, you will have a hard time convincing your friends to trust you.

When another friend has another moving day, to salvage your reputation, you're the first to volunteer to help. You give your solemn vow that, no matter what, you'll be there. Your friend is skeptical. To convince your friend that you mean what you say, you offer to pay the cost of his rental truck if you don't show up and he can't move on time. Your options are narrowed even more than before, but your friendship is strengthened.

The ability to make a binding promise is essential to earn the trust of other people, especially people you don't know or don't know very well. Instead of helping a friend move out of kindness and generosity, say that you have started a moving business. For a reasonable and affordable fee, you and a handful of strong men will show up and move people out of their apartments. You have the muscle and the truck, but there's just one problem. Your potential customers need to be convinced that you will do the job they're paying you to do and not disappoint them when they need you.

You can offer reassurances all day long, but what your customers want and what you want to give them is something more than empty promises. What you want is a contract. A contract is a binding promise that is enforceable in court. If you make a contract and then don't do what you promised to do, the courts will punish you. It sounds bad, but really it's a good thing.

It is obviously beneficial to have someone tied to you by a binding a contract. In that case, the force of the law stands behind you to compel the person making the promise to keep his or her word or face the consequences. But equally important is the ability to bind yourself through a contract to other people. It's the most reliable way to earn trust.

When you are bound by a contract to keep your promises, your customers will have confidence that you will really do the work. As a business owner, you don't want to work unless you are going to get paid. Likewise, your customers don't want to pay you unless they are sure you will do the work. A contract that binds you and your customers makes it possible to do business. You get to make a little money, and they have their things moved. The fact that you are both bound by the contract gives you both the confidence to make the transaction possible.

Accepting the legal commitment that comes with making a contract is not altruism or self-sacrifice. No one likes punishments, but by signing up to be punished under the law for failing to perform your promises, you and your customers establish the trust you need to do business.

Every day, in countless ways, the law of contracts makes it possible for us to live in the modern world. Electricity lights up cities, trucks roll into groceries stores, and banks safeguard our savings—all tied together by the binding legal promises in contracts. Our highly compartmentalized and specialized economy can only function if promises are made, kept, and enforced.

The law of contracts is vital because only by trusting each other to keep our promises are we able to achieve the benefits that come from the countless trades and transactions among people who often know little or nothing about each other. The chains that we assume under the law of contracts free us to do business. We can place our confidence in people we have never met and whom we have no particular reason to trust. The reassurance we need comes from the legal system ready to enforce promises if people break their word.

HAIRY HANDS AND EXPECTATION DAMAGES

When someone makes a contract, we expect that person to live up to that binding, legal commitment. But this world is full of disappointment, and sadly, too often promises are broken, much to our sorrow and dismay. What happens then?

In the 1920s, electric power lines were going up all across the country. George Hawkins was a New Hampshire electrician in those early days of the electric age.[205] He made decent money and enjoyed his work, but electricity is dangerous, and one day an electrical wire burned his hand, leaving it scarred and disfigured.

Dr. Edward McGee was a doctor in Hawkins's neighborhood who had recently learned about a new surgical technique that involved cutting skin from one part of a person's body and grafting it onto another. Dr. McGee told Mr. Hawkins that by using the skin grafting technique, he could repair the deformed hand by taking skin from Hawkins's chest and grafting it onto his hand. Dr. McGee promised that Hawkins would have a "one hundred percent good hand" after the surgery.

Eager to remove the scars, Hawkins quickly agreed to the surgery. Dr. McGee was as good as his word. He successfully removed the skin from the chest and grafted it onto the hand, covering up the unsightly scars. Hawkins was thrilled, and this story looked like it would have a happy ending despite the grisly beginning.

After a few days, Hawkins began to notice small hairs sprouting from the palm of his hand. A few days later, the hairs had thickened and darkened. A few days after that, the palm of Hawkins's hand had become a furry monstrosity, covered in the same thick hair that covered his chest.

Hawkins sued Dr. McGee. Far from getting the "one hundred percent good hand" he was promised, Hawkins was left with an inhumanly hideous, hairy hand. Dr. McGee readily confessed his error. Skin grafts were a new surgical technique, and he was only a novice. The question was: how should the court compute the damages that Dr. McGee should pay to poor Mr. Hawkins?

One possibility might be that, since Hawkins didn't get what he paid for, he could just get his money back for the surgery. A refund might seem too little because Hawkins was not just out of pocket for the surgery. He was worse off than when he started. Before the surgery, his hand was merely scarred. After the surgery, it was grotesque and repulsive. In a different case, returning the money paid might be the right remedy, but Hawkins's damages were more extensive.

Another possibility would have been to award Hawkins the cost of repair. Hawkins's hairy hand was "broken," and under this view, the remedy for something that is broken is the cost of fixing it. Hawkins could obtain estimates from other surgeons who were able to mend the defective hand, and Dr. McGee could be compelled to pay Hawkins the fees and costs for a second, hopefully successful, surgery.

Another possibility would be to return Hawkins to the place from where he started. Before the surgery, Hawkins had a hand that was deformed with ugly scars. After the surgery, Hawkins had a hand that had no scars but was deformed by thick chest hair growing out of his palm. He started with a deformed hand and ended with a deformed hand. Assuming that a hairy hand was a worse deformity than a scarred one, Hawkins could have been paid the difference in value between the hand he had started with and the hand he ended with. (Figuring out that value is a difficult question in itself, but let's assume that a reasonably accurate way of making that computation existed.) Since the hand he had started with wasn't that great to begin with (because of the scars), the amount Hawkins would receive would be reduced as well.

A fourth possibility would be to start not with Hawkins's injured hand, but rather with what Dr. McGee promised and Hawkins expected. Dr. McGee enticed Hawkins to undergo the experimental, skin-graft surgery with the specific promise that, after it was all over, Hawkins would have a "one hundred percent good hand." That promise was not fulfilled. Hawkins's hairy hand was a far cry from what anyone would call "one hundred percent good." Using this measure of damages, Hawkins should be paid the difference in value between the perfect hand he was promised and the hairy hand he received.

Take a moment and think about which of these four possible measures of damages is the right one for Mr. Hawkins. When you're done, compare your answer to the decision of the Supreme Court of New Hampshire.

The New Hampshire Supreme Court picked option four; Hawkins was entitled to the difference between what he was promised and what he received. Hawkins had fulfilled his side of the bargain by paying Dr. McGee's fee. Dr. McGee, in turn, was obligated to fulfill his side of the bargain by delivering a "one hundred percent good hand" to Hawkins. Dr. McGee's work did not live up to his promise. The only way for the law to give Hawkins the full benefit of the bargain he had struck was for Dr. McGee to pay the value that he had failed to deliver.

This measure of damages is called **expectation damages** because it is based on the expectations of the parties to the contract. Expectation damages make the most sense when the parties to the contract share a common understanding of the benefits of the agreement, so they both know what the other is expecting. Expectation damages most closely approximate what the state of the world would have been if the contract's promises had not been broken.

Computing damages as the difference between what was promised and what was delivered is common in a wide variety of contract cases. If you hire a gardener to mow your lawn for $50 per week for ten weeks, but turn the gardener away when she shows up to work, you can expect to pay expectation damages. The gardener expected to be paid $500 under the contract, and you can expect to pay the full $500 because you prevented the gardener from doing the job.

Conversely, if the gardener fails to show up and you have to hire another company to tend your lawn at $60 per week, the neglectful gardener will owe you $100. You expected to have your lawn mowed for $500. Your lawn was mowed, so that part of your expectations was fulfilled, but because of the breach of contract by the gardener, you paid $600 instead of $500. The gardener will have to pay you the difference between what you expected to pay and what you wound up paying.

Nevertheless, expectation damages can sometimes have awkward consequences. In some cases, a small sum is paid with the expectation of a large benefit, so if something goes wrong, like Hawkins's unfortunate skin graft, the person making the promise can wind up paying more than they received, sometimes a lot more. In other cases, it is difficult to determine what exactly the parties expected, or even if their expectations are understood, what the value of those expectations might be. The proud father who sees his daughter's wedding ruined by a feckless caterer who had promised a "perfect" night is going to have a hard time proving the value of a perfect wedding.

Because of some of their limitations and drawbacks, expectation damages are not the only possible way of computing damages in a breach of contract case.

ZSA ZSA GABOR, HOLLYWOOD FANTASY, AND RELIANCE DAMAGES

Zsa Zsa Gabor was a socialite, movie star, and heartthrob of the 1950s and 1960s. Among other things, she was famous for marrying and divorcing nine husbands and commenting that she "never hated a man enough to give him his diamonds back."[206] By the 1990s, Gabor's most celebrated days of stardom were well behind her, but her fame could still draw a crowd. In 1991, she was approached by Leonard Saffir—an entrepreneur who was trying to create what he called a fantasy vacation, where the well-to-do could make a movie and pretend to be Hollywood movie stars for a week.[207] Saffir called his weeklong adventure Hollywood Fantasy.

To make the fantasy complete and to generate media interest to sell more tickets, Saffir wanted to hire Gabor to spend three days at the retreat, act in a few scenes in the vacationers' movies, and have lunch and dinner with the guests. Saffir also wanted to use Gabor's famous name in advertising and have her give interviews to the media while she was there. Saffir offered to pay Gabor $10,000 for the work, plus $1,000 for expenses. Gabor signed a letter agreeing to the job.

A month before the Hollywood Fantasy vacation was set to start, Gabor and Saffir got into an argument, and Gabor backed out. Saffir tried to find a replacement movie star, but couldn't. Hollywood Fantasy had to cancel the vacation and went out of business.

Saffir and his company, Hollywood Fantasy, sued Gabor for breach of contract, and because Gabor had abandoned the job without a good reason, they won. The question was how much should Saffir and Hollywood Fantasy receive as damages.

Saffir asked for his expectation damages. It was true that Hollywood Fantasy was a new venture, but Saffir had big plans for the company. If Gabor had performed her part of the contract and appeared at the Hollywood Fantasy vacation as promised, Saffir expected that the publicity from the event would launch the company to great success. He expected that he would hold ten future fantasy vacations, making $25,000 each, and he expected that he would be able to sell a bloopers and outtakes video of Gabor's acting for a profit of $1,000,000. He wanted the court to require Gabor to pay the full $1,025,000 of his expectation damages.

Despite his high hopes, Saffir had no evidence that he had any chance of achieving his exalted ambitions. Without any facts to support Hollywood Fantasy's claims for lost profits, the court could not award expectation damages.

But Gabor had breached the contract, and Saffir had won his case, so the law would not leave him without a remedy if a reasonable remedy could be found. While Saffir did not have evidence that money would flow like water if Gabor had only showed up at the fantasy vacation as promised, Saffir had spent a fair amount of money getting ready for the event. He had printing costs for brochures and press releases, marketing costs for mailings and advertising, travel expenses, script-writing costs, telephone calls, logo T-shirts, and other out-of-pocket expenses. All of this added up to $57,500. Not the millions Saffir was hoping for, but not nothing either.

The $57,500 that the court ultimately awarded Saffir was based on a measure of damages very different than the expectation damages we previously discussed. These damages are called **reliance damages**; they are calculated based on the losses incurred by relying on the other party to perform the contract. The purpose of reliance damages is to put the person who relied on the unfulfilled promise in the same position she would have been had the promise not been made.

Say your neighbor hires you to paint his house and promises to pay you $10,000 and you go out and spend $4,000 on supplies and equipment. If your neighbor reneges and doesn't pay, reliance damages will return to you the $4,000 you spent, so you are not out of pocket any money because of the broken promise. You are no better off than before the contract was made, but you are no worse off either.

In general, plaintiffs will prefer to receive expectation damages, and defendants will prefer to pay reliance damages. Expectation damages give the plaintiff the full benefit of his or her bargain and approximate the position of the parties if the contract had been faithfully and fully performed. Reliance damages are a fallback if expectation damages cannot be had (as was the case for Hollywood Fantasy where its expectations were too speculative).

Reliance damages can be cold comfort when plaintiffs (like Saffir) have high hopes for the future if the contract is performed, but the law must base its decisions on evidence. While expectation damages may be preferred, if the evidence just isn't there—if the expectations are just another empty Hollywood fantasy—then reliance damages are better than none at all.

CONSEQUENTIAL DAMAGES

Imagine that you are fresh out of high school. School was never your thing, so you don't want to go to college, but you do want to earn a little money. You don't have a car, but you have a bicycle, so you decide to open a messenger business. For a reasonable fee, you will deliver packages around town on your bike. You'll get to be outside, get good exercise, make some money, and be your own boss.

For your business, you have the simplest of contracts. You promise to deliver the packages on time and in good condition. Your clients promise to pay your delivery fees. Success comes quickly. Soon you have a dozen clients, and your future is looking great.

Then one day a car gets too close and clips you as it rushes by. You are thrown from your bike. You tumble by the side of the road. Miraculously, you're not hurt, and your bike is also unscathed, but the package you were carrying flew out of your backpack, rolled down a hill, and disappeared into a lake.

Knowing that you have to face the consequences, you call up your client and tell him that the package he had entrusted to your care was lost. The client erupts in anger. Inside the package was a critical part for the machinery in his factory. Now he will have to order a new part from China, which will mean several weeks' delay before his factory can be up and running again. You immediately hear from your client's lawyer, who sues you for breaking your promise to deliver the package. Again, the question is what damages should you have to pay.[208]

Naturally, the client wants his expectation damages. He expected you to deliver the package, and you didn't. If you had delivered the package, he would have his part, and his factory would be up and running. For starters, he demands that you pay for the cost of replacing the part you lost. That sounds expensive but seems fair, seeing as how you were the one who lost the part.

Then the lawyer drops the big bombshell. Because the part was lost, a new part had to be ordered from overseas. The factory was idled for several weeks, during which time the client had to turn away orders from customers who couldn't wait an extra month for their products. The lawyer wants you to pay for the money the client lost because his factory couldn't operate because you lost the critical part.

The lawsuit has taken on a whole new meaning.

Consequential damages are damages that flow as a consequence of a breach of contract. In this example, the impact of the lost part on the client's factory was a consequential damage. The harm did not flow naturally and directly from failing to make a delivery. It flowed from the special consequences of failing to make this particular delivery of this specific part for a customer with these special circumstances. If the part had not been a critical one, or if a replacement had been readily available, or if the factory had not gotten any orders, or if some alternative factory had been available, if any of these and many other possible circumstances had occurred, then there would have been no (or only minimal) damage.

When is it fair to make someone who breaches a contract pay for the consequential damages of the breach? In the messenger example, consider two possible preludes to the accident. In the first, the package is wrapped in a plain, brown paper bag. The messenger is given no special instructions and no warnings about the value of the package or the importance of making the delivery on time.

In the second, the package is in a steel box marked "vital," "critical," and "urgent" in red, capital letters. The client tells the messenger that this part is critical to the survival of his company and that without it his factory will shut down and he will lose lots of money. He asks the messenger if he is up to the task. The messenger says he is. The client asks the messenger if he understands that if he fails to deliver the part, the client's company will be ruined. The messenger says that he understands. The client asks the messenger if he is fully prepared to make a delivery this valuable and critical. The messenger says that he is. After these questions are asked and answered, the client solemnly hands the package over into the messenger's care.

In the first scenario, the messenger has no reason to think that this particular package is any more important than any other. The client said nothing about the package being particularly special. The package itself did not suggest any unusual importance. Making the messenger pay for consequential damages when he had no notice that he was carrying such precious cargo is unfair.

If the messenger had known the risk he was assuming, he might have taken special precautions, like using a car instead of a bike, or he might have refused the job entirely. But since the client didn't tell him about the potential consequential damages, the messenger didn't have an opportunity to protect himself from those heavy losses.

In the second scenario, the client went out of his way to communicate the critical importance of the part and its timely delivery. The messenger accepted the job with full knowledge and appreciation of the gravity of the undertaking. If the messenger harbored any doubts about his ability to perform, he had the opportunity to speak up, but he did not. If the risks were too great, the messenger could and should have declined the work.

Under the law, consequential damages are recoverable if they are reasonably foreseeable or the breaching party was made aware of the possibility of the damages. This rule strikes a balance between breaching and non-breaching parties. The breaching party shouldn't be exposed to risks of losses that he had no idea were possible when he undertook the job. The non-breaching party shouldn't have to bear losses that he had every reason to expect the other party would guard against.

Consequential damages have the potential to be very large. The old saying about how for want of a nail the kingdom was lost illustrates how a seemingly small undertaking can generate enormous damages if things go wrong. That can be a lot of risk to shoulder, especially when the amount being paid for the service is relatively small, like when a package is entrusted to a company for delivery. To manage that risk, people and businesses will demand limitations on their liability, a subject to which we turn next.

LIMITATIONS OF LIABILITY

Delivery companies would not last long if every time they lost a package or delivered one late they had to pay not only the value of the package but also all of the consequences of a wayward delivery. The same is true for virtually any important product or service that doesn't cost very much.

If there were no way to avoid consequential damages, businesses would have to live in fear of massive losses. A seller might be held responsible for losses if

• A car breaks down and the buyer misses a business opportunity.

• A software program crashes and a potentially best-selling novel is lost.

• A camera malfunctions at a movie shoot and a multi-million dollar scene needs to be re-shot.

Vendors could go out of business very quickly if they were exposed to such large and unpredictable liabilities. Luckily, the law has a solution. Sales and purchases are just contracts, and contracts are just agreements, and the parties to agreements can agree to pretty much whatever they want (within certain outer bounds—no agreements to commit fraud, no agreements to sell illegal substances, etc.). The solution is a limitation of liability.

A limitation-of-liability clause puts a cap on the damages that one party has to pay the other in the event of a breach of contract. In many cases, a seller will limit its liability to the sales price of the product—in other words, a refund.

In some ways, limitation-of-liability clauses can seem unfair. If you entrust an important and valuable package to someone who promises to deliver it, and the person you trusted breaks that promise, a limitation of liability means that you would suffer the catastrophic loss—even though you acted perfectly innocently—and the person who caused the loss—the person who broke the promise—would shoulder only a negligible amount of the pain.

Without limitation-of-liability clauses, however, it might be very difficult to find anyone willing to deliver packages or sell software or engage in any other business where the product prices are low but the potential for losses are unknowably high. And even if someone were willing to make a go of those businesses, the prices they charged would have to be significantly higher to cover the legal claims that would come when something, at some point, inevitably, went wrong.

A limitation of liability will sometimes leave some individual buyers without much of a remedy, but the limitation confers a benefit on buyers as a group in the form of lower prices and greater availability of products and services.

Sellers don't have to purchase expensive insurance or demand intrusive information about how exactly a buyer will use their products before making a sale or providing a service.

Imagine how you would feel if a store refused to sell you a camera unless they were sure that you would use it exclusively for relatively damage-proof activities like taking pictures of your food to post on Facebook. If you wanted to use the camera to make a movie or run a business, the seller might refuse to sell to you at all.

The limitation of liability allows the buyer to assume the risk that the camera will not work and take precautions that are proportional to the potential consequences of the camera not working. If a defective camera just means that you won't be making your Facebook-posting quota for the day, then (maybe) no precautions are needed. If you are a wedding photographer and camera failure could cost you your business, then you might have more than one camera with you, just in case. Either way, the seller doesn't need to know your business or charge different prices to different users. Their exposure is limited to just replacing the camera.

For most buyers, nothing will go wrong. For those where something does go wrong, only a fraction will be seriously damaged. The small group of buyers who dearly depend on a product or service can find protection by buying insurance or by entering into special contracts with select vendors who are willing to provide greater, but more expensive, guarantees of performance.

Limitation-of-liability clauses underscore the flexibility of the law of contracts. Since the obligations of a contract come only from agreement, the parties can structure their relationship however they like. The parties' consent is king.

CONTRACTS OF ADHESION AND UNCONSCIONABILITY

The classic paradigm of a contract is two people haggling over terms and then finally coming to a mutual agreement. For many consumers, this kind of contract is something like the unicorn; it's something everyone has heard of but no one has ever seen.

Next time you go to a store, as an experiment, try to negotiate the store's return policy. If the store's policy says you have thirty days to return an item, ask the manager if you could have ninety days. Odds are you will receive a polite, or not-so-polite, refusal.

In many cases, consumers don't even have anyone to talk to before they make a purchase. If you buy software for your computer, a screen pops up with a multi-page, end-user license (which chances are you've never read). You can click "I agree" and start using the software or you can click "I do not agree," in which case the software simply fails to start up. You have a choice, such as it is, but no opportunity to negotiate.

Car mechanics, insurance companies, credit card issuers, and mortgage lenders all have lengthy, standard forms for their contracts drafted by their lawyers and refined over decades to benefit the sellers. These contracts, for the most part, are non-negotiable. Companies expect consumers either to take or leave the deal as presented.

Contracts that are presented to consumers on a take-it-or-leave-it basis with no opportunity to negotiate are called **contracts of adhesion**. In the twenty-first century, for most consumers, most of their contracts are contracts of adhesion over which buyers exercise no meaningful influence.

Form contracts have their benefits. If a storeowner had to negotiate individual agreements with every potential customer who wandered into his or her shop, business would never get done. Imagine if General Motors tried to negotiate custom contracts with all of the millions of people who buy its cars and trucks. You would have to wait a long time to get to the front of the negotiating line.

Businesses especially like form contracts because, when the business writes the contract, the business can put things in the agreement that favor itself, like, for example, a limitation-of-liability clause. These business-friendly terms can be fair, or in some cases, they can be grossly unfair, taking advantage of unsophisticated consumers who don't have the time or expertise to read and understand the fine print of everything they have to sign to get the products and services that they need or want. And even if consumers did have the time and expertise, would they have the bargaining power to get things changed? Not likely.

Long ago, the law recognized that great disparities in bargaining power—where one party dictated the terms of an agreement—could lead to contracts that were so unfair and one-sided that no reasonable person would ever agree to the terms if he or she had any possible alternatives. From this observation was born the doctrine of **unconscionability**.

The doctrine of unconscionability is a departure from the general rule of respecting the freedom of consenting adults to enter into whatever agreements that they think best and advantageous with whatever terms that they are willing to agree to. The classic case that announced the willingness of courts to wade into the world of consumer protection from bad deals is *Williams v. Walker–Thomas Furniture Co.*[209]

The Walker-Thomas Furniture Company was a small furniture store in the District of Columbia. It operated on the poor side of town, and many of its customers had very little money to spend on furniture or anything else. Many customers didn't have steady jobs, and they often had bad credit or no credit at all. To make it easier for people in this poor neighborhood to make purchases, Walker-Thomas allowed customers to buy furniture, take it home, and use it, while paying the full price a little at a time in installments. The installment contract was printed on a form that Walker-Thomas required customers sign in order to buy the furniture.

The installment contract was written in a way to give the furniture company the maximum amount of security. If you bought more than one piece of furniture from the store (say a table and chairs or a sofa and a lamp), each payment you made was spread across all of the furniture you had ever purchased from the store, so none of the furniture would be paid off until all of the payments due for all of the furniture you ever purchased were paid in full. Until all the furniture was paid off, Walker-Thomas retained the right (*i.e.*, a security interest) to repossess all of the furniture it had sold to the customers who defaulted on their payments.

On April 17, 1962, Ora Lee Williams went to the Walker-Thomas store and bought a stereo for $514.95. For her prior purchases, Ms. Williams owed Walker-Thomas $164. With the stereo purchase, her total debt was $678 (about $5,250 in 2013 dollars). Ms. Williams defaulted on her payments, and the furniture store, as provided in its contract, tried to repossess not only the recently purchased stereo, but also all of the furniture purchases Ms. Williams had ever made at the store.

The court that heard Ms. Williams's case was appalled at the store's draconian and one-sided remedy. The court noted that Ms. Williams was given no choice about the terms of the furniture sale and no opportunity to negotiate any aspect of the transaction. This lack of meaningful bargaining power is known as *procedural unconscionability*.

In addition, the court felt that the terms of the contract were "commercially unreasonable," meaning that the terms were so unfair and one-sided that rational people who knew and understood the terms would reject them out of hand. This deep unfairness in the terms is known as *substantive unconscionability*.

The installment contract in *Williams* was suspect because the procedural and substantive unconscionability together called into question whether the contract was really an agreement at all. A contract depends upon the consent of the parties, but if the terms of a contract are excessively one-sided, that one-sidedness itself is evidence that there could not possibly have been true, free, and voluntary consent. "[W]hen a party of little bargaining power, and hence little real choice, signs a commercially unreasonable contract with little or no knowledge of its terms," reasoned the court in *Williams*, "it is hardly likely that his consent, or even an objective manifestation of his consent, was ever given to all the terms."[210]

In the opinion of the *Williams* court, no one would ever agree to a bad deal if the terms were really, really bad. On the other hand, in some cases, for some people, they may already be in a pretty bad situation, and for them it's possible that a bad deal is better than no deal at all.

For example, a common consumer protection statute is a cap on lending money at very high interest rates. Making loans with sky-high interest rates is called *usury*, a nasty and pejorative word, and frankly, nobody likes paying interest to moneylenders.

If no one likes paying even reasonable interest, why would anyone agree to a loan with an exorbitant interest rate? The consumer-protection point of view would be that those people have been taken advantage of. Another way of looking at the fact that people do indeed agree to extremely higher interest rates might be that people understand the risks of the debt, but they desperately need the money, so they agree to terms that people with a less desperate need would never dream of accepting.[211]

Lenders are no saints; they loan money to make money. Lending is their business, their livelihood. If there is no profit in the business, they will want no part of it. The biggest risk to a lending business is the risk of not getting paid back. The poorest, most desperate people are the ones most likely to default on a loan, leaving the lender without her money. From the lender's point of view, high interest rates make loans to the poor possible. The risk of default and total loss for the lender is high, but so is the reward—in the form of high interest payments—if the lender can successfully pick borrowers who make their payments.

When the government intervenes to disrupt a contract that two adults are willing and wanting to consent to, the risk is that the government will do more harm than good. So, while the government limits the interest rates that can be charged on loans, limited interest rates mean fewer lenders willing to extend credit to risky debtors. The riskiest debtors tend to be the poorest people, and so the consumer-protection statute meant to protect the poor from exploitation, in some cases, leaves the beneficiaries of the protection without access to the money that they would prefer to have. The downstream consequences of interference with the freedom of contract must be considered against the hoped-for benefits.

In modern times, state and federal legislatures have stepped in to help protect consumers in many different situations. They have enacted statutes that regulate the terms of certain contracts, require certain disclosures, and prohibit contracts written in print that is too fine to read or in foreign languages. These consumer-protection statutes also usually allow consumers to bring lawsuits against companies that fail to follow all of the law's regulations.

At their best, consumer-protection statutes restore a modicum of the balance that existed in the traditional contracting model of two equal parties bargaining over terms. As sellers increasingly are large corporations without the interest, or the ability really, to enter into individual negotiations with their thousands or millions of customers, consumers have largely lost any ability to influence the contracts they are offered. They must take the terms offered or forgo the product or service.

At their worst, consumer-protection laws impose excessive costs on transactions, leaving some people without access to the goods and services that they want and are willing to buy but can't because the government has outlawed the contract terms that would bring buyers and sellers together.

The doctrine of unconscionability and consumer-protection statutes are just two examples of the fact that the freedom to contract is not completely free. The law recognizes inequities in bargaining power and tries to establish a modicum of fairness. Yet even this modest and seemingly laudable goal is not without potential pitfalls because fairness can be very much in the eye of the beholder and consequences can be very much unintended.

8

Accidents: The Law of Torts

On the whole human beings want to be good, but not too good and not quite all the time.

—George Orwell

RIGHTING WRONGS

The Buddha is said to have observed that all life is suffering. While that bleak assessment may go a bit far in its denial of joys and happiness, injuries are unavoidable. Accidents happen. Often, too often, we are careless, inattentive, remiss, neglectful, and negligent. And other people get hurt as a result. When accidents happen, the world is made worse. Something that was whole is broken. It could be as small as a dented bumper or as cataclysmic as a shattered life.

Even more regrettable, some injuries are not accidents. People will hurt others on purpose for love, for money, for revenge, or sometimes just for spite or any other of a host of reasons. These wounds cry out for mending, and the law does its best to respond.

The area of the law that deals with accidents and intentional injuries is called **torts**. The word comes from an old French word that means something twisted or turned. A tort is a wrongful act, an act that is twisted or turned into something

247

that it should not be. The law of torts is the law of injuries and accidents and their legal remedies.

The animating purpose behind the law of torts is to compensate victims for the wrongful injuries they have suffered. The past cannot be changed. It is beyond the law's power to make right an injury by erasing its occurrence from history. While the damage to victims, and hence the loss created in the world, cannot be undone, the legal system attempts to transfer the loss onto the shoulders of the person who caused it.

The traditional remedy offered by the law of torts is damages. The person who caused the injury pays money to the person who suffered it. For some injuries, a transfer of cash is the perfect remedy. If someone wrecks your car, the law awards you money—damages—to buy a new one. For other injuries, money is a most imperfect substitute. If you lose your hand, leg, or a loved one's life to an accident, cash is cold comfort. Nevertheless, the legal system has no alternative remedy to offer, so in the absence of alternatives, money is the standard remedy for injuries as diverse as a scratch in your paint to the death of your child.

Not all injuries fall within the purview of the law of torts. Some injuries are the inevitable bumps and scrapes of living in the world, like broken hearts and disappointed dreams, a cruel illness or an unfair disability. For those hurts and sorrows, the law offers no remedy. The law of torts encompasses only the acts of people and only when people hurt each other in ways prohibited by law. There is no remedy for a critic's vicious review that sinks a movie or a competitor opening up shop next to a store and drawing away its customers. While these injuries are real, they are not wrongful in the eyes of the law, and only wrongful conduct can be a tort.

The law of torts is called upon to answer two major questions. The first is what conduct is wrongful in the eyes of the law. The second is how much compensation should be given to victims of that wrongful conduct.

Before exploring the law's answers to those questions, we should clarify the relationship between intentional torts—actions where one person deliberately injures another—and crimes.

Intentional torts, such as battery (hitting people), conversion (taking what is not yours), and fraud (tricking someone out of their money or property), look just like crimes because they are crimes as well as torts. Even though the same act (for example, punching someone in the nose) can be both a tort and a crime, the purposes of the law of torts and the criminal law are quite different. The object of the law of torts is to compensate victims for their injuries—to make them whole. In contrast, criminal law at its core focuses on punishment and deterrence by making an example of the wrongdoer. These different purposes lead to very different legal regimes. Because the law of torts governs private disputes, it is our focus here.

The law of torts exists because people hurt each other, sometimes by accident, sometimes on purpose. Victims who suffer injury at the hands of other people through no fault of their own should not have to bear the injury if there is some way to transfer it to the wrongdoers who caused the harm. The law of torts is the legal system's way of identifying when to transfer losses and how much.

THE REASONABLE PERSON

Imagine that you and your spouse are taking a weekend getaway and leaving your teenage son behind. You give him firm instructions not to throw a party—that's a given—but the ways he can get in trouble in the forty-eight hours that you will be gone defy enumeration. So you tell him on your way out the door not to do anything that you wouldn't do and hope he can figure out from that time-honored admonition where the lines are drawn by modeling his behavior on your own. You don't want your son to live like a hermit; you just want him to be reasonable, which can be a tall order for hot-blooded teens.

The number of ways people can injure each other is beyond anyone's ability to catalog and define. The challenge for the law is guiding people toward doing the right thing in a world where actually describing what is right and what is wrong in every possible situation is impossible. For this task, like the parents admonishing their teenager, the law sets up a theoretical role model for all of us to follow: the reasonable person of ordinary prudence.

The reasonable person always exercises the exact amount of care of a person of prudence. No more, no less. She always buckles her seat belt, changes the batteries in her smoke detectors every six months, and like clockwork, takes her car in for the scheduled maintenance recommended by the manufacturer. She eats her vegetables, flosses her teeth twice a day, and never, ever crosses a street without looking both ways—twice. She does not live completely sheltered from danger and risk, but for every danger and every risk, she takes precautions and care to prevent injury to herself and to others. She is a model citizen—and she does not exist.

Nevertheless, the law compares our daily conduct with this artificial construct and requires us to match the reasonable person's reasonableness step for step. If injury or harm results from our failure to act as the reasonable person would, then the law holds us liable in tort, and we must pay for the damage we've caused.

The duty to act reasonably is universal and inescapable but also largely undefined. Its vagueness is both its strength and its weakness. The strength of the standard is its infinite flexibility and adaptability to novel situations. No rule is prescribed in advance. On the contrary, what is reasonable and what is not is determined only after the fact.

The weaknesses of the reasonable person standard is the mirror image of its strengths. Because of its vagueness, the standard provides little guidance in specific situations. It leads to disputes over what is reasonable and what is not. And because it is determined after the fact, it lends itself to hindsight bias where risks that have materialized seem more likely because they actually happened. When dice come up snake eyes, the other possible outcomes are all-too-easily forgotten.

If this sounds familiar, that's good! It means that you're starting to think like a lawyer, and you remember our discussion about the benefits and flaws of standards and bright-line rules. The reasonable person is a standard. Even standards, however, need some point of reference. In many cases, reasonableness boils down to an appeal to the common sense of judges and jurors. Common sense will usually be informed by comparisons against what everyone else is doing. If most doctors perform an EKG when patients complain of chest pain, then every doctor will want to run the same test on patients with the same complaint. Reasonableness often means running with the crowd. If things go wrong, going your own way risks judges and juries, influenced by hindsight bias, finding that your conduct wasn't reasonable.

The name for the degree of caution exercised by the reasonable person is **the standard of care**. While it is not defined as a matter of law by the actions of others (because it is possible that everyone is neglecting an obvious precaution), the standard of care takes its cues from how others act in similar situations, on the assumption that it is unlikely that a mass of people are all unreasonable. We may celebrate idiosyncrasy and individuality, but when it comes to being reasonable, it pays to take precautions and stick with the herd.

BLAMEWORTHINESS AND THE CURIOUS CASE OF HELEN PALSGRAF

On August 24, 1924, it was a hot day at the East New York Long Island Rail Road station on Atlantic Avenue in New York City. No one knew it, but legal history was about to be made.

The platform was crowded with people coming and going. A whistle blew its last call for passengers, and a train slowly began to pull out of the station. At that moment, two men rushed onto the platform. They were late, and this was their train, slipping slowly away.

Panicked, the two men pushed their way through the crowd as quickly as they could, jostling and apologizing as they went. The train was moving away from them, but they were rapidly closing in. It looked like they just might make it, but the train was beginning to pick up speed. It was going to be close.

A guard on the train, seeing the distress of the late-coming passengers, held the door open and urged the men forward, waving his arms for them to hurry. The train continued its slow but steady acceleration. The first man came within jumping distance and leapt. It was close, but the man made it onto the moving car and moved safely inside.

His companion was close behind but struggling to keep up. He was carrying a package and was trying hard not to drop it as he rushed for the train. The man's face turned red. His breath came hard and fast. He was close, but not quite there. In one final effort to make his train, the second man lunged forward, off-balance, arms outstretched, fingers grasping for the rail.

A guard on the platform rushed in to help. The guard on the train holding the door and the other guard on the platform saw that the man seemed like he was about to fall. Together, the two guards—the one on the train and the one on the platform—reached out, laid hands on the would-be rider, and simultaneously pulled and pushed to get him onto the accelerating cars.

Then something unexpected happened.

The push and pull of the guards caused the passenger to drop the package he was holding. The package hit the railroad tracks hard. Unbeknownst to the guards, the package, which was wrapped in plain newspaper, was filled with fireworks. The fireworks in the package caught a spark from the tracks and exploded, sending shock waves down the tracks and over the platform.

Meanwhile, on the far end of the platform stood Mrs. Helen Palsgraf, patiently waiting for her train to arrive and blissfully unaware of what was about to happen next. She had arrived early and was in no particular hurry. She was looking to beat the heat by catching a train to Rockaway Beach and taking in the cool, refreshing ocean air. While she waited, she had taken refuge from the heat of the day in the shadow beneath two giant scales. Nothing in the scene alerted her to the possibility of danger—until the fireworks exploded.

The shock waves from the blast rocked the platform, causing the immense scales to teeter and then fall—with calamitous results. The scales collapsed onto the unsuspecting Mrs. Palsgraf, crushing her beneath their massive weight. She was rushed to a hospital. Her injuries were severe.

She sued.

The strange case of Mrs. Palsgraf, the exploding fireworks, and the collapsing scales made its way through the New York courts, as New York's brightest legal minds struggled with the question of whether the railroad company should have to pay for Mrs. Palsgraf's injuries. Four years later, in 1928, the case finally reached the highest court in the state, the New York Court of Appeals, where the judges had to decide when is it fair to hold one person responsible for the injury of another.

Sometimes it seems that the law of torts is a contradictory beast. On the one hand, the focus of the tort system is to compensate injured parties for their injuries. At the same time, not all injuries are considered compensable under the law. Injuries inflicted by bad fortune, for example, like being struck by cancer or being swallowed up by an earthquake or washed away by a tsunami, will find no redress in the courts. Terrible as those afflictions are, they are beyond the reach of the law because the law can only shift losses, not eliminate them, and whom would the legal system hold responsible for injuries caused by nature? If no one did anything wrong that led to the injury, then there is no one to blame and no one to whom to shift the loss of the injury. This same principle applies when people are involved in the injury. If the people involved have done nothing wrong, if they are not *blameworthy* in some way, then the legal system will not find them liable for another person's injury.

The *Palsgraf* case exquisitely posed the question of when should the law intervene to shift the loss of an injury.[212] The sequence of events that led to Helen Palsgraf's catastrophe began when the two railroad employees attempted to help the late-coming passenger catch the moving train. If the railroad guards had not intervened, if they had decided to simply let the latecomer miss his train, they would not have jostled his arm that held his package; the package would not have slipped from the passenger's grasp and fallen onto the rails; the package, which turned out to be fireworks, would not have exploded; the shock waves from the explosion never would have happened and never would have rattled the scales at the other end of the platform; and the scales would not have fallen on the unsuspecting Mrs. Palsgraf. Because the railroad employees set in motion the cascade of events that ended with her injury, Mrs. Palsgraf argued, the railroad should be held responsible and should have to pay for the damages that she suffered.

As sympathetic as the innocent Mrs. Palsgraf was, the New York high court did not support her cause, albeit by the margin of a single vote.[213] In an opinion written by Chief Justice Benjamin Cardozo, who would later be elevated to the Supreme Court of the United States, the New York Court of Appeals concluded that the railroad could not be held responsible for Mrs. Palsgraf's injuries because its employees had done nothing that any reasonable person could have believed would lead to Mrs. Palsgraf getting hurt.

The railroad employees were only trying to help a passenger onto a train, reasoned Chief Justice Cardozo. They had no way of knowing that the wad of newspaper that the running latecomer had tucked under his arm was, in reality, a dangerous package of highly volatile explosives. According to Cardozo, a person's duty is not simply to avoid causing injury to another. Rather, a person's duty is to avoid taking actions that unreasonably increase the risk of injuries to others.

Cardozo supported his argument with the example of a driver racing down the streets at a reckless speed. Everyone would agree that driving on public roads at high speeds is wrongful, but why is it wrongful? According to Cardozo, speeding is wrong because it creates an obvious risk of injuring people or property. Because the wrongfulness of speeding lies in the elevated and unnecessary risks that speeding creates, speeding is wrong even if no one is injured.

In contrast, if the same car drives at the same speed, but is on a racetrack instead of a public street, there is no longer anything "wrongful" about careening at high speed. Pedestrians, parked cars, and unsuspecting motorists populate public streets, all of which are highly vulnerable to speeding cars. In contrast, we expect speeding cars on a racecourse, which should only have other cars going at comparable speeds piloted by drivers who are fully aware of the situation and its dangers.

Using this example, Cardozo concluded, "The risk reasonably to be perceived defines the duty to be obeyed, and risk imports relation; it is risk to another or others within apprehension." In other words, your duty to avoid causing injury is limited to avoiding risks that a reasonable person could foresee as having a significant chance of hurting another person. If the sequence of events is too improbable—if it is too unforeseeable—there is no duty and no liability.

In the *Palsgraf* case, the actions of the railroad employees—helping a passenger onto a train—were innocent and harmless. Nothing about the situation alerted them or would have alerted any reasonable person that helping this passenger catch this train was putting other people in danger, especially not people standing on other end of the train platform, far from the action. Because the railroad employees didn't know and couldn't know about the fireworks, they had not done anything wrong, and their employer could not be blamed or held responsible. And so, Mrs. Palsgraf lost her case, but she gained immortality in the annals of legal history and law school casebooks.

The teaching of the *Palsgraf* case is that you are only responsible for another person's injuries if you violate a *duty* owed to that other person. This duty, in turn, is defined by the risks of your conduct. If you engage in dangerous or risky conduct, then you can expect to pay for any resulting injuries. If, on the other hand, you engage in conduct that is ordinary and prudent, without any reasonably foreseeable risk, and yet by some freak turn of events, someone gets hurt, the loss will fall where it lands and will not be shifted to you.

With a few exceptions,[214] this concept of duty is the cornerstone of the law of torts and understanding it is the key to understanding how the legal mind thinks about our relationships with each other.

HEROICS, RISK, AND DUTY

A man in a faded, oversized army jacket waits in line for the next available bank teller. A baseball cap is pulled low over his face, his hands are stuffed deep in the pockets of his jacket, and he shifts his weight nervously from leg to leg as he advances through the line. The man approaches the counter and passes the teller a note. Just four words.

"I have a gun."

The man nods at the cash drawer. The teller hesitates. The man gives the teller a glimpse of a metal object stuffed in his pocket and pointing at the teller's chest. The teller sees that the man is deadly serious.

The robber is not a big man, and the deep creases in his face betray that he is not particularly young. He leans in to tell the teller to hurry.

This is a mistake.

Seeing an opportunity, the teller leaps across the counter and grips the would-be robber's shoulders, twisting his body to pull him to the ground. The robber struggles to keep his footing against the teller's greater height and weight and strength. He reaches for the gun in his pocket. Freeze frame.

The teller and the robber are locked in a physical confrontation. The robber's gun is in his hand. This battle has a number of possible endings, some good and some very, very bad.

Let's start with the Hollywood ending. The teller, seeing the gun as their bodies twist towards the ground, knocks it out of the robber's hand with a swift blow to the wrist. The gun skitters harmlessly away. With the gun gone, the teller leverages his superior size to subdue the robber. The other patrons of the bank burst into applause for the teller's heroism. The police take the robber away. The mayor gives the teller a medal.

But it is possible that the teller does not get his Hollywood ending. Return to the frozen frame. Teller and robber struggle for the gun. In the fight, the gun goes off—who knows who caused it to discharge—the bullet ricochets off the wall straight into the heart of a woman who had come with her husband to apply for a loan to buy their first house. Distracted by the gunshot and the screams of the others in the bank, the teller slips. The robber does not hesitate. He slams the metal barrel of the pistol across the teller's face, knocking out a tooth and leaving the teller dizzy and disoriented. The robber flees. The police and paramedics arrive too late. The woman is dead.

Other endings to this story exist, but they are merely variations. For happy endings, the robber is subdued. No one is hurt. For tragic, the fight injures or kills a bystander or bank employee or someone else. So rewind the tape to the moment the robber leans in and puts himself within the teller's grasp. What is the teller's duty under the law?

To begin, it is obvious that the robber bears the primary responsibility for initiating the sequence of events with a strong probability of ending in injury or death. He came to the bank to steal, and he brought with him a weapon to carry out his wicked plan. But banks live in a world of robbers, and while they may take precautions such as having security guards, surveillance cameras, and panic buttons and keeping limited cash on hand in strong vaults with police protection close by, armed robbers are a reality that no amount of precaution can erase.

The bank has an indisputable right to protect its property and a duty to protect the assets of its depositors, but at the same time, the bank should not put other people in danger while it is doing so. The bank-robber hypothetical is a hard case because the bank teller did not do anything obviously wrongful. On the contrary, at great personal risk, he tried to stop a crime, and if he succeeds, he is a hero. If he fails, and someone is hurt, the story is very different.

If the teller had not engaged the robber, then it is highly likely that no one would have been injured. The robber said that no one would be hurt, and he would have had no reason to injure anyone after he had the money he came for. The teller's heroism vastly increased the risk that someone would get hurt. By taking on the armed robber, the teller risked not only his own life, but also the lives of everyone else in the bank that day. And in the second possible unfolding of events, an innocent woman paid the price with her life.

Confronted with an armed robber, the bank and its teller have another path available to them, one that does not carry the same high risks. The teller could simply hand over the money as asked, and after the robber has fled the premises, the teller could call the police. The bank has surveillance tapes to identify the perpetrator. The bills handed over can be marked and traced. A fleeing robber is also highly conspicuous, so there is a reasonable chance that the police—who are trained in pursuing, confronting, and subduing bad guys—will capture the robber and return the stolen money. Letting the crime unfold might be frustrating, but it also could save lives.

And so, when the murdered woman's husband sues the bank for negligence, the courts will have to determine whether the bank should pay for the teller's heroics.

The bank will raise the defense that it was the robber who fired the gun. The widowed husband will argue that the bank teller unreasonably heightened the risks of an already dangerous situation, recklessly risking lives and costing his wife's hers to save what at most was a few thousand dollars.

Courts considering these conflicting arguments must weigh the consequences for the parties to the lawsuit, but also for other people who will look at the rule the courts lay down and modify their behavior accordingly.

If the courts rule for the husband, banks will instruct their tellers not to resist robbers. This will protect future husbands and wives from stray bullets in future robberies.

But banks are not the only part of the equation. If robbers know that bank employees will not resist their demands if bank patrons are at risk, robbers will plan their thefts for when the bank is full of bystanders. Robbers might be encouraged to take hostages, which would put more people in danger.

This is a close case, with good arguments for both the bank and the widowed husband. For the majority of courts that have tackled this problem, the danger of encouraging would-be robbers to plan their attacks for when bystanders are present has tipped the scales in the bank's favor.[215]

The law of torts attempts to fashion rules that minimize the risks of accidents and injuries. When the teller tackled the robber, he created a risk of injury. Forbidding tellers from tackling robbers, however, would also create a risk of injury by encouraging more dangerous robberies. When two risks compete, the law attempts to deter the greater risk and tolerate the lesser, even if doing so means that when the lesser risk comes to pass, the injured go without compensation.

DEFINING DUTY

The law of torts can seem, at times, to be nothing but a dizzying circle. A person is liable to another for injuries he or she causes when he or she breaches a legal duty not to injure that person. But where do these duties come from? How can you tell the difference between an injury that the law will compensate (punching someone in the nose) and an injury that the law will not compensate (breaking someone's heart)?

As we've discussed, the core of the law of torts is making the blameworthy pay for the damage they do. The *Palsgraf* case gives the classic formula of duty as the obligation to take no actions that unreasonably increase the foreseeable risks of injury to other people.

Even with the *Palsgraf* rule as a guide, blameworthiness and duty can be slippery and very much in the eye of the beholder.

It is possible that if we were to dig down to the buried roots of our thinking about torts, we would not find pure logic, but rather a visceral, primitive intuition of right and wrong.

Nevertheless, the law likes to think of itself as ruled by reason and not intuition. It recoils from explanations that appeal only to our guts and not our minds. When considering whether a legal duty should or should not exist, courts will weigh (or claim that they will weigh) factors like the following:[216]

- The foreseeability of harm to the injured party.
- The degree of certainty that the plaintiff suffered injury.
- The closeness of the connection between the defendant's conduct and the injury suffered.
- The moral blame attached to the defendant.
- The policy of preventing future harm.
- The extent of the burden to the defendant.
- The consequences to the community of imposing a duty.
- The availability, cost, and prevalence of insurance for the risk involved.

This is an impressive list of considerations, but they can be hard to apply in practice. Consider the following example.

Carlos is in a business meeting when his cell phone rings. It's one of those long-winded, meandering meetings, the kind that start late and end late, with no agenda and no focus, so Carlos excuses himself and takes the call. He immediately regrets his decision and wishes that he had sent the call to voicemail.

It's Harriet, his crazy ex-girlfriend, the one Carlos is trying very hard to forget. The meeting only numbed Carlos's mind. The thought of talking to Harriet makes his head hurt.

Before he can hang up, something in Harriet's voice catches Carlos's attention. Something is wrong. He can hear the sounds of cars honking in the background, and her voice is hard to hear over gusts of wind.

Cautiously, Carlos asks Harriet where she is. She says she is standing on a guardrail on a freeway overpass. She tells him that below her cars are flying at breakneck speeds, and she's thinking about taking a step to join them on the asphalt fifty feet below.

Carlos breaks into a cold sweat. This is exactly the reason he broke up with Harriet. She was unstable, dramatic, and manipulative. Harriet begs Carlos to drive out and see her. Carlos says he can't do that. She cries, and then abruptly she stops and says that she will do whatever he says. If Carlos tells her to come down from the bridge, she will. If he tells her to jump, she will.

Carlos rolls his eyes. He's certain that he's being played, and this conversation is going nowhere, just like his relationship with her. He is done wasting time on psychotic ex-girlfriends, so he says, "Jump" and hangs up.

The world turns, and Carlos finds that Harriet's parents have sued him for the wrongful death of their child. The tort of wrongful death is causing the death of another through negligence, and an essential element of negligence is the existence of a legal duty. Did Carlos have a legal duty to prevent Harriet's suicide? Let's run through the factors.

Foreseeability. Was it foreseeable that Harriet would jump if Carlos told her to do it? Some facts point to yes. Harriet told Carlos she would jump if he told her to. Carlos knew that Harriet was unstable; that was one of the reasons he broke up with her. Harriet had gone a long way toward committing the final act. She was standing on a freeway overpass. Someone who had gone that far could easily take the one last, fatal step.

Other facts suggest no. Carlos thought that Harriet was being dramatic and manipulative. She had made dramatic claims in the past without harming herself. It is one thing to take steps to prepare for a suicide and another thing to go through with it. Suicide is (thankfully) rare, so the odds were that Harriet would climb down from the overpass and just go home.

Degree of certainty of the injury. Harriet is dead. The injury is incontrovertible.

Connection between defendant's conduct and the injury. In one sense, one might think Carlos set the wheels in motion when he broke up with Harriet and sent her into a dark spiral of depression, but that act by Carlos seems fairly remote from Harriet's suicide weeks later. Carlos, however, was on the phone with Harriet right before she died. Not only did he not try to stop her, he callously uttered the word "jump" right after she told him that if he told her to jump, she would. Carlos's lack of sympathy to Harriet's pleas is chilling.

At the same time, although Carlos spoke a hurtful word to a vulnerable person, he did not push her off of the bridge. Harriet had brought herself to that point on her own, and there is no way to know that she wouldn't have gone through with the suicide no matter what Carlos said.

Moral blame. Carlos acted like a heartless jerk. His ex-girlfriend reached out to him with a desperate cry for help, and he coldly turned his back on her. On the other hand, Carlos had broken up with Harriet and wanted to move on without her. She called him and tried to drag him back into her life against his will. He didn't mean to cause any harm. He just wanted to communicate that their relationship was definitively and irrevocably over.

Preventing future harm. If Carlos is held liable for Harriet's death, future Carloses will be more likely to attempt to intervene to help future Harriets. On the other hand, given how close she was to killing herself, it is not clear that Carlos could have done anything that would have prevented what happened. Harriet was too far away physically and possibly too far away mentally and emotionally. Whether intervention by ex-boyfriends would prevent suicides by rejected girlfriends teetering on the edge of freeway overpasses is uncertain.

Burden on the defendant. If Carlos is responsible for Harriet's death, there may be no way for him ever to end his relationship with her. If the law requires that Carlos run to Harriet's side anytime she threatens to harm herself, Carlos might never be free to go on with his own life without her. Then again, perhaps there is a difference between responding to multiple calls and responding to just one. And perhaps there is a difference when the call comes in and it seems that the caller is very close to harming herself.

Consequences to the community. It is not clear what the consequences to the community would be of imposing a duty on Carlos in this case.

Availability of insurance. There is no insurance against suicide. If Carlos is required by law to bear the liability for Harriet's death, he will have to bear it on his own.

So, having run through the factors, is the answer any clearer to the question of whether a legal duty should exist to prevent (or maybe refrain from encouraging) the suicide of another person? Some of the factors point one way, some the other. Even within factors, different facts point in opposite directions.

For good or for ill, the law does not have the option of throwing up its hands and giving up. The plaintiffs have asked for relief. If the courts deny it, then effectively they will be ruling that Carlos had no legal duty. If the courts grant it, then effectively they will be ruling that Carlos did have a legal duty.

Consider another example. Many states have enacted laws that prohibit drivers of motor vehicles from sending text messages while driving.[217] It seems clear enough that a driver who causes an accident because he is distracted by texting while driving will have breached a legal duty and will be liable in tort to any person the driver injures. But what about the person who sends the text message to the driver? Is there a legal duty to refrain from sending a text message to someone you know is driving a car?

The question is tricky. The statutes banning texting while driving don't settle the issue because they make no reference to the person with whom the driver is communicating. At the same time, it takes two to tango, as the saying goes, and every text message has a sender and a recipient. By responding to text messages, the remote texter aids and encourages the driver to break the law by reading and responding to those texts while driving. On the other hand, it is reasonable to expect other people to obey the law, so it is hard to see how just sending a text, without something more, could generate legal liability even if the person who reads and responds to it is driving.

Whether a person who communicates electronically with a driver should be legally responsible if the driver has an accident is not obvious, and reasonable minds can disagree. One court in New Jersey answered the question by concluding that "the sender of a text message can potentially be liable if an accident is caused by texting, but only if the sender knew or had special reason to know that the recipient would view the text while driving and thus be distracted."[218] Did the court go too far in defining the scope of legal duty? The answer depends on how you weigh the different factors of duty, but that is not very different than saying the answer depends on whether you agree or disagree with the court's decision.

Legal duty is not a law of nature that is discoverable through careful measurement and the process of experimentation. Legal duty is a judgment. Sometimes the judgment is made by the legislature in the form of a statute; more often it is made by courts in the form of legal precedents. This judgment can be, and is, informed through analysis, but at the same time, the analysis only guides legal thinking. Rarely does the analysis compel one and only one conclusion.

In the case of Carlos, despite his boorish behavior, the law would likely not find him responsible for Harriet's suicide. Carlos had no special relationship to care for and protect Harriet from harm. He may have had a moral duty to help her, but likely not a legal one.[219]

In the case of remote texters, one court has held that, under some circumstances, they can be held liable for injuries caused by drivers who answer their texts. Other courts will one day weigh in, and a consensus will emerge, but until that happens, the scope of the remote texters' duty under the law remains cloudy.

The struggle to define when a person has a legal duty and when a person does not is at the heart of the law of torts. The definition of duty draws upon our most visceral intuitions about right and wrong. Sometimes the answers are obvious. Other times we just have to make do with our best guess.

THE ACCIDENT THAT DIDN'T HAPPEN

Accidents are bad. That seems obvious enough, but it's worth considering for a moment why they are bad. Consider the following hypothetical sequence of events.

Imagine you are dusting and you accidentally knock over an antique vase that has been in your wife's family for generations. You watch in horror as priceless porcelain tumbles end over end, hurtling toward the hard floor and imminent destruction.

But then, by some incredibly lucky stroke, the vase makes impact, not on the floor, but on your foot, which absorbs the force of the fall, and the vase rolls away unharmed. You pick up the vase as fast as you can, inspect it for damage, and seeing none, put it back in its place safe and sound, chastising yourself that this is why you shouldn't be dusting in the first place. In these circumstances, how much should you pay for this accident?

To be sure, an accident undeniably occurred. By your carelessness, you knocked an expensive and fragile item off of a shelf where it had been safely sitting until clumsiness intervened. The vase's destruction was all but certain, and only the freakiest of flukes averted the disaster. Yet disaster was averted. In these circumstances, the law holds that the accident—real and certain as it was—has no legal consequence. No damages resulted from the accident, and so no compensation is due the owner of the vase. The risky, neglectful, careless conduct goes unpunished.

Now let us return to the moment before the careless hand caught the edge of the precious porcelain and consider a less happy outcome. All unfolds as before, the dusting, the inadvertent but fateful collision of hand and vase, the dramatic fall, but this time the inevitable is not miraculously avoided.

The vase hits the floor with fatal force and loudly shatters into a thousand pieces.

This time, the law will take a very different view of the carelessness. This time, you will be required to pay the owner the value of the vase. Yet here again, it is worth pausing for a moment to question why.

In both scenarios, the actions that set events in motion were identical. The difference between the scenarios rests entirely in the outcome of those actions. In one, nothing was broken. In the other, the vase shattered.

The differences in these outcomes are nothing but the product of chance. If the law focused on the wrongdoer and the wrongdoer's actions alone, the legal consequences in both cases should be the same because the actions were the same. But the wrongdoer's intentions and the wrongdoer's actions are not the principal concern of the law of torts—the outcome is. The main objective of the law of torts is to *compensate* the injured and not to *punish* the injurers. This is an important distinction.

In the case where the vase does not break, there is no injury to compensate. Before the accident, the owner had a priceless heirloom sitting stately on her shelf. After the accident, the heirloom continues in its place of honor. In the case where the vase breaks, the loss is tangible and obvious. While money may be a poor and unwanted substitute for the vase, the legal system will do its best to award a sum that will compensate the owner for her loss. The law will offer nothing for the injury that didn't happen

In the tort system, the wrongfulness of the action manifests in the consequences of the action. Wrongs without consequences are not wrongs that the law of torts will address.

BLAMEWORTHINESS, STATE OF MIND, AND MORAL LUCK

Consequences play a big role in our assessment of the blameworthiness of different actions. Rebecca Saxe, a neuroscientist at the Massachusetts Institute of Technology, devised an experiment to assess how human brains respond to different situations where the blameworthiness of another person's actions is in question. The experiment's design raises questions about our deepest intuitions about right and wrong and goes something like this.[220]

Grace and her friend are on a tour of chemical factory when they decide to take a break from the tour and stop for coffee. The friend sits down in a seating area while Grace goes to the break room and finds the coffee. Next to the coffeepot are two containers filled with white powder. One container is labeled sugar. The other container is labeled deadly poison. Grace scoops two spoonfuls of white powder from the jar labeled sugar into her friend's coffee cup. Her friend drinks the coffee and thanks her for the sweet refreshment. All is well.

This is the world as it should be. Grace intends to sweeten her friend's coffee with sugar, and she does. It would be hard to find anyone who thinks that Grace has done anything morally or legally wrong. Now let's consider what happens as we move away from this happy scenario.

Returning to the moment Grace enters the break room in search of coffee, she sees the same two jars of white powder with the same labels "sugar" and "deadly poison." Grace scoops two spoonfuls from the sugar jar into her friend's coffee. Her friend drinks and immediately chokes and dies. The white powder, it turns out, was not sugar at all, but deadly poison. The two containers were tragically mislabeled.

The world is no longer right. In this version, Grace killed her friend. She scooped poison into her friend's drink, and her friend died. But Grace did not know that she was poisoning her friend's drink. The jar was labeled sugar, and that's what Grace thought the white powder was. Her actions led to a terrible consequence, but her intentions were innocent. Nevertheless, despite her good intentions, her friend is dead. Is Grace morally and legally innocent or guilty?[221] Before you answer, consider another variation on this theme.

Grace goes to the break room to fetch the coffee and again finds the jars with the same white powder and the same labels. This time the labels are correct. Poison is in the poison jar and sugar in the sugar jar. Wanting to get back to her friend before the coffee cools, Grace is rushed and distracted, and without realizing it, she scoops the powder from the poison jar. Her friend promptly dies.

As in the previous scenario, Grace has killed her friend by putting poison in her drink, and as in the previous scenario, Grace innocently intended to put sugar into her friend's coffee. In other words, Grace's physical actions and her state of mind are exactly the same in both scenarios. In the first, Grace scooped poison out of a jar that she mistakenly believed to be sugar. In the second, Grace scooped poison out of a jar that she mistakenly believed to be sugar.

You didn't read that wrong; the scenarios are identical—almost. Although Grace acted innocently in both scenarios, most people will put much greater blame on Grace in the scenario where she made a mistake by rushing too quickly than in the scenario where she made a mistake by relying on the erroneous labels. But why?

The difference lies in the reasonableness of the different errors. In the first case, Grace had no reason to know that she was poisoning her friend. The jar of poison was labeled sugar. Nothing warned her of the danger. In the second case, the danger was plain, but Grace missed it because she was in a rush.

In theory, in the first case with the mislabeled jar of poison, Grace could have discovered that the white powder wasn't sugar. She was in a chemical factory, after all, and could have had it tested before she scooped it into her friend's drink. Yes, the danger would have been difficult to discover, but it would not have been impossible.

The amount of effort required to avoid the error, however, would have been enormous. Grace would have had to conduct a chemical analysis to detect the poison. If she were that paranoid, she would have to test the coffee, the cup, and the spoon as well to make sure that none carried dangerous chemicals. That amount of precaution without some sign of heightened risk is unreasonable.

In contrast, in the case where the jars were correctly labeled, Grace could have avoided poisoning her friends without much effort by simply reading the labels more carefully. Requiring Grace to read the labels isn't much of a burden considering that a life was at stake.

Before we leave Grace and her friend, let us consider two more variations. Grace goes for the coffee and again sees the two jars and the two labels. This time, Grace reaches past the sugar jar, and fully aware of what she is doing, she scoops two large dollops of powder from the poison jar into her friend's coffee. She hands the coffee to her friend (although "friend" isn't really the right word anymore), and her friend promptly chokes and dies.

At this point, Grace has crossed a significant line. This was no accident. With full knowledge of what she was doing, Grace scooped poison into her friend's drink. She planned to kill her friend, and she succeeded. This is murder, pure and simple. Grace is clearly morally blameworthy, but how does her blameworthiness compare if she takes the same actions with a different outcome?

In this scenario, Grace goes for the coffee and again sees the two jars. Grace again bypasses the sugar jar and scoops the powder from the poison jar into her friend's drink. This time, nothing happens. The jars were mislabeled. The poison jar contained only harmless sugar. How blameworthy is Grace?

In the first variation, Grace scoops from the poison jar, and her friend dies. In the second, Grace scoops from the poison jar, and her friend lives. The outcomes of the two cases could not be more different. Grace's state of mind, however, is the same. In both cases, she intended to poison her friend's drink.

The second variation—in which Grace pours what she mistakenly thinks is poison into her friend's drink—would be considered in criminal law to be an *attempt*. Criminal attempts are something of an oddity because an attempt to commit a crime is punishable even if no one is actually hurt. Putting sugar into a friend's drink is not a crime, and that is what Grace did, but Grace *intended* to put poison in the drink. The crime is not the deed, but her intentions.

In both the completed and attempted poisonings, Grace's state of mind was murderous. Should her punishments be the same for both the murder and the attempt, or should they be different because in one case, through a happy accident, her friend lived?

If we judge the morality of the person based on his or her thoughts and intentions, treating failed attempts differently from successful ones seems strange. The person who fires a gun and misses has committed exactly the same blameworthy act as the superior marksman who fires a gun and hits.

If we care about people's deeds and not their inner thoughts, then punishing attempts at all is strange. Grace's actual act was to put sugar in her friend's drink. She may have *thought* that it was poison, but it wasn't, and no harm was done.

At the intersection of thoughts and deeds, the law of torts and the criminal law diverge. The criminal law punishes both completed crimes and attempts, although the punishment for completed crimes is more severe than the punishments for attempted, but uncompleted, crimes. In contrast, for the most part, tort law does not provide a remedy for attempts. The goal of the law of torts is to compensate victims for actual losses—not merely imagined or possible losses. If there are no losses, there is nothing to compensate.

The five scenarios we've considered are summarized in this table.

	Label	Actual	Injury	Tort	Crime
1	Sugar	Sugar	None	No	No
2	Sugar (mislabel)	Poison	Death	No	No
3	Sugar (wrong jar)	Poison	Death	Yes	No
4	Poison	Poison	Death	Yes	Yes
5	Poison	Sugar	None	No	Yes

What these examples illustrate is that our intuitions about blameworthiness depend on a combination of thoughts and outcomes, but they are not always consistent.

Scenario number three in the table—the one where Grace mistakenly scoops powder from the poison jar when she meant to scoop powder from the sugar jar—is a prototypical example of **negligence**, the most common wrongful act covered by the law of torts. Negligence is causing an injury by failing to take reasonable care. In the example, if Grace had been paying more attention, she would have seen that she was scooping from the wrong jar, and her friend would not have been injured.

In the law's terminology, Grace owed her friend a duty of care when she was preparing the coffee, and she breached that duty of care when she did not pay enough attention to what she was doing. Because her friend was injured by Grace's breach of the duty of care, Grace incurred liability under the law of torts.

The disaster that befalls Grace's friend and the legal liability that falls on Grace's shoulders is very much the product of bad luck. Grace didn't mean any harm. She just wasn't paying attention—a lapse that everyone is guilty of from time to time, the only difference being the severity of the consequences.

By chance, Grace scooped from the poison jar. If, by chance, Grace had scooped from the sugar jar, Grace would have been just as guilty of not paying attention, but no harm would have come from her carelessness, and she would have had no liability in the eyes of the law.

Negligence cases illustrate what philosophers call **moral luck**. Moral luck is when the rightness or wrongness of a person's actions (i.e., the *morality* of what they have done) is judged, at least in part, on circumstances outside of the person's control.[222] The classic example is two drivers who speed through a red light without stopping. For one, the intersection is empty, and the driver reaches the other side without incident or injury. For the other, an elderly couple is in the crosswalk. The car hits the couple.

Both drivers committed the same wrong (running the red light), but because of circumstances outside of their control—because of *luck*—the consequences of the wrongs were radically different. If the law catches up with these drivers, the different consequences will give them radically different fates.

The driver who ran the light but had the good fortune to have the crosswalk empty at the time would, at most, get a ticket and pay a modest fine. The first driver, blameworthy as he may be, will owe nothing in tort to anyone. The second driver who ran the light and hit the couple will have to pay costly damages to the couple's family for the injury and will likely find himself looking at a lengthy prison sentence for vehicular manslaughter,[223] all because he had the misfortune of having his crosswalk occupied.

It is not unreasonable to hold the view that, as a moral matter, both drivers are equally blameworthy to equal degrees. Their states of mind were the same. Their actions were the same. Their actions both created the same risk of severe injury in equal measure.

The law's approach to problems is more practical than philosophical. The purpose of the law of torts is not to pass moral judgments—although it does pass those judgments when defining the extent a person's legal duties—but rather, the purpose is to compensate people for their losses when they are injured by other people who have done something wrong. There are enough actual injuries to keep the courthouses full without the courts getting involved when no one gets hurt.

UNQUANTIFIABLE LOSSES

It is all well and good to say that the law aims to compensate for injuries, but moving from concept to application can be very difficult. Losses from accidents can be thought of like holes in the ground. Before the accident, the surface is flat and unbroken. The accident gouges a hole in the victim's land. The law attempts to fill the hole, but the dirt has to come from somewhere, so the law turns to the wrongdoer to fill the hole. The total loss in the world is the same. A hole was made and cannot be unmade, but the victim's land is restored to the way it was before—at least that's the idea.

Of course, the injured person—the one with the hole—is entitled only to a repair of what he or she has lost, and nothing more. If you drive a beat-up truck that gets smashed in a collision that was not your fault, the law will award you the value of the beat-up truck you lost, but not the value of the shiny new model you've had your eye on. If you want to upgrade your wheels, you're going to have to come up with the money yourself, just as you would have had to do if the accident had never happened. You lost your old, beat-up truck in the accident, and you should have it back. Your hole should be filled. No less and no more.

So far, so good, and if the injuries of the world could be reduced to holes to be filled, then a measuring tape and a dump truck would be all we'd need to set things right. For real injuries, figuring out how big the hole actually is can be extraordinarily complex. Consider the following accidents:

• A friend accidentally breaks a family heirloom.

• A newspaper mistakenly publishes your picture over a caption referring to a convicted child molester.

• A surgeon drops a scalpel, which severs your spinal cord, paralyzing your legs and confining you to a wheelchair.

In each of these cases, the only way to truly restore the injured party would be to build a time machine, go back in time, and ensure that the accident never happened in the first place. Since time machines are unlikely to be available anytime soon (or any time really),[224] money is the only remedy the law can offer.

The true values of these losses defy reduction to a dollar amount. What is the price to be placed on a sentimental heirloom that connects a person to his or her ancestors? What is the value of being free from the misinformed suspicion of friends and neighbors? What amount makes a person whole for losing the ability walk?

Since an award of damages in tort must be limited to the amount that would restore the injured party to his or her circumstances before the injury, a value for those injuries must be established. Here, for the most part, the legal system simply leaves it up to the people who find the facts in the trial courts— usually juries—to use their judgment and common sense to make their best guess of a number that will put things as right as they can be put.

Relying on people's best guesses feels somewhat arbitrary. Two different decision-makers looking at objectively comparable situations can come to very different conclusions about what amount of money would be appropriate for an injury that in any other setting would be unthinkable and incalculable.

While no one likes arbitrariness, the alternative is even less palatable. If definitive certainty were strictly required to award damages, many of the most grievously injured plaintiffs could never meet that standard. The result would be that the people most deserving of a legal remedy would recover no damages at all. It would be strange if the unjustly injured received nothing precisely because their losses were so staggering that they could not be computed with certitude, and at the same time, wrong-doers who inflicted these staggering losses would pay nothing to compensate for the harms they caused.

As between wrongdoers and victims, the moral balance tips in favor of offering something to victims even if that means exposing wrongdoers to some element of arbitrariness and unfairness.

THE EGGSHELL PLAINTIFF

A boy of fourteen sits in a classroom at his desk.[225] He's bored. He wants to be outside, but school won't get out for what seems to him to be just this side of eternity. He turns his head and sees his classmate sitting at the desk next to his. The classmate is younger and totally absorbed by the teacher's lecture. The boy shakes his head in disgust. The teacher turns her back to write something on the chalkboard. On an impulse, the boy swings his leg and kicks his classmate in the knee. It's not a violent kick, but certainly more than enough to get his attention and to sting.

Then something unexpected happened.

The classmate doubles over in pain and lets out a horrific scream. He rolls onto the floor, hands wrapped over his knees, his face contorted in anguish. The teacher rushes over and cries out for someone to go for help. An ambulance comes. The classmate is rushed to a hospital. A surgeon is called. Hours later, the boy emerges from the operating room; his leg has been amputated at the knee.

It turns out that the classmate has a rare, degenerative muscle condition, susceptible to activation by sudden impacts. For an ordinary boy of ordinary resilience, the kick that was delivered would have had much more emotional than physical impact. But for this boy, with this muscle condition, the kick took his leg and with it his ability to walk.

So what is to be done? The boy who kicked his classmate did something wrong, that much is plain. One student shouldn't kick another at his desk in school. It is more than foreseeable that kicking will hurt. That was the intended purpose. Avoiding hurting other people is a legal duty, and under the law anyone who purposely causes injury to another person can be held responsible for the injuries that resulted when he breaches this duty.

There is only one reason for a schoolboy to kick his classmate in class, so the intent to injure is clear, but what was the injury that was intended? Consider for a moment the case from the boy's point of view. He did something he knew was wrong, yes, but in his mind what he did—a kick in the leg—fell within the realm of harmless pranks, and in virtually any other classroom with any other boy, that is how the law would have treated it. This wasn't the mischief-maker's first experience with the rough and tumble of the schoolyard. Many times had he exchanged hits and kicks and bumps and bruises with other boys on other occasions, receiving as much as he had given, and in none of those encounters were the consequences any greater than minor scrapes and hurt feelings. He had no idea—he couldn't have had an idea—that this time this same act with this particular boy would have such a catastrophic outcome. Should this boy be punished for the relatively insignificant harm that he intended or the extremely grave harm that resulted?

Let's recall the lessons from the case of Mrs. Palsgraf and the fireworks.

In the *Palsgraf* case the *fact* of injury was unforeseeable. When Mrs. Palsgraf attempted to hold the railroad company liable for her injuries, the law refused her pleas because the railroad company could not foresee that attempting to help a passenger catch a train could lead to an explosion which would lead to scales falling at the other end of the train platform which would lead to Mrs. Palsgraf's injury. Foreseeability, in other words, was the limiting principle for liability. Does foreseeability impose the same limits on damages? Is the case of the two classmates like *Palsgraf* or is it fundamentally different?

In the classmates case, the *extent* of the injury is what is unforeseeable, and this, it turns out, is a crucial difference. As *Palsgraf* explained, it is the duty of every person to avoid actions that create unreasonable risks of foreseeable harm to other people. If you breach that duty, you act at your peril. You assume the risk of having to pay for any damage that follows naturally from the actions that breached the duty of care, even if the damages are improbable, surprising, and yes, unforeseeable.

This point of law is sometimes referred to as the eggshell-skull rule.[226] The metaphor comes from the idea that a particular person might have a very thin skull, like an eggshell. A blow to the head that would be harmless for any other person causes severe injury to the eggshell plaintiff. Even though no one could have anticipated the extent of the injury, the defendant must pay for all of the damages the plaintiff suffers, not just the damages that would be normally expected for people with greater resistance to harm.

Making a boy who did a small and stupid thing (or more precisely in this case, the boy's family) pay for the other boy's loss of a leg may seem extreme. He didn't intend to make his classmate lose his leg. If he had known that his kick would mean amputation, he certainly wouldn't have done what he did. Why should he shoulder such a massive loss when all of the other schoolchildren who have done comparable acts of minor mischief escape without paying anything at all?

In the end, the law cannot solve the philosophical morality of the question. All the law can do is recognize that a loss has come into the world, a loss that cannot be undone, no matter how much every party to this tragedy may wish it. Two people stand before the courts: one who breached his duty and one who did not. The one who did not breach any duty is crippled for life. As between these two boys, someone must bear the loss, and so the law will shift the loss (to the extent that it ever can for a permanent, physical injury) from the blameless to the blameworthy, even if the loss is far greater than anything that could have been foreseen.[227]

RUSSIAN ROULETTE

In the examples we've used so far, we have talked about wrongdoers and victims as if these groups were fans of rival sports teams decked in opposing colors and positioned on opposite sides of a stadium, each waving flags and rooting for their team. The world is not so simple.

As we discussed in the chapter on the Problem of Proof, knowing who did what is challenging under the best of circumstances and in the worst can be fraught with profound uncertainty. People called into the court system know, either from hard experience, advice received from learned counsel, or simple intuition informed by how tough it is to make decisions in everyday life, that this uncertainty in decision-making is an inherent part of the legal process. And this scares the living daylights out of them.

Imagine for a moment that you have been accused of a heinous crime, a crime that you did not commit. Call it murder, rape, child molestation, whatever the worst crime you can think of might be. A prosecutor comes to you and offers you a deal.

If you plead guilty and admit in open court that you did this terrible thing—which you did not do—the prosecutor will make sure that you get a light sentence, a few years behind bars at most. If you do not take this generous offer, the prosecutor warns, you will proceed to trial and one of two things will happen.

One possibility is that you will win and be found not guilty on all counts. In that case, you will walk out of the courthouse free and clear. The other possibility is that a jury will convict you of something, and you will spend the rest of your life in prison. The life you have known, the people you have loved, the hopes and dreams you have harbored will all be permanently and irrevocably lost. The only line between these two fates is the judgment of twelve average people you have never met and who have never met you. Is this a risk that you are willing to take?

You might think that you would be strong and stand up for truth and justice and not bow to crass pressure from the prosecutor. And maybe you would. The experience of other people who have faced this situation in real life is not so cheerful.

According to the Innocence Project, there are at least twenty-eight documented cases of people who pled guilty to rapes and murders they did not commit to escape the possibility of much greater penalties that would have been imposed after a trial.[228] This is a number worth pausing over. Twenty-eight *innocent* people who had done nothing wrong preferred long prison sentences to trusting the legal system to avoid imposing even longer prison sentences.

No one knows how many innocent people are in jail who confessed to crimes they did not commit but for whom exonerating evidence was sadly never found. The University of Michigan tracks exonerations in its National Registry of Exonerations. Of 1,281 exonerations from the last twenty-five years, 11 percent involved cases where the accused falsely confessed to a crime they did not commit. For youth under 18, the number of exonerations that involved a false confession was a frightening 38 percent.[229]

Litigants in civil cases also must confront the inherent riskiness of trials. They face demands and accusations. They did nothing wrong. (Or at least let's say for the sake of argument that that they honestly believe that they did nothing wrong.) If they present their case and are believed, they will not have to pay the plaintiff anything. If they are not believed, however, they will have to pay large sums of money. Even in the best of cases, the risk of losing is real and frightening.

People believe many things with little or no evidence. Some of these beliefs cannot be proven one way or the other (*e.g.,* religion). Some are highly dubious (*e.g.,* the belief that the dangers of vaccines outweigh the benefits).[230] Some are demonstrably false (President Obama is, in fact, a U.S. citizen).[231] Cognitive scientists have found substantial evidence that "[p]eople are credulous creatures who find it very easy to believe and very difficult to doubt."[232]

Any time your fate is in the hands of other people, it is impossible to think about all of the false, silly, and downright outlandish things that other people believe and not worry that even if truth and justice are on your side, you might lose anyway. There is always the chance that the people deciding your case might believe the wrong side.

Imagine you are embroiled in a lawsuit. Your adversary's case is built on lies and misrepresentations. Your lawyer is confident that if you take the case to trial, you will win. You are feeling pretty good, so you ask your lawyer, "How likely am I to win?"

The lawyer pauses, considers, and then says, "Eighty to eighty-five percent."

You smile, feeling even better. You understand that no one can guarantee victory, but if your lawyer is right, the odds are heavily tilted in your favor.

But then you think, "If I have an eighty to eighty-five percent chance of winning, then I have a fifteen to twenty percent chance of losing."

That doesn't sound as good. What else has a fifteen to twenty percent chance of happening? The odds of rolling a seven with two dice are one in six, which is about seventeen percent. How many times have you seen someone roll a seven with two dice?

Russian Roulette is a game where one bullet is loaded into a revolver with six chambers, and the cylinder holding the bullet is spun so no one knows where the bullet is. The player then points the gun to his head and pulls the trigger. Most people would never consider playing Russian Roulette, even though the odds are that five out of six times—about eighty-three percent—no harm would come.

What if the Russian Roulette game were played with a revolver with ten chambers and the odds of winning rose to ninety percent? Would you play if there were twenty chambers and the odds of winning were ninety-five percent? If there were thirty-six chambers, ninety-seven percent of the time you would be safe. That's a pretty safe bet, but one in thirty-six is also the chance of rolling double-sixes with two dice. Would you bet your life that the dice would not fall that way? What would it take to get you to take your chances on a spin of the pistol's cylinder? If you were forced to play, how much would you pay to get out of pulling the trigger and finding out whether fortune is in your favor?

Defending a lawsuit can seem as reckless as a game of Russian Roulette. The consequences of a loss can be devastating. Even with highly favorable chances, many people will prefer to part with a significant amount of money to avoid the possibility of terrible and irreversible losses.

Now consider one additional element of risk. In Russian Roulette, you can calculate the chances of success and failure with precision and make a decision about what risks you're willing to run with the odds firmly in mind. In lawsuits, however, there is the additional risk that you have not calculated the risks correctly. In other words, you're playing with a gun that you might think has a hundred empty chambers, but might really only have one, and there is no way to know because you only get to spin the barrel once.

In addition to the risk of losing, defending against a meritless claim is not costless. Lawyers must be paid. Likely, there are experts and consultants who also must be paid. Your time is valuable, and if you are a business, so is the time of your employees. Finally, there is the intangible but real cost of anxiety and distraction that comes from worrying about the case. Losing a lawsuit is awful, but in many cases, winning is not much better.

Between the risks and the out-of-pocket costs, litigation is highly unappetizing. To be fair, plaintiffs face the same risk of losing a case they should win, but this just underscores the pressure that comes from the uncertainties of resolving disputes in the legal system.[233] The difficulty of assembling conclusive proof about past events compounded by the difficulty of establishing the right amount of compensation for injuries is a recipe for unpredictable outcomes. Not knowing what will happen in a lawsuit scares plaintiffs and defendants alike towards settlement, irrespective of whether their causes are just or unjust.

What this means is that being exposed to a lawsuit is no small thing. It is tempting to think that the solution to any potential dispute is to let the courts figure it out, but that ignores the costs created by the risks inherent in the legal system. Once a dispute is tossed into the legal arena, the justice of the case will often matter less than the relative costs and risks of the parties. Businesses will often pay millions of dollars to settle weak cases against them to avoid the risk of paying tens of millions of dollars if they were to lose.

If you are afraid that you might lose a lawsuit—and no matter how strong your case may be, losing is almost always a possibility—then you must at least consider taking steps you would not otherwise take to mitigate misfortune. Money will be paid where it should not have been paid. Businesses will hire lawyers instead of new employees. Insurance will be purchased and precautions installed in the name of managing and reducing risk.

In some cases, these costs and expenses will be money well spent. Products will be better designed. Drugs will be safer and more effective. Public statements will be more carefully crafted so as not to mislead.

In other cases, these costs and expenses will be wasted efforts that produce no benefit for anyone other than the service providers who sell solutions to manufactured problems. Warning labels will be printed to alert people to the dangers of falling off ladders or submerging hair dryers in bathtubs.

In chess, there is a saying that "the threat is stronger than the execution" because a player will often weaken his or her position to fend off a threat. In law, a similar thing can be said. The threat of unpredictable outcomes at trial pushes litigants and potential litigants to compromise. Merely exposing a person to the threat of litigation will change behavior. Sometimes the change will be welcome. Other times, the change will have negative consequences when people try to steer well clear of the litigation line or pay large sums of money to avoid even remote risks of devastating losses.

Before a legal rule is established, the possible negative consequences of exposing people to a system where settlement is the dominant means of resolution need to be carefully considered, lest the legal system become less a means of vindicating justice and more a system for transferring wealth to the least scrupulous who are most willing to abuse the system.

TORTS AND CRIMES

No part of the legal system holds greater fascination for the public than the criminal justice system. Crime shows, crime movies, and crime novels all regularly top their respective entertainment charts. True crimes can occupy thousands of hours, as pundits in all mediums exchange their speculations about what is really happening in the criminal case and why.

Because of the ubiquity of stories about crime, it may be surprising to learn that it is difficult to define precisely what is a crime and what isn't. It is clear enough that crimes are wrongful acts, but that's the exact same definition given to torts, which are civil wrongs, not criminal ones.

In fact, many torts are also classified as crimes. Battery, which we've seen earlier, is both a tort and a crime. Traditionally, crimes are divided into two categories. The first consists of acts that are inherently and always wrong, like murder, rape, and theft. When Latin terms for legal concepts were popular, this was called **malum in se**, which means wrong or evil in and of itself.

The second category of crimes consists of acts that are wrong only because people have said that they are wrong. In this category are things like smoking marijuana. The only way to know what a person can or can't smoke is for the law to tell you. Naturally, there is a Latin term for this category as well: **malum prohibitum**, which means prohibited wrong. Many regulations are *malum prohibitum*. Speed limits, minimum drinking ages, and mandatory business licenses are all examples of rules for acts that are not inherently wrong, but rather only wrong because the law says so.

The distinction between crimes that are wrong in and of themselves and crimes that are wrong only because they are prohibited is not hard and fast. Many crimes that are *malum prohibitum* are prohibited because they hurt people or create excessive risks of hurting people. There was a time in the not-so-distant past when dumping toxic waste into rivers was a perfectly legitimate business practice. Eventually, people figured out that poisoning the drinking supply caused other people downstream to get sick, and the law stepped in to prohibit the practice.

One way to think about the distinction between crime and torts is to concentrate on the person's intent. The more sinister the intent, the more likely the act will be defined as a crime, and not simply a civil wrong. In the criminal law, this evil intent is known as the *mens rea*, which literally translated means guilty mind.

Although exceptions exist, for the most part crimes almost all require some *mens rea*—that is, some showing that the person meant to harm another person. This purposefulness in causing harm is what justifies stigmatizing and punishing an act as a crime.

Perhaps the most distinctive feature that separates crimes from torts is the remedies available and their purposes. If a person commits a crime, the law has the power to put them in jail, take away their money and possessions, or in the most extreme cases, put them to death. Criminal punishments put in jeopardy the most sacred rights of citizens: their life, liberty, and property.

In contrast, because torts are civil (as opposed to criminal) wrongs, the remedies for torts are limited to damages. A person's property may be at stake in a torts case, but their life and liberty are secure.

The purpose of criminal remedies differs from the purpose of tort remedies. Crimes are especially odious, and so the object of criminal remedies is to punish the wrongdoer and to deter others from doing the same thing. A subsidiary but related goal of criminal punishment is to incapacitate the wrongdoer and protect others by keeping him or her off the streets for a period of time. Finally, in the ideal case, the criminal punishment will help rehabilitate the offender and transform the one-time criminal into a law-abiding citizen.

In some cases, the goals of criminal law can be inconsistent. Punishment is simply the law inflicting pain and suffering on the wrongdoer. Generally, it is considered wrong to intentionally inflict pain and suffering on another human being, but in the case of crimes, the offender has inflicted pain and suffering on others. While the pain felt by crime victims cannot be unfelt any more than the crime itself can be undone, one view of justice requires that the perpetrator share some measure of that pain to restore balance to society.

To be just, the punishment must fit the crime. There must be some proportional relationship between the pain the criminal caused and the pain the law imposes. Too light a punishment demeans the suffering of the victim. Too heavy a punishment suggests wanton cruelty. Different people in different places and in different times have held very different views about what a proportional punishment is for a crime.

Deterrence has a completely different character. The punishment is no longer aimed solely at the criminal offender, but also at the citizenry as a whole to learn from the offender's painful example.

For a punishment to achieve deterrence, it must be sufficiently severe and visible that other people considering the illegal conduct will be aware of the penalty and afraid enough of it that they decide it's better to obey the law than run the risk of getting caught. The amount of punishment necessary for deterrence is dictated by what is needed to scare people straight. This amount can differ from the amount of punishment that might be considered proportional. If deterrence alone were the sole goal of the criminal law, all sorts of vicious and grotesque punishments might be devised that would discourage people from breaking the law. Being buried in the ground up to your neck in the hot sun near an anthill might be an effective way to get people to think twice about crossing a street against the light, but it would also be unspeakably cruel.

The incapacitation goal of criminal law flows naturally from the most typical punishment in our criminal justice system: incarceration. Locking someone up in jail necessarily means that person isn't on the streets and able to commit more crimes, at least until the jail sentence is over.

Rehabilitation is a controversial goal. For those who see the criminal law as primarily a vehicle to mete out punishment on criminals, rehabilitation can seem weak and even in some ways a benefit, especially if it involves additional education or job training at taxpayers' expense. At the same time, most crimes don't carry life sentences, and so convicts will eventually be released into a civilian world that would much prefer them not to fall back into a life of crime.

In contrast to the criminal law's goals of punishment, deterrence, incapacitation, and rehabilitation, the law of torts aims primarily to compensate injured people for the damages they have sustained. The goal is to make the injured person whole. This means putting the injured person in the same position (or as close an approximation as the law can achieve) that he or she was in before the accident occurred.

The tortfeasor (the person who commits the tort) is obligated to pay only for the damages he or she caused, and no more. While the law of torts plays a deterrence role, it is only indirect, operating through the natural desire to avoid having to pay money for something that confers no direct benefit on the person paying. It is not the same as the criminal law, which might set a stiff penalty for something with small damages to provide extra deterrence.

Although the distinctions in the remedies between torts and crimes are the clearest dividers between the two categories, even these lines are blurry. For certain torts, the law authorizes **punitive damages**. As the name implies, the purpose of punitive damages is not to compensate the victim, but rather to punish the wrongdoer.

The punishment meted out by the civil law through punitive damages can far exceed any punishment that the criminal law might have imposed. Punitive damages can reach nine or ten times the actual damages suffered, which can be tens of millions of dollars or more. In the case of the oil spill by the Exxon Valdez, the jury awarded five billion dollars in punitive damages, spawning years of litigation over whether that eye-popping award was unduly excessive.[234]

At the same time, the criminal law is often used to compensate victims. Orders of restitution are now quite common, making a criminal case a convenient venue for victims to receive civil compensation without having to go through the time and expense of filing lawsuits on their own.

Torts and crimes share the quality that they both represent society's judgment about what conduct should not be permitted. They differ in how they deal with misconduct. Torts focus on helping victims. Crimes focus on punishing wrongdoers. Together they reflect our values and powerfully shape all of our actions.

Part Five

Final Thoughts

TWO FISH ARE peacefully swimming together in the ocean when they are passed by an older fish going in the opposite direction. As he swims past the young pair, the older fish asks, "How's the water?" The two young fish make no reply, and the older fish continues on his way. A few moments pass in silence, and then the two young fish frown at each other with looks of deep confusion. One fish asks the other the question that they're both thinking: "What the hell is water?"[235]

The legal system is at once a strange and familiar thing. It is a constant presence in all of our lives, like the air we breathe, and often it is just as invisible. The law sustains us by providing order, stability, and predictability to the social system. But from time to time, the law buffets and rocks us when we bump against its strictures.

The story of the law is the story of human life itself. It represents the field where people meet to pursue their passions and their dreams—sometimes in symphonic cooperation, sometimes in fierce opposition. To resolve the conflicts that inevitably arise among us, the law must contend with powerful forces that define our existence, but often go unnoticed.

The goal of this book has been to make visible the invisible parts of the legal system and the disputes that the legal system exists to resolve. If there is any lesson to be learned from the legal system and the way the law thinks about problems, it is this: our grasp on the past is tenuous in the best of circumstances. When the fragility of our memories clouds our recollection of our most significant experiences, what chance do the everyday incidents that make up our daily routines have of making a permanent mark? Our disputes are often confused contests of misremembered snippets that like a kaleidoscope change each time we examine them.

Even when our memories are clear and true, the past can still remain elusive. We are social animals and the truths of our lives are often defined by what the people around us believe or don't believe. The memories and perceptions of others can differ radically from what we thought we heard or saw. Sometimes these differences can be chalked up to the quirks of the mind. Other times, differences may be the product of outright deception.

Even if we personally are convinced that we know the truth, other people will not accept our convictions as facts without substantial proof. And so the false account is weighed in the same basket as the true one, because truth or falsity cannot be known except in the weighing. Outright falsehood receives equal consideration as honest truth because both arrive at justice's door wearing the same clothing.

These clashes of uncertain memory, hazy perceptions, false logic, and bald-faced lies are the battleground upon which legal disputes are fought, won, and lost. They also occupy a central place in our relationships with the people around us.

Law schools delight in telling their students that they will train them to "think like lawyers." If you have made it this far, you will know that thinking like a lawyer is not significantly different from just thinking. The genius of the law is not its novel insights, but rather its methodical nature, breaking down large and unwieldy questions to smaller more manageable pieces, until the image of a coherent whole emerges. The legal mind provides scaffolding that permits the construction of imposing structures, but the scaffolding itself is just plain wooden planks and metal poles.

In *One Hundred Years of Solitude*, the Nobel-prize-winning novel by the Colombian writer Gabriel García Márquez, the people of the fictional town of Macondo come under a spell that causes them to forget the names of all the things in the world. To fight against this mass amnesia, the people hang signs on every object, like "this is a cow" and "this is a pig," but soon the spell of forgetting becomes so powerful that the people forget the meaning of the written marks that spell out the words "cow" and "pig." To survive the plague of forgetting, the people must re-learn the words and establish a common understanding of what things mean.

The law is like Macondo recovering from the forgetting spell. Everything that comes before it must be defined, classified, and categorized. Sometimes this is easily done, but the hard questions, the ones that occupy the courts the most, are sometimes so seemingly impossible that judges and courts are left wide open to the charge that they just invent solutions as they go along.

What the law's struggle with definition teaches is that the meaning of things is not fixed, not exact, and not knowable by simple reference to a dictionary or a measurable law of nature. The true meanings of the most important words and concepts in our vocabulary—like reasonableness, best efforts, and good cause, to say nothing of the hallowed Constitutional phrases of liberty, freedom of speech, and due process—are revealed one case at time through the actions with which we, by our collective judgment, associate them.

The law's struggles are not that different from our own. The sum of our experiences defines us and the people around us. The legal mind demands we ask whether what we think we know and what others would have us believe are really true. The sources of our knowledge should be scrutinized, our intuitions questioned, and our assumptions probed. Nothing should be taken for granted.

The lessons of the law—its logic, its structure, and its approach to the fundamental problems of proof and rules—can be applied not just in legal settings, which are their natural habitat, but also in our relationships with the people around us, whether they be family or friends, colleagues or competitors. The legal mind is the mirror of our own. It faces the same problems of deception, perception, forgetting, and ambiguity that we face. Thinking like the law thinks, solving problems as the legal mind does, helps us understand our world, our legal system, and if we're lucky, ourselves.

Acknowledgements

There's an old story about a man who asks a street artist to draw him a sketch. The artist sets to work and soon presents the man with a finished portrait. The man is impressed and asks, "How much do I owe you?"

The artist says, "Twenty dollars."

"Twenty dollars!" cries the man. "It only took you five minutes to draw the sketch."

The artist replies, "Five minutes, plus a lifetime of study and practice."

This book took longer than five minutes to write, but like the artist's sketch, it represents the synthesis of my twenty years in the legal world, as a student, practitioner, and educator. I have tried to cite my most immediate sources in the endnotes, but that does not begin to acknowledge and express my indebtedness and gratitude for the wisdom and insights of the many teachers, thinkers, and writers who have taught, informed, and inspired me. Any attempt to list them all would be doomed to failure, so I will say only that I am deeply thankful for having so many generous teachers, colleagues, and friends.

Most of all, I owe an immeasurable debt to my family for their love and support. Writing is lonely and challenging work with few oases of inspiration as cursor and text make their slow journey across the long, white desert of page after page. Without my wife Deborah and my sons Andrew and Eric to sustain me and their generous willingness to endure countless nights and weekends without their husband and dad, nothing would be possible. I am immensely grateful that you are in my life.

Endnotes

1. Maria Popova, "The Secret of Life from Steve Jobs in 46 Seconds," *Brain Pickings*, http://www.brainpickings.org/index.php/2011/12/02/steve-jobs-1995-life-failure/ (http://bit.ly/17o0U0t); http://www.youtube.com/watch?v=kYfNvmF0Bqw.

2. Oliver Wendell Holmes, Jr., *The Common Law* (1881), p. 1.

3. This is the so-called BOLD imaging, which stands for blood oxygenation level dependent. Essentially, brain activity is measured by the amount of oxygenated blood in a particular area and a point in time. *See* Oliver R. Goodenoug and Micaela Tucker, "Neuroscience Basics for Lawyers," 62 Mercer L. Rev. 945, 949 (Spring 2011).

4. Marcus E. Raichle, "A Paradigm Shift in Functional Brain Imaging," *The Journal of Neuroscience*, 14 Oct. 2009, 29(41): 12729-12734; doi: 10.1523/JNEUROSCI.4366-09.2009 (available at http://www.jneurosci.org/content/29/41/12729.long#xref-ref-17-1) (http://bit.ly/1aX0ZpD).

5. http://www.goodreads.com/author/quotes/1771.Sun_Tzu.

6. http://en.wikipedia.org/wiki/Homunculus.

7. http://law2.umkc.edu/faculty/projects/ftrials/salem/SALEM.HTM (http://bit.ly/1frigtY).

8. http://www.cnn.com/2010/WORLD/africa/08/25/nigeria.child.witches/index.html (http://bit.ly/18PenrG).

9. Ilya Somin, "Assessing our Moral Beliefs in Light of Predicted Future Moral 'Progress'" *Volokh Conspiracy* (March 26, 2007) (http://www.volokh.com/2007/03/26/assessing-our-moral-beliefs-in-light-of-predicted-future-moral-progress/ (http://bit.ly/172cy0B).

10. John Stuart Mill, *On Liberty* (1869), available at www.bartleby.com/130/.

11. Peter Tiersma and Matthew Curtis, "Testing the Comprehensibility of Jury Instructions: California's Old and New

Instructions on Circumstantial Evidence," Journal of Court Innovation, Vol. 1, p. 231, 2008; Loyola-LA Legal Studies Paper No. 2009-43. Available at SSRN: http://ssrn.com/abstract=1505010.

12. Megan Garber, "How to Catch a Liar on the Internet," *The Atlantic* (Sept. 2013), http://www.theatlantic.com/magazine/ archive/2013/09/the-way-we-lie-now/309431/ (http://bit.ly/18jGaEn).

13. Jochen Mecke, *Cultures of Lying*, p.8 (2007) (cited in *United States v. Alvarez*, 638 F.3d 666, 675 (9th Cir. 2011) (Kozinski, J., concurring in the denial of rehearing en banc).

14. See Aldert Vrij, Detecting Lies and Deceit: Pitfalls and Opportunities, p. 22 (2008).

15. *Id.*

16. *United States v. Alvarez*, 132 S. Ct. 2537, 2553 (2012) (Breyer, J., concurring).

17. Madeline R. Conway, Cordelia F. Mendez, "Freshman Survey Part III: Classes, Clubs, and Concussions," *Harvard Crimson* (Sept. 5, 2013), http://www.thecrimson.com/article/2013/9/5/ freshman-survey-academics-extracurriculars/ (http://bit.ly/1b50LQJ).

18. Megan Garber, "How to Catch a Liar on the Internet," *The Atlantic* (Sept. 2013), http://www.theatlantic.com/magazine/archive/ 2013/09/the-way-we-lie-now/309431/ (http://bit.ly/18jGaEn).

19. http://www.amazon.com/Pogo-We-Have-Met-Enemy/dp/ 0671212605

20. M. O'Sullivan, "Home Runs and Humbugs: Comment on Bond and DePaulo," *Psychological Bulletin* 134(4):493-497 (2008); *see also* Andrew Shelton, "Deception: Do you swear to tell the whole truth and nothing but the truth, so help you God?" *The Jury Expert*, 2009, 21(3), 46-50. Available at http://www.thejuryexpert.com/wp-content/uploads/DeceptionMay2009Volume21No3.pdf (http://bit.ly/1gPWM7X).

21. *See* Jesse Bering, "18 Attributes of Highly Effective Liars", *Scientific American Blog* (2011), http://blogs.scientificamerican.com/

bering-in-mind/2011/07/07/18-attributes-of-highly-effective-liars/ (http://bit.ly/1eAouZq).

22. http://en.wikiquote.org/wiki/Jean_Giraudoux.

23. CF Bond, "International Deception," *Personality and Social Psychology Bulletin*, Vol. 26, No. 3, 385-395 (2000).

24. Andrew Shelton, "Deception: Do you swear to tell the whole truth and nothing but the truth, so help you God?" *The Jury Expert*, 2009, 21(3), 46-50. Available at http://www.thejuryexpert.com/wp-content/uploads/DeceptionMay2009Volume21No3.pdf (http://bit.ly/1gPWM7X).

25. *See, e.g.,* Richard Wiseman, Caroline Watt et al. "The Eyes Don't Have It: Lie Detection and Neuro-Linguistic Programming," PLoS ONE 7(7): e40259. doi:10.1371/journal.pone.0040259 (2012) (http://bit.ly/15UCa9E).

26. Aldert Vrij, Detecting Lies and Deceit: Pitfalls and Opportunities, p. 4 (2008).

27. Jorge Luis Borges, "Funes the Memorious," *Labrynths*, translated by James E. Irby. Available at http://www.srs-pr.com/literature/borges-funes.pdf.

28. Robert A. Burton, On Being Certain: Believing You Are Right Even When You're Not (2008), p. 10.

29. Robert N. McCauley, "Bringing Ritual to Mind", in *Ecological Approaches to Cognition: Essays in Honor of Ulric Neisser*. p. 296 (1999).

30. Douglas Martin, Ulric Neisser Is Dead at 83; Reshaped Study of the Mind, New York Times, Feb. 25, 2012 (available at http://www.nytimes.com/2012/02/26/us/ulric-neisser-who-reshaped-thinking-on-the-mind-dies-at-83.html?pagewanted=all&_r=0) (http://nyti.ms/1b514uV).

31. Alison George, "I Could Have Sworn ...: An interview with false-memory expert Elizabeth Loftus," Slate.com (Sept. 8, 2013), http://www.slate.com/articles/health_and_science/new_scientist/2013/09/elizabeth_loftus_interview_false_memory_research_on_eye witnesses_child_abuse.html (http://slate.me/16SRzeG).

32. This example is taken from Christopher Chabris and Daniel Simons, *The Invisible Gorilla* (2010), pp.45-47.

33. *See* M.H. Sam Jacobson, Paying Attention Or Fatally Distracted? Concentration, Memory, and Multi-Tasking In A Multi-Media World, 16 Legal Writing 419, 423-424 (2010) ("Conventional wisdom has been that working memory can only hold seven bits of information, plus or minus two. However, subsequent studies indicate it may be significantly less than that, perhaps three to five, depending on the type and complexity of information and the degree of chunking, or recoding, of the information.")

34. Patrick Lynch, Short-Term Memory ("Short-term memory decays rapidly and usually disappears from a person's mind within 30 seconds.") (http://explorable.com/short-term-memory) (http://bit.ly/1b51dhZ).

35. *See* Daniel Goldberg, "The Detection of Constructed Memories and the Risks of Undue Prejudice", American Journal of Bioethics, p. 24 (Jan. 2008).

36. Christopher Chabris and Daniel Simons, *The Invisible Gorilla* (2010), p.45.

37. *Id.* at 46.

38. *See* http://www.usamemorychampionship.com.

39. Talarico, J.M., & Rubin, D.C. (2003). Confidence, Not Consistency, Characterizes Flashbulb Memories. Psychological Science, 14, 455–461

40. Medina, John (2010-07-06). Brain Rules: 12 Principles for Surviving and Thriving at Work, Home, and School (p. 83). Pear Press. Kindle Edition

41. Medina, John (2010-07-06). Brain Rules: 12 Principles for Surviving and Thriving at Work, Home, and School (p. 100). Pear Press. Kindle Edition

42. Daniel Gilbert, *Stumbling on Happiness* (2007), p. 88 (citing, M.K. Johnson and S.J. Sherman, "Constructing and Reconstructing the Past and the Future in the Present," in *Handbook of Motivation and Cognition: Foundations of Social Behavior*, ed. E.T. Higgins and R.M. Sorrentino, vol. 2 (New York: Guilford Press 1990), 482-526; and M.K. Johnson and C.L. Raye, "Reality Monitoring," *Psychological Review* 88:67-85 (1981)).

43. Paul Simon, "The Boxer," *Bridge Over Troubled Waters*, Columbia Records (April 1969).

44. http://www.youtube.com/watch?v=M8LNEq1EeEw.

45. *See* http://en.wikipedia.org/wiki/Retina.

46. *See* http://en.wikipedia.org/wiki/Blind_spot_(vision).

47. Clarke DD, Sokoloff L (1999) in Basic neurochemistry. Molecular, cellular and medical aspects, Circulation and energy metabolism of the brain, eds Agranoff BW, Siegel GJ (Lippincott-Raven, Philadelphia), Ed 6, pp 637–670.

48. John C. Russ, *The Image Processing Handbook, Sixth Edition*, CRC Press (2011), p.85 (available at http://bit.ly/16zMSCk).

49. Richard Gregory, Brainy Mind, British Medical Journal, 19 December 1998, issue 317: pp. 1693–1695.

50. John Locke, An Essay Concerning Human Understanding (1689).

51. Richard Gregory, Brainy Mind, British Medical Journal, 19 December 1998, issue 317: pp. 1693–1695.

52 Robert T. Gonzalez, "Wine Tasting is Bullshit: Here's Why," The Daily Explainer (May 8, 2013) http://io9.com/wine-tasting-is-bullshit-heres-why-496098276 (http://bit.ly/1bg3dDt), citing Frédéric Brochet, "Chemical Object Representation In The Field Of Consciousness" (http://bit.ly/1c2TnTT).

53. Robin Lloyd, False ID: Face Recognition on Trial, LiveScience (March. 14, 2005) (available at http://www.livescience.com/6897-false-id-face-recognition-trial.html) (http://bit.ly/1eF52uH).

54. My wife Deborah served as one of the attorneys for Arthur Carmona after his conviction, but this account is exclusively from sources in the public record, the most important of which are a series of articles by Dana Parsons printed in the Los Angeles Times. *See, e.g.*, Can Justice Be Blinded by Eyewitnesses? (http://lat.ms/1f8qbyA); A Guilty Plea to Obsession With Injustice (http://lat.ms/18jZDTs); *see also* Bob Emmers, "Eyewitness Blues: How a Baseball Cap Derailed Justice," *Orange Coast Magazine* (Sept. 1999), p.133-135 (available at http://bit.ly/18N47WH); *see also* http://en.wikipedia.org/wiki/Arthur_Paul_Carmona.

55. *See* Saundra Davis Westervelt, John A. Humphrey, *Wrongly Convicted: Perspectives on Failed Justice* (2001).

56. Leon Friedman, "The Problem of Convicting Innocent Persons: How Often Does It Occur and How Can It Be Prevented?" 56 N.Y.L. Sch. L. Rev. 1053, 1056 (2011/12).

57. *See* Loftus et al., *Eyewitness Testimony: Civil and Criminal* § 2-2, at 13 (4th ed. 2007)

58. Wells, G. L., and E. F. Loftus. 2003. Eyewitness memory for people and events. In Handbook of Psychology: Vol. 11, Forensic Psychology, eds. A. M. Goldstein, and I. B. Weiner. Hoboken, NJ: John Wiley & Sons, Inc.

59. *See* Brigham & Bothwell, The Ability of Prospective Jurors to Estimate the Accuracy of Eyewitness Identifications, 7 Law & Hum. Behav. 19, 22-24, 28 (1983) (nearly 84% of study respondents overestimated accuracy rates of identifications); *see also*, e.g., Sigler & Couch, Eyewitness Testimony and the Jury Verdict, 4 N. Am. J. Psychol. 143, 146 (2002).

60. The description of this experiment is from Dan Simon and Christopher Chabris, *The Invisible Gorilla* (2009).

61. Wells, G. L., & Bradfield, A. L. (1998). "'Good, you identified the suspect': Feedback to eyewitnesses distorts their reports of the witnessed experience. Journal of Applied Psychology, 83, 360-376 (cited by Castelle, George and Loftus, Elizabeth, "Misinformation and Wrongful Convictions", in Saundra Davis Westervelt, John A. Humphrey, *Wrongly Convicted: Perspectives on Failed Justice* (2001).

62. *See* Brigham & Bothwell, The Ability of Prospective Jurors To Estimate the Accuracy of Eyewitness Identifications, 7 Law & Hum. Behav. 19 (1983).

63. See Cutler & Penrod, *Mistaken Identification*, at 181-209; Lindsay, Wells, & Rumpel, "Can People Detect Eyewitness-Identification Accuracy Within and Across Situations?" 66 J. Applied Psychol. 79, 83 (1981).

64. *See* Brewer, Feast, & Rishworth, The Confidence-Accuracy Relationship in Eyewitness Identification, 8 J. Experimental Psychol. Applied 44, 44-45 (2002) ("average confidence-accuracy correlations generally estimated between little more than 0 and

.29"); see also, e.g., Sporer, Penrod, Read, & Cutler, Choosing, Confidence, and Accuracy: A Meta-Analysis of the Confidence-Accuracy Relation in Eyewitness Identification Studies, 118 Psychol. Bull. 315 (1995).

65. For more about this chilling story, *see* Jennifer Thompson-Cannino, Ronald Cotton, and Erin Torneo, *Picking Cotton* (available at http://amzn.to/16TObMD).

66. Mark Hansen, Forensic Science: Scoping out eyewitness Ids, 87 A.B.A.J. 39, April, 2001, http://nersp.osg.ufl.edu/~malavet/evidence/notes/thompson_cott on.htm).

67. Gary L. Wells, Amina Memon, and Steven D. Penrod, Eyewitness Evidence: Improving Its Probative Value, p. 52, http://www.psychology.iastate.edu/~glwells/Wells_articles_pdf/ps pi_7_2_article[1].pdf (http://bit.ly/19C6YwU); *see also* John P. Rutledge, They All Look Alike: the Inaccuracy of Cross-racial Identifications, 28 American Journal of Criminal Law 207-228, 211-214 (Spring 2001)

68. Fiona Gabbert, Amina Memon, and Kevin Allan, Memory "Conformity: Can Eyewitnesses Influence Each Other's Memories for an Event?" Appl. Cognit. Psychol. 17: 533–543 (2003)

69. *Perry v. New Hampshire*, 132 S.Ct. 716, 727 (2012).

70. *Perry v. New Hampshire*, 132 S.Ct. 716, 729-30 (2012).

71. Oliver Wendell Holmes, Natural Law, 32 Harvard Law Rev. 40, 41 (1918).

72. The literature in this area is vast. Two accessible introductions are Dan Ariely's *Predictably Irrational* and Daniel Kahneman's *Thinking, Fast and Slow*.

73. "Pauling Honored by Scientists at Caltech Event," *Los Angeles Times* (1 March 1986).

74. *See* https://en.wikipedia.org/wiki/Linus_Pauling.

75. *See* "The Clinton-Gore Administration Record of Progress," http://clinton5.nara.gov/WH/Accomplishments/ eightyears-06.html (http://1.usa.gov/1eAqSPZ).

76. Government Accountability Office, "Community Policing Grants: COPS Grants Were a Modest Contributor to Declines in Crimes in the 1990s," http://www.gao.gov/new.items/d06104.pdf.

77. *Id.* at 13.

78. Including the U.S. Supreme Court: *Norfolk & W. Ry. Co. v. Ayers*, 538 U.S. 135, 173 (2003).

79. *Tarasoff v. Regents of the University of California*, 17 Cal. 3d 425, 431 (1976).

80. *See, e.g.,* "Hindsight Bias," http://en.wikipedia.org/wiki/Hindsight_bias.

81. http://en.wikiquote.org/wiki/Niels_Bohr. This quotation has also been attributed to Yogi Berra, but apparently Bohr said it first. *See* http://www.peterpatau.com/2006/12/bohr-leads-berra-but-yogi-closing-gap.html.

82. *Tarasoff* at 438.

83. Susan J. LaBine and Gary LaBine, "Determinations of Negligence and the Hindsight Bias," 20 Law and Human Behavior 501 (1996).

84. Jeffrey J. Rachlinski, "A Positive Psychological Theory of Judging in Hindsight," in *Behavioral Law and Economics* (Cass Sunstein, ed.) Cambridge Univ. Press (2000), p. 96 (available at http://bit.ly/16S7jxM).

85. Harry Plotkin, "Why Your Jurors' Hindsight Is 20/20," http://www.litcounsel.org/commentary/plotkin0110.htm (http://bit.ly/1b9yQf4) (citing, Kamin and Raschlinski, Ex Post is Not Equal to Ex Ante: Determining Liability in Hindsight, 19 Law and Human Behavior 89 (1995); *see also* Kahneman, Daniel, *Thinking, Fast and Slow*, Macmillan, 2011.

86. *See, e.g.,* Matt Groebe, "Does Bifurcation Eliminate the Problem? A Closer Look at Hindsight Bias in the Courtroom," *The Jury Expert*, 2011, 23(1), 17-22 (available at http://bit.ly/1bA2m06) (citing, Hastie, R., Schkade, D.A., & Payne, J.W. (1999). Juror judgments in civil cases: Hindsight effects on judgments of liability for punitive damages. Law and Human Behavior, 23(5), 597-614.)

87. *See, e.g.,* Merrie Jo Pitera. "Managing Hindsight Bias," *The Jury Expert* (August 1, 2013) (available at http://www.thejuryexpert.com/2013/08/managing-hindsight-bias/).

88. *The Onion.* "Winning Lottery Numbers So Obvious In Hindsight." (Aug. 8, 2013) (available at http://www.theonion.com/

articles/winning-lottery-numbers-so-obvious-in-hindsight,33413/)
(http://onion.com/16S7FV1).

89. Tversky, A. & Kahneman, D. (1974). "Judgment under
uncertainty: Heuristics and biases". Science, 185, 1124–1130; *see
also* Daniel Kahneman, *Thinking, Fast and Slow* (2009).

90. *See* Edward Teach, "Avoiding Decision Traps: Cognitive
Biases and Mental Shortcuts Can Lead Managers into Costly Errors
of Judgment," CFO Magazine (June 2004) (available at
http://www.cfo.com/article.cfm/3014027); *see also* Dan Ariely,
Predictably Irrational.

91. *See* http://www.cnbc.com/id/100909829; *see also*
http://nbcnews.to/1f950wp.

92. *Id.*

93. Quoted in Edward Teach, "Avoiding Decision Traps:
Cognitive Biases and Mental Shortcuts Can Lead Managers into
Costly Errors of Judgment," CFO *Magazine* (June 2004) (available at
http://www.cfo.com/article.cfm/3014027).

94. John Malouf and Nicola Schutte, Shaping Juror Attitudes:
Effects of Requesting Different Damages Amounts in Personal
Injury Trials, 129 J. Soc. Psych. 491, 495 (1989) ("when more
money was requested for damages by the plaintiff's attorney, the
jurors awarded more"); Gretchen B. Chapman and Brian H.
Bornstein, The More You Ask for the More You Get: Anchoring in
Personal Injury Verdicts, 10 Applied Cognitive Psychol. 519 (1996)
("plaintiffs would do well to request large compensation awards").

95. Ward Farnsworth, *The Legal Analyst*, p.231 (2007),
describing Verlin B. Hinsz and Kristin E. Indahl, Assimilation in
Anchors for Damage Awards in a Mock Civil Trial, 6 J.
Experimental Psycho. 91 (2000).

96. http://www.federalregister.gov/uploads/2011/01/
fr_facts.pdf (http://1.usa.gov/15NIJy3).

97. The first census was not taken until 1790. The 3.9 million
figure included slaves (who were counted as 3/5 of a person) but
excluded Native Americans. *See* http://www.infoplease.com/ipa/
A0905361.html.

98. The U.S. Census Bureau maintains an updating count on the U.S. population at http://www.census.gov/main/www/popclock.html.

99. *See* http://faculty.washington.edu/qtaylor/a_us_history/1700_1800_timeline.htm (http://bit.ly/17VCV56).

100. *See* U.S. Census Bureau, "Age and Sex Composition: 2010," http://www.census.gov/prod/cen2010/briefs/c2010br-03.pdf

101. *See* http://inventors.about.com/library/inventors/blfarm4.htm.

102. "Too Few Farmers Left to Count, Agency Says", *New York Times*, Oct. 10, 1993, http://www.nytimes.com/1993/10/10/us/too-few-farmers-left-to-count-agency-says.html (http://nyti.ms/15k2kaK).

103. *See, e.g.*, the Book of Leviticus, among others.

104. Leonard Read. "I, Pencil". (Dec. 1958), http://www.econlib.org/library/Essays/rdPncl1.html (http://bit.ly/18ki8ao).

105. 15 U.S.C. § 1.

106. Fed.R.Civ.Proc 4(a)(1)(A).

107 *See, e.g.*, Cal. Veh. Code 23152; for an interesting discussion of how blood alcohol levels are computed, *see People v. Vangelder*, 2013 Cal. LEXIS 9442 (Cal. 2013).

108. *See, e.g.*, 17 C.F.R. § 240.10b-5 (prohibiting any "device, scheme, or artifice to defraud").

109. *See* http://student-of-life.newsvine.com/_news/2010/11/21/5502595-thomas-jefferson-supported-rewriting-the-constitution-every-19-years-equated-not-doing-so-to-being-enslaved-to-the-prior-generation-what-do-you-think-about-that (http://bit.ly/1bAl1ZM).

110. U.S. Const. Art. V.

111. Lewis Carroll, *Through the Looking Glass* (1871). Available at http://www.gutenberg.org/files/12/12-h/12-h.htm.

112. U.S. Census Data, http://www.census.gov/compendia/statab/2012/tables/12s0209.pdf.

113. *See* http://www.averagemaleheight.com/

114. Upton Sinclair famously wrote "It is difficult to get a man to understand something, when his salary depends on his not understanding it." (http://bit.ly/19vrUW7).

115. Abraham Lincoln, Address at a Sanitary Fair (April 18, 1864), http://teachingamericanhistory.org/library/document/address-at-a-sanitary-fair/.

116. This example is adapted from Frederick Schauer, Thinking Like A Lawyer (2009), p. 152, who borrowed it from H.L.A. Hart, "Positivism and the Separation of Law and Morals," 71 Harv. L. Rev.593 (1958).

117. *See* http://www.merriam-webster.com/dictionary/vehicle.

118 *Harris v. City of Santa Monica*, 56 Cal.4th 203 (2013).

119. Brown v. Entertainment Merchants Ass'n, 131 S. Ct. 2729 (2011).

120. *See* http://www.scotusblog.com/?p=108116.

121. *People v. Nelson*, 200 Cal.App.4th 1083 (2011).

122. Stan Lee and Steve Ditko, *Amazing Fantasy #15*, p. 11 (Aug. 1962).

123. *See generally* https://en.wikipedia.org/wiki/Fourth_Council_of_the_Lateran.

124. *Id.*

125. John H. Langbein, Reneé Lettow Lerner, Bruce P. Smith, History of the Common Law, p.44 (2009).

126. John H. Langbein, Reneé Lettow Lerner, Bruce P. Smith, History of the Common Law, p.52 (2009).

127. This account is compiled from Wikipedia, "My Sweet Lord" (http://en.wikipedia.org/wiki/My_Sweet_Lord); George Harrison's "My Sweet Lord" Copyright Case (http://performingsongwriter.com/george-harrison-my-sweet-lord/) (http://bit.ly/16s22Q2); and Famous Copyright Infringement Cases in Music (http://www.fairwagelawyers.com/most-famous-music-copyright-infringment.html) (http://bit.ly/1aqgkOr).

128. Mark Twain. *Following the Equator* (1897).

129 Sebastian Anthony, "How long do hard drives actually live for?" Extremetech.com (Nov. 12, 2013) (http://bit.ly/1g8zawA).

130. http://rationalwiki.org/wiki/Extraordinary_claims_ require_extraordinary_evidence (http://bit.ly/1i9xXEq); *see also* Carl Sagan (writer/host) (Dec. 14, 1980). "Encyclopaedia Galactica," Cosmos: A Personal Voyage. Episode 12. Minute 01:24. PBS.

131. Guri C. Bollingmo, Ellen O. Wessel, Dag Erik Eilertsen and Svein Magnussen (2008). Credibility of the emotional witness: A study of ratings by police investigators. Psychology, Crime & Law 14(1): 29 – 40.

132. This assumption is codified in the law of evidence in the exception to the hearsay rule for "statements against interest." *See, e.g.,* Fed. R. Evid. 804(b)(3).

133. For a list of digital forensic tools, *see* http://en.wikipedia.org/wiki/List_of_digital_forensics_tools.

134. Upton Sinclair, I, Candidate for Governor: And How I Got Licked (1935).

135. Joseph DeGiuseppe, Jr., "The Effect of the Employment-At-Will Rule on Employee Rights to Job Security and Fringe Benefits," 10 Fordham Urb. L.J. 1, 2 (1981) (available at http://ir.lawnet.fordham.edu/cgi/viewcontent.cgi?article=1175&co ntext=ulj&sei-redir=1) (http://bit.ly/1aqg8yQ).

136. *See, e.g.,* Charles H. Muhl, "The Employment At-Will Doctrine: Three Major Exceptions," Monthly Labor Review (Jan. 2001), at 4. (available at http://www.bls.gov/opub/mlr/ 2001/01/art1full.pdf) (http://1.usa.gov/1bdzrzD).

137. 42 U.S.C. § 2000e-2(a) (http://www.eeoc.gov/laws/ statutes/titlevii.cfm).

138. *McDonnell Douglas Corp. v. Green*, 411 US 792 (1973).

139. *See* https://en.wikipedia.org/wiki/Precedent.

140. 3 Cai. 175 (N.Y. Sup. Ct. 1805). For an interesting account of the backstory behind this famous case, *see* Bethany R. Berger, "It's Not about the Fox: The Untold History of Pierson v. Post," Duke L.J. (Apr. 2006).

141. *See* Robert C. Elickson, *Order Without Law*, p.42 (1991).

142. *Citizens United v. Federal Election Com'n*, 130 S. Ct. 876 (2010) (Roberts, C.J., concurring) (citing Payne v. Tennessee, 501 U.S. 808, 827 (1991)).

143. *See, e.g.,* Alexander Hamilton, Federalist No. 78 ("The interpretation of the laws is the proper and peculiar province of the courts. A constitution is, in fact, and must be regarded by the judges as, a fundamental law. It, therefore, belongs to them to ascertain its meaning, as well as the meaning of any particular act proceeding from the legislative body. If there should happen to be an irreconcilable variance between the two, that which has the superior obligation and validity ought, of course, to be preferred; or, in other words, the Constitution ought to be preferred to the statute, the intention of the people to the intention of their agents.")

144. 5 U.S. 137 (1803).

145 *Marbury,* at 177.

146. *Planned Parenthood of Southeastern Pa. v. Casey,* 505 US 833 (1992).

147. *See* http://en.wikipedia.org/wiki/Homer_Plessy.

148. *Plessy v. Ferguson,* 163 U.S. 537 (1896).

149. *See* http://en.wikipedia.org/wiki/Jim_Crow_laws (last visited May 26, 2013).

150. *See* Justice Harlan's eloquent dissent in *Plessy.*

151. 347 U.S. 483 (1954) .

152. *Citizens United v. Federal Election Com'n,* 130 S. Ct. 876 (2010) (Roberts, C.J., concurring), citing *Plessy v. Ferguson,* 163 U.S. 537, 16 S.Ct. 1138, 41 L.Ed. 256 (1896), overruled by *Brown v. Board of Education,* 347 U.S. 483, 74 S.Ct. 686, 98 L.Ed. 873 (1954); *Adkins v. Children's Hospital of D. C.,* 261 U.S. 525, 43 S.Ct. 394, 67 L.Ed. 785 (1923), overruled by *West Coast Hotel Co. v. Parrish,* 300 U.S. 379, 57 S.Ct. 578, 81 L.Ed. 703 (1937); *Olmstead v. United States,* 277 U.S. 438, 48 S.Ct. 564, 72 L.Ed. 944 (1928), overruled by *Katz v. United States,* 389 U.S. 347, 88 S.Ct. 507, 19 L.Ed.2d 576 (1967).

153. *Casey* at 854-855.

154. *Citizens United v. Federal Election Com'n,* 130 S. Ct. 876 (2010) (Roberts, C.J., concurring).

155. http://en.wikiquote.org/wiki/Charles_Evans_Hughes.

156. This discussion focuses on the procedures for civil cases, that is, private disputes that do not involve the social issues of

crimes and the criminal law. Some of the logic of the criminal law is briefly explored in the Section "Why Crimes?"

157. *See, e.g., Bell Atlantic Corp. v. Twombly*, 550 U.S. 544 (2007); *Ashcroft v. Iqbal*, 56 U.S. 662 (2009).

158. 347 U.S. 483 (1954).

159. The phrase "remedies at law" alludes to a historical division in the courts of England and early America where "courts of law" were empowered to award damages and "courts of equity" were empowered to issue injunctions, and a litigant could not go to a court of equity unless the courts of law offered no adequate remedy. It is a testament to how slow the legal profession is to change that the phrase "no adequate remedy at law" persists long after the historical distinction between courts of law and equity has been largely erased.

160. *See, e.g.,* Federal Rule of Civil Procedure 26(b)(1).

161. *See* http://www.emc.com/collateral/analyst-reports/idc-extracting-value-from-chaos-ar.pdf (http://bit.ly/19H5DF7).

162. *See* http://www.marketingcharts.com/wp/direct/18-24-year-old-smartphone-owners-send-and-receive-almost-4k-texts-per-month-27993/ (http://bit.ly/15VagOK).

163. *See* http://news.cnet.com/8301-32973_3-57409792-296/how-much-is-that-patent-lawsuit-going-to-cost-you/ (http://cnet.co/1b7AptK).

164. *See* http://about.bloomberglaw.com/practitioner-contributions/federal-circuits-model-e-discovery-order/ (http://bit.ly/1bdzUlo).

165. *See, e.g.,* http://www.krollontrack.com/publications/onesmallstep.pdf (http://bit.ly/15vgCp8).

166. *See, e.g., United States v. Alvarez*, 132 S. Ct. 2537 (2012) (First Amendment prohibits prosecution for falsely claiming to have won medal of honor).

167. Emily Dickinson's beautiful poem is worth reading in its entirety:

Tell all the truth but tell it slant,
Success in circuit lies,
Too bright for our infirm delight

The truth's superb surprise;

As lightning to the children eased
With explanation kind,
The truth must dazzle gradually
Or every man be blind.

Source: http://www.poemhunter.com/poem/tell-all-the-truth.

168. *See* http://www.gallup.com/poll/1891/snakes-top-list-americans-fears.aspx.

169. *See* Fredrick Schauer, "Can Bad Science Be Good Evidence? Neuroscience, Lie Detection, And Beyond", 95 Cornell L. Rev. 1191 (2010); Aldert Vrij, Detecting Lies and Deceit: The Psychology of Lying and the Implications for Professional Practice (2000); Jeremy A. Blumenthal, A Wipe of the Hands, a Lick of the Lips: The Validity of Demeanor Evidence in Assessing Witness Credibility, 72 Nebr. L. Rev. 1157, 1190-97 (1993); Olin Guy Wellborn III, Demeanor, 76 Cornell L. Rev. 1075, 1082-88 (1991).

170. *See, e.g.*, Fed. R. Civ. Proc. 33.

171. Douglas C. Rennie, The End Of Interrogatories: Why Twombly And Iqbal Should Finally Stop Rule 33 Abuse, 15 Lewis & Clark Law Rev. 192 (2011).

172. In some states, notably California, a motion to dismiss is known as a **demurrer**. The principles described in the text are the same.

173. *See* Federal Rule of Civil Procedure 12(b). Rule 12(b)(6) authorizes motions to dismiss for failure to state a claim.

174 Fed.R.Civ.Proc. 56(a).

175. Kevin M. Clermont & Stewart J. Schwab, How Employment Discrimination Cases Fare in Federal Court, 1 J. Empirical Legal Stud. 429, 440 (2004).

176. Theodore Eisenberg and Charlotte Lanvers, What is the Settlement Rate and Why Should We Care?, 6 J. Empirical Legal Stud. 111 (2009).

177. *Id.*

178. http://en.wikiquote.org/wiki/George_Carlin.

179. *See, e.g.*, Cal. Evid. Code § 1115 *et seq.*

180 Douglas A. Henderson, "Mediation Success: An Empirical Analysis,"11 Ohio St. J. on Disp. Resol. 105, 132 (1996).

181. *See* John H. Langbein, Reneé Lettow Lerner, Bruce P. Smith, History of the Common Law, p.41 (2009) ("The medieval presentment jury was expected to come to court already knowing that it thought someone 'notoriously suspect.'")

182. This facet of the American jury trial may be changing. Some courts have conducted research into what happens when jurors are allowed to ask questions and found generally positive results. *See* Should Jurors Ask Questions in Criminal Trials (available at http://www.courts.state.co.us/userfiles/File/Court_Probation/Supreme_Court/Committees/Jury_System_Standing_Committee/dodgereport.pdf (http://bit.ly/1b7AGNB); *see also* Steve Chapman, "When Jurors Talk Back" (http://reason.com/archives/2009/04/13/when-jurors-talk-back) (http://bit.ly/1846Vf8).

Some states already allow jurors to ask questions, but the practice is fairly limited, at least at this point in time. *See* American Judicature Society, Statutes for Juror Questions to Witnesses (available at https://www.ajs.org/judicial-administration/jury-center/jury-system-overview/jury-improvement-efforts/improving-trials/juror-questions-witnesses/juror-questions-statutes/) (http://bit.ly/1dKIKVn).

One problem with letting jurors ask questions is that the process is often very cumbersome. Concerned about the injection of prejudice, courts will generally require jurors to write their questions down and then will have to go over the proposed questions with the attorneys for both sides in private and only if the judge agrees that the question is permissible will it be read to the witness who then answers the question. Obviously, this process means that one question can take a very long time.

183. *See* Josh Voorhees, Zimmerman's Legal Team Kicked Off Its Defense With a Knock-Knock Joke (June 24, 2013) (available at http://slate.me/191TZDy).

184. *See, e.g.,* Hillary Burgess, Deepening The Discourse Using The Legal Mind's Eye: Lessons from Neuroscience and Psychology that Optimize Law School Learning, 29 Quinnipiac L. Rev. 1

(2011); *see also* M. H. Sam Jacobson, Paying Attention Or Fatally Distracted? Concentration, Memory, And Multi-Tasking In A Multi-Media World, 16 Legal Writing 419 (2010).

185. Carol Tavris and Eliot Aronson, Mistakes Were Made Made (But Not by Me) (2007), p. 136 (citing, Deanna Kuhn, Michael Weinstock, and Robin Flaton (1994), "How Well Do Jurors Reason? Competence Dimensions of Individual Variation in a Juror Reasoning Task," Psychological Science, 5, p.289-296.)

186. *See, e.g.,* Federal Rule of Evidence 702.

187. *People v. Kelly*, 549 P.2d 1240 (Cal. 1976).

188. If the question is so one-sided that no opposing expert can be found, then the dispute likely would never reach the courts because the person with the losing side of the argument would simply surrender without the trouble of a lawsuit.

189. Daniel C. Murrie, Marcus T. Boccaccini, Lucy A. Guarnera, Katrina A. Rufino, "Are Forensic Experts Biased by the Side That Retained Them?" Psychological Science (August 2013). (available at http://pss.sagepub.com/content/early/2013/08/21/09567976134 81812.full) (http://bit.ly/15uA7c5).

190. *See* Dow Chemical held liable in breast-implant case, Baltimore Sun, Feb. 16, 1995 (available at http://articles.baltimoresun.com/1995-02-16/news/1995047027_1_dow-corning-dow-chemical-force-dow (http://bit.ly/1bHjnFE).

191. *See* Breiting VB, Holmich LR, Brandt B, Fryzek JP, Wolthers MS, Kjoller K, McLaughlin JK, Wiik A, Friis S (2004). "Long-term Health Status of Danish Women with Silicone Breast Implants". Plastic and Reconstructive Surgery 114 (1): 217–226 (http://dx.doi.org/10.1097%2F01.PRS.0000128823.77637.8A) (http://bit.ly/18476HB); Villenueve PJ et al. (June 2006). "Mortality among Canadian Women with Cosmetic Breast Implants". American Journal of Epidemiology 164 (4): 334–341 (http://dx.doi.org/10.1093%2Faje%2Fkwj214) (http://bit.ly/18qU9X5).

192. David L. Faigman, Legal Alchemy: The Use and Misuse of Science in the Law, p. 59 (1999).

193. *Lilly v. Virginia*, 527 U.S. 116 (1999).

194. *See, e.g.*, Judicial Council of California Civil Jury Instructions, No. 200 ("A party must persuade you, by the evidence presented in court, that what he or she is required to prove is more likely to be true than not true. This is referred to as 'the burden of proof.'") (http://www.courts.ca.gov/partners/documents/caci_2013_edition.pdf).

195. *See, e.g.*, California Criminal Jury Instructions, No. 220 (available at http://www.legapedia.org/state-by-state/california/jury-instructions/calcrim-220.-reasonable-doubt).

196. *See, e.g.*, Frederick Schauer, *Thinking like a Lawyer*, p. 220 (Harvard University Press 2009).

197. *See, e.g.*, http://injury.findlaw.com/torts-and-personal-injuries/wrongful-death-overview.html (http://bit.ly/16s2NJ5).

198. *See* Brian H. Bornstein, Judges vs. Juries, Court Review 56, 57 (available at http://aja.ncsc.dni.us/courtrv/cr43-2/CR43-2Bornstein.pdf); *see also* Brian Palmer, How Accurate Are Juries, Slate (July 18, 2013) (http://www.slate.com/articles/news_and_politics/explainer/2013/07/zimmerman_trial_how_accurate_are_juries.html) (http://slate.me/1h34yLE).

199. Lee F. Peoples, "The Citation of Wikipedia in Judicial Opinions," 12 Yale J.L. & Tech. 1 (2009) (noting that Wikipedia has been cited in over 400 judicial opinions as of 2009).

200. *Muller v. Oregon*, 208 U.S. 412 (1908).

201. *Muller*, 208 U.S. at 421.

202. *Id.* at 421-22.

203. For a more extended discussion of fact-finding in judicial opinions, *see* David L. Faigman, Legal Alchemy: The Use and Misuse of Science in the Law, p. 90-121 (1999).

204. This phrase has been attributed to numerous people, including Oliver Wendell Holmes, Jr., but it appears that it was first used in Zechariah Chafee, "Freedom of Speech in Wartime", 32 Harvard Law Review 932, 957 (1919).

205. The source of this anecdote is the famous case of *Hawkins v. McGee*, 84 N.H. 114, 146 A. 641 (N.H. 1929).

206. *See* http://www.goodreads.com/author/quotes/311501.Zsa_Zsa_Gabor.

207. This anecdote is taken from *Hollywood Fantasy Corp. v. Gabor*, 151 F. 3d 203 (5th Cir. 1998).

208. In this example, you might object that you lost the package through no fault of your own. The careless driver was the cause of both your and the package's accident. Breaches of contracts, however, are measured by whether promises are performed. With only rare exceptions, if the promise is not performed, the person who failed to fulfill the contract must pay damages to the person who did not breach. If you could find the driver, you could shift the consequences to him or her under the law of torts, but for now, assume that the driver sped away, never to be seen or heard from again, leaving you holding the proverbial bag.

209. 350 F.2d 445 (D.C. Cir. 1965).

210. *Id.* at 449.

211. *See, e.g.,* Lisa J. Servon, "The Real Reason the Poor Go Without Bank Accounts," The Atlantic Cities (Sept. 11, 2013) ("When I interviewed my customers, however, I learned that for many lower income people, commercial banks are ultimately more expensive. The rapidly increasing cost of bounced checked fees and late payment penalties has driven many customers away from banks, particularly those who live close to the edge, like many of my RiteCheck customers. A single overdraft can result in cascading bad checks and hundreds of dollars in charges.") (http://www.theatlanticcities.com/jobs-and-economy/2013/09/why-poor-choose-go-without-bank-accounts/6783/) (http://bit.ly/19AYrLX).

212. It might be more precise to say that the *Palsgraf* case analyzed when the law will shift the *economic* loss, because the loss itself—the injury suffered by Mrs. Palsgraf—could not be shifted. The pain she suffered and the crippling aftereffects were hers to bear alone. The law of torts can only make money change hands. Each person's experiences are, and can only be, theirs and theirs alone.

213. *Palsgraf v. Long Island Railroad Co.,* 162 N.E. 99 (NY CA 1928).

214. There are cases where duty is not the primary basis for tort liability, and instead, strict liability is imposed. Liability is "strict" because the law shifts the losses even though the defendant may not

have done anything wrongful or blameworthy. Strict liability comes up in cases of products liability, for example, and the reason for shifting the losses is because businesses that sell goods and services are in the best position to insure against the losses that arise from their businesses, certainly in a better position than the individual consumers who purchase their goods and services.

215 *See, e.g., Boyd v. Racine Currency Exchange*, 306 N.E.2d 39 (Ill. 1973); Ward Farnsworth, *The Legal Analyst* (2007), p.3-6.

216. *See, e.g., Rowland v. Christian*, 69 Cal.2d 108 (1968).

217. *See, e.g.,* Cal. Veh. Code § 23123.5; N.J.S.A. 39:4-97.3.

218. *Kubert v. Best* (N.J. App. Div. 2013), available at http://www.judiciary.state.nj.us/opinions/a1128-12.pdf.

219. *See, e.g., Adams v. City of Fremont*, 68 Cal.App.4th 243 (1998) (police officer has no duty to prevent armed person who is threatening suicide from carrying out the threat); *Nally v. Grace Community Church*, 47 Cal.3d 278 (pastor has no duty to prevent suicide of person he is counseling).

220. A video of Professor Saxe describing her research is at http://www.ted.com/talks/rebecca_saxe_how_brains_make_moral _judgments.html (http://bit.ly/16KrKcL).

221. We focus here on Grace and her blameworthiness. It is a separate question whether the chemical factory should be held liable for Grace's friend's death because it allowed deadly poison to be stored next to a pot of coffee in a container labeled sugar.

222. Stanford Encyclopedia of Philosophy, http://plato.stanford.edu/entries/moral-luck.

223. *See, e.g.,* Cal. Penal Code § 192(c)(1) (defining "vehicular manslaughter" as "driving a vehicle in the commission of an unlawful act, not amounting to felony, and with gross negligence; or driving a vehicle in the commission of a lawful act which might produce death, in an unlawful manner, and with gross negligence.")

224. On June 28, 2009, physicist Stephen Hawking threw a party for time travelers. To ensure that only legitimate time travelers attended, Professor Hawking didn't publish the invitations until after the event. He waited and waited—and no one arrived. It seems that if time travel becomes possible in the future, the intrepid time travelers will have no interest in partying with a famous physicist at

the beginning of the 21st century. Alternatively, time travel is, and forever will be, impossible. *See* Eddie Wrenn, "The party that didn't go off with a Big Bang: Stephen Hawking held a party for time-travellers — but no one turned up...," The Daily Mail, July 3, 2012 (http://www.dailymail.co.uk/sciencetech/article-2168178/Stephen-Hawking-held-party-time-travellers--turned-.html) (http://dailym.ai/1h356Ba).

225. *See, e.g., Vosburg v. Putney,* 50 N.W. 403 (Wisc.1891).

226. Black's Law Dictionary 593 (9th ed. 2009).

227. Not everyone agrees with the eggshell-skull rule. Some have argued that the rule misaligns incentives, subjects injurers to unfair surprise, and creates other problems. *See, e.g.,* Steve P. Calandrillo & Dustin E. Buehler, "Eggshell Economics: A Revolutionary Approach to the Eggshell Plaintiff Rule," 74 Ohio State Law Journal 375 (2013).

228. The Innocence Project, http://bit.ly/HB8Cbj.

229. University of Michigan, Exonerations in 2013: The National Registry of Exonerations (Feb. 4, 2014), http://www.law.umich.edu/special/exoneration/Documents/Exonerations_in_2013_Report.pdf (http://bit.ly/LJF8tp); Zusha Elinson, "False Confessions Dog Teens," *The Wall Street Journal* (Sept. 8, 2013) http://online.wsj.com/news/articles/SB10001424127887324906304579036901493013302) (http://on.wsj.com/1g7iohy).

230. *See* http://www.cdc.gov/vaccines/; *see also* http://antiantivax.flurf.net/; Phil Plait, Anti-Vaccine Megachurch Linked to Texas Measles Outbreak, Slate.com (Aug. 26, 2013) (http://slate.me/1cl7F3X).

231. *See* http://hawaii.gov/health/vital-records/News_Release_Birth_Certificate_042711.pdf (http://1.usa.gov/1fTfQHh); *see also* http://www.snopes.com/politics/obama/birthers/birthcertificate.asp (http://bit.ly/GHlQU3).

232. Daniel T. Gilbert, "How Mental Systems Believe," American Psychologist, Vol. 46, No. 2, February 1991.

233. The resolution of disputes will always involve uncertainty because we humans are by our nature fallible and imperfect.

234. Sharkey, Catherine M., The Exxon Valdez Litigation Marathon: A Window on Punitive Damages (April 13, 2010). University of St. Thomas Law Journal, Vol. 7, No. 1, 2010; NYU Law and Economics Research Paper No. 10-15; NYU School of Law, Public Law Research Paper No. 10-25. Available at SSRN: http://ssrn.com/abstract=1588961.

235 This anecdote is adapted from David Foster Wallace's 2005 commencement address to Kenyon College. A transcript of the talk is available at http://moreintelligentlife.com/story/david-foster-wallace-in-his-own-words (Sept. 19, 2008) (http://bit.ly/1cfverA).

Made in the USA
San Bernardino, CA
20 December 2014